REDUNDANCY
LAW IN EUROPE

European Labour Law in Practice

VOLUME 1

The titles in this series are listed at the back of this volume.

KLUWER LAW INTERNATIONAL

REDUNDANCY LAW IN EUROPE

Edited by

Maarten van Kempen

Lisa Patmore

Michael Ryley

Robert von Steinau-Steinrück

Co-ordinated by

Paul Bartelings

 Wolters Kluwer

Law & Business

AUSTIN   BOSTON   CHICAGO   NEW YORK   THE NETHERLANDS

Published by:
Kluwer Law International
PO Box 316
2400 AH Alphen aan den Rijn
The Netherlands
Website: www.kluwerlaw.com

Sold and distributed in North, Central and South America by:
Aspen Publishers, Inc.
7201 McKinney Circle
Frederick, MD 21704
United States of America
Email: customer.care@aspenpubl.com

Sold and distributed in all other countries by:
Turpin Distribution Services Ltd.
Stratton Business Park
Pegasus Drive, Biggleswade
Bedfordshire SG18 8TQ
United Kingdom
Email: kluwerlaw@turpin-distribution.com

ISBN   978-90-411-2764-8

© 2008 Kluwer Law International BV, The Netherlands

TABLE OF CONTENTS

Estonia   **55**
Maksim Greinoman
Daisy Tauk

Finland   **65**

Riitta Sedig
Pavel Koivistoinen
Petteri Viljakainen

Germany   **89**

Robert von Steinau-Steinrück
Alexander von Vogel

The Netherlands   **159**
Wouter Engelsman
Hannagnes Faber
Maarten van Kempen
Dave Sieler

Poland   171
Lukasz Kuczkowski

Russia   **203**
Nadezhda Bulatova
Nadezhda Serova
Sergey Stefanishin

Slovak Republic   **213**
Tomáš Čermák
Zuzana Majerčáková
Karin Šturdíková

Slovenia **223**

Ralf Pescheck
Melanie Taufner

Spain   **231**
Jesús Domingo Aragón
Eva Sainz Cortadi

Sweden   **239**
Jessica Stålhammar

Switzerland 247
Andrea Bantle
Andrea Kaiser
Sara Licci

EDITORS AND COORDINATOR

Maarten van Kempen (1968) graduated with a degree in law from Erasmus University Rotterdam in 1993. During his career as an employment lawyer he has worked for several respected law firms such as Loeff Claeys Verbeke, Price-WaterhouseCoopers and Holland Van Gijzen, where he became a partner in 2005. On 1 April 2008, Maarten joined national law firm Dijkstra Voermans, which has a strategic alliance with BDO CampsObers. Maarten advises a wide range of clients on all aspects of employment law. He has a significant experience in multi-jurisdictional reorganizations. He has published articles in law reviews and newspapers on employment law and workers' participation. He is a panel member on Holland's only legal radio show, broadcast on BNR Nieuws Radio.

Lisa Patmore (1972) graduated with a degree in law and economics from the University of Central Lancashire in 1993. She joined Pinsent Masons LLP in 2000 and is currently a partner in the firm's Employment Group, based in London. Lisa specializes in all aspects of employment law (both contentious and non-contentious), and has significant experience in trade union and collective issues. Lisa acts mainly for employers, though occasionally she acts for executives. She regularly advises employers on high-level terminations, collective redundancies and reorganizations, imposition of new terms and conditions of employment and other strategic issues. Lisa also has considerable experience working on corporate transactions, both domestic and multi-jurisdictional.

Michael Ryley (1960) graduated with a degree in law from Oxford in 1982. Save for a period spent working in Tokyo, Michael has spent his entire career to date in the City of London, advising a wide range of clients on all aspects of employment law and human resources strategy. He is a well-known speaker and writer on employment law issues. His extensive bibliography includes 'Employment Law

Aspects of Mergers and Acquisitions: A Practical Guide', 'TUPE: Law and Practice', 'Employment Law for the Construction Industry' and many articles for professional journals.

Dr Robert von Steinau-Steinrück (1964) graduated from Bonn University in 1991. He received a doctorate in law in Bonn. He has been a solicitor since 1996, and a specialist in labour law since 2001. Robert specializes in restructuring, transactions, collective and individual labour law, service-contract law, expats and international labour law. He is co-author of *Compendium of Mergers and Acquisitions*, 2005, *Employment & Labour Law in Germany* (2nd edition), 2008 and many other publications. He is a member of the Working Group for Specialized Labour Law Solicitors of the German Bar Association, the German Association of Labour Courts, the German-British Lawyers' Association, the German-British Association, the International Bar Association and the European Employment Lawyers' Association. He is a partner in the Berlin office of Luther Rechtsanwaltsgesellschaft mbH.

Coordinator

Paul Bartelings (1962), graduated (law degree) from the Free University Amsterdam in 1989. He has worked as a knowledge manager in professional services firms for more than fifteen years. He is currently Head of Knowledge Management and Training at Holland Van Gijzen Attorneys at Law and Civil Law Notaries and Director of The Holland Law School.

LIST OF CONTRIBUTORS

Austria

- Leonhard Reis   KWR Karasek Wietrzyk Rechtsanwälte GmbH

Belgium

- Hans Arnold   Ernst & Young Tax Consultants

Bulgaria

- Anelia Dinova   PI Partners
- Todor Kakchev   PI Partners

Cyprus

- Achilles C. Emilianides   Achilles & Emile C. Emilianides

Czech Republic

- Tereza Kadlecová   Weinhold Legal
- Eva Svobodová   Weinhold Legal

Denmark

- Ewa Ljung Rasmussen   Maqs Law Firm

Estonia

- Maksim Greinoman   Advokaadibüroo Greinoman & Co.
- Daisy Tauk   Advokaadibüroo Glikman & Partnerid

Finland

- Pavel Koivistoinen   Ernst & Young Oy
- Riitta Sedig   Ernst & Young Oy
- Petteri Viljakainen   Ernst & Young Oy

France

- Etienne Pujol   Granrut Avocats
- Roselyn Sands   Ernst & Young Société d'Avocats
- Laurent-Paul Tour   Ernst & Young Société d'Avocats

Germany

- Robert von Steinau-Steinrück   Luther Rechtsanwaltsgesellschaft mbH
- Alexander von Vogel   Luther Rechtsanwaltsgesellschaft mbH

Greece

- Ioannis Meimeteas   PI Partners

Hungary

- Imre Krisch   Gobert, Fest & Partners Attorneys at Law
- Norá Kürti   Gobert, Fest & Partners Attorneys at Law

Ireland

- Kevin Langford   Arthur Cox

Italy

- Maria Teresa Iannella   Studio Legale Tributario
- Stefania Radoccia   Studio Legale Tributario

Latvia

- Imants Jansons   Kronbergs & Cukste Law Firm

Lithuania

- Ieva Povilaitienė   Jurevičius, Balčiūnas and Bartkus

Luxembourg

- Guy Castegnaro   Castegnaro Cabinet d'Avocats
- Ariane Claverie   Castegnaro Cabinet d'Avocats

Malta

- Matthew Brincat   Ganado & Associates, Advocates

Netherlands

- Wouter Engelsman   Holland Van Gijzen
- Hannagnes Faber
- Maarten van Kempen
- Dave Sieler   Holland Van Gijzen

Poland

- Lukasz Kuczkowski   Domanski Zakrzewski Palinka sp.k.

Portugal

- Luís Miguel Monteiro   Morais Leitão, Galvão Teles, Soares da Silva & Associados
- Joana Almeida   Morais Leitão, Galvão Teles, Soares da Silva & Associados

Romania

- Cristina Bazilescu   PI Partners

Russia

- Nadezhda Bulatova   Ernst & Young (CIS) B.V.
- Nadezhda Serova   Ernst & Young (CIS) B.V.
- Sergey Stefanishin   Ernst & Young (CIS) B.V.

Slovakia

- Tomáš Čermák   Weinhold Legal v.o.s.
- Zuzana Majerčáková   Weinhold Legal v.o.s.
- Karin Šturdíková   Weinhold Legal v.o.s.

Slovenia

- Ralf Peschek   Wolf Theiss
- Melanie Taufner   Wolf Theiss

Spain

- Jesús Domingo Aragón   Ernst & Young Abagados
- Eva Sainz Cortadi   Ernst & Young Abagados

Sweden

- Jessica Stålhammar   Maqs Law Firm

Switserland

- Andrea Bantle   Ernst & Young AG
- Andrea Kaiser   Ernst & Young AG
- Sara Licci   Ernst & Young AG

United Kingdom

- Ben Doherty   Pinsent Masons LLP
- Catherine Johns   Pinsent Masons LLP

INTRODUCTION

Despite the fact that more and more European countries are united within the European Union, it must be understood that each European country is still a sovereign state with its own legislation and judicial system. From an employment law perspective, HR directors and legal counsel often have to deal with different legal criteria regarding timing, information and consultation, risks and costs when it comes to restructuring companies in different countries.

This book is intended to present an overview of the most relevant legislation regarding redundancy schemes within the European Union as well as in Russia and Switzerland. One chapter describes the European directive regarding mass redundancies. Further, it contains twenty-nine reports written by one or more experienced employment lawyers from each particular country. Each report includes an overview of the relevant legislation of the country in question regarding timing, information and consultation, risks and costs, as well as advice for legal practice.

This book should be helpful to all professionals dealing with employment law in one or more countries in Europe.

As editors, we wish to thank all contributors for their contributions. Further, we wish to thank the law firms Luther and Pinsent Masons, both member firms of PMLG, Holland Van Gijzen Attorneys and Civil Notaries and its Holland law school, who have made this book possible.

REDUNDANCY

European law regarding redundancy has its origins in the European Union's Social Action Programme 1974-1976. At that time, the Union had recently been enlarged from the six founding states to nine Member States, with the prospect of further enlargement. Pursuant to the Programme, three key directives were introduced: the Directive on Collective Redundancies (75/129), the Acquired Rights Directive (77/187) and the Insolvency Directive (80/987). In promoting this legislation, the European Commission was reacting to the actualization of the common market and the gradual enlargement of that market as the Union grew in membership. Its objective was to assist in the restructuring of enterprises throughout the Union so as to encourage the emergence of a stronger group of enterprises, more attuned to the needs of the market.

In compiling the Redundancy Directive, the Commission avoided restricting the rights of management to organize and reorganize its businesses as it saw fit. Its approach was that management should be free to adapt as the market developed, and that there would be no restriction on management's ability to dismiss workers. However, the social consequences of restructuring were not forgotten by the Directive, which enhanced employee rights to counterbalance management's freedom to restructure. The Directive's objective is to promote industrial democracy, allowing employee participation in the decision-making process (albeit limited to a consultative role) and providing a level of protection to those employees who are displaced. With the enlargement of the market, a fresh Directive (92/56) was published, and this has now been consolidated into Directive 98/59.

Though the Directive is commonly known as the 'Collective Redundancies Directive', its definition of redundancies is wider than what is generally understood, as it refers to 'dismissals effected by an employer for one or more reasons not related to the individual workers concerned'.[1] Typically, of course, this relates

---

1. Article 1(1)(a).

to circumstances where fewer jobs are required within the enterprise, where skills are no longer needed or where there is a change in location. However, it is wider in that it can include voluntary redundancy and voluntary early retirement programmes, as well as circumstances in which the employer proposes to effect a change of terms and conditions of employment.[2]

The Directive allows Member States a choice of two models to determine when collective consultation is required; both models involve an analysis of the number of dismissals proposed. The first model (adopted, for example, by Denmark) is essentially a 10% rule, relating the number of redundancies proposed to the total workforce. Accordingly, the larger the workforce within the enterprise, the greater the number of redundancies that need to be proposed before obligations arise. By contrast, the other model (used, for example, in the UK), which is focused on the aggregate number of redundancies to be declared, increases the amount of protection afforded to employees, as the enterprise is defined more broadly.

Considerable difficulty has arisen in relation to the thresholds for determining when the collective consultation requirements come into play. These hinge on the definition of 'establishment'. The numbers of proposed redundancies are analyzed by establishment for the purpose of applying the thresholds in the Directive. An enterprise seeking to avoid the application of the Directive will wish to argue for a wide definition of 'establishment' in a country where the Danish model has been used (to 'dilute' the number of redundancies proposed as a proportion of the whole), whereas an employer faced with the UK model will wish to see a narrow interpretation so as to count the smallest number of redundancies. However, in *Rockfon*,[3] the European Court held that it was necessary to have a European-wide definition of this term. One of the problems is that the terminology varies considerably in translations of the Directive into the languages of the Member States. When trying to adopt a purposive approach, the Court had some difficulty because whereas a narrow definition of establishment was helpful to the employees in the Rockfon case, in countries where the other model of applicability of the Directive is applied, a more expansive test of establishment would be beneficial to the employees. It is clear from the case of *Athinaiki*[4] that the courts are to be encouraged to focus primarily on adopting a purposive approach (used, for example, in the UK). The Court suggested that there is sufficient flexibility in the definition to permit the concept of establishment to be considered in a way favourable to employees so as to promote the need for collective consultation, whilst at the same time doing little for legal certainty in this area.

The Directive incorporates a number of exceptions relating to fixed-term contracts, contracts which are task related and where the task has been completed,

---

2. See, for example, the case of *GMB v. Man, Truck & Bus* [2000]. All ER 868 in the UK, where the scope of the Directive (or, in this case, the derivative provisions of English law) extended over a project to change employee terms and conditions.
3. [1995] ECR 1-4291.
4. C-270/05.

public administrative bodies, establishments governed by public law and the crews of sea-going vessels.

The required timetable for consultation is not specifically defined. The Directive provides that the employer 'shall begin consultation with the workers' representatives in good time with a view to reaching agreement'.[5]

It should be noted that although this is essentially a consultative obligation, there is some blurring of the boundary between the concept of consultation and bargaining. If the employer is to consult with the employee representatives with a view to reaching an agreement, then it follows that it must put forward proposals that are objectively likely to promote an agreement. It does not have the option of simply 'going through the motions' by putting forward its own proposals, which have little chance of employee endorsement.

Consultation will ordinarily need to start shortly after proposals are submitted so as to allow sufficient time for the process to take place before implementation. Clearly, the consultation must take place before firm decisions are reached, or it will have little purpose. Consultation may take place with whatever the local law provides by way of employee representatives. In countries such as the Netherlands and Germany, this will be the local works councils; in France, the *Comité d'Entreprise*. In the UK, consultation will be done with recognized trade unions where these exist or, where they do not, groups specifically elected for the purpose.

The consultation agenda must deal first with the ways and means of avoiding redundancies or of reducing the numbers affected, and second, with the ways of mitigating the consequences and appropriate social measures (though the discussion required by the Directive is likely to fall well short of the level of discussion needed in many countries relating to social plans).

There is a requirement that the employer make all relevant information available to support the information and consultation process.[6] In particular, the following items must be provided to the employee representatives in writing:

- reasons;
- the number and categories of workers to be made redundant;
- the number and categories of workers normally employed;
- the period over which redundancies are to be effected;
- selection criteria; and
- payment.

Several obligations will require that the relevant 'competent public authority' be notified of the impending redundancies. The role of the relevant authorities can vary considerably from country to country. In the UK, for example, notification may amount to little more than forewarning the local job centre of the impending redundancies in a particular area. By contrast, in countries such as the Netherlands, the authorities have the power to prohibit redundancies from taking place at all.

---

5. Article 2(1).
6. Article 2(3)(a).

It is clear from the case of *Junk*[7] that redundancies may not be effected within the notification period, although there is nothing to prevent notices of redundancy being issued during that period, provided that they take effect after the end of the period.

---

7. [2005] IRLR 310.

AUSTRIA

Leonhard Reis

1   OVERVIEW

Redundancy schemes in Austria must cope with several labour law and employment law provisions, since different laws apply to collective bodies representing the interests of employees and to individual employment relationships,.

Austrian collective labour law is laid down in the Labour Constitution Act (*Arbeitsverfassungsgesetz*), which governs, inter alia, collective bargaining and the rights of the most important collective body, the works council.

If an employer has more than four permanent employees over the age of eighteen working in a plant (or any organizational unit), a works council (*Betriebsrat*) may be established (section 40 of the Labour Constitution Act). Works councils have participation rights regarding proposed changes in operations that vary in extent. These rights range from rights to information and rights to consultation with respect to changes and to the enforcement of social compensation plans. Collective labour law imposes important information requirements that must be addressed in redundancy schemes.

The most essential instruments of collective labour law are the collective bargaining agreement (*Kollektivvertrag*) and the plant agreement (*Betriebsvereinbarung*). Collective bargaining agreements apply to all employees of an employer who is a member of an employer's association (mainly the Austrian Chamber of Commerce), regardless of the employee's membership in a trade union. As membership in an employer's association is, for the most part, mandatory, almost all employees (and employers) are subject to a collective bargaining agreement. Such an agreement may not alter the statutory rights of employees to the detriment of employees. The most essential tool of the works council is the plant agreement. Plant agreements may regulate employment issues for a particular plant of a company or for the entire company. They are written contracts concluded between the employer company and the works council and can only regulate those issues reserved to plant agreements by law or by a collective bargaining agreement (section 29 of the Labour Constitution Act).

As far as individual employment law is concerned, the Act on White-Collar Workers (*Angestelltengesetz*) is applicable to all employees performing office work or activities of a commercial character or more complex activities of a non-commercial character that require particular training. All other employees are regarded as blue-collar workers. This distinction has lost much of its former significance, because the rights of blue- and white-collar employees have been aligned. Nevertheless, different rules (such as notice periods) may apply. In addition, the relationship between the employer and the employee is regulated by an individual employment contract. This contract may not alter the provisions of a plant agreement, collective bargaining agreement or most statutory provisions to the detriment of the employee. In the case of termination, the provisions of all of these sources may be examined and fulfilled.

2   MAJOR LEGAL REGULATIONS

As a general rule, under Austrian law, no grounds are required for termination. Nevertheless, notice periods must be observed. Furthermore, employees are entitled to seek general protection against groundless termination in plants (*Betrieb*) having more than four employees. The employee is entitled to contest the termination as being unjust on social grounds. The consequence may be reemployment, but in practice a high percentage of lawsuits result in lump sum compensation payments.

2.1   INDIVIDUAL TERMINATION OF EMPLOYMENT

2.1.1   Sections 20 and 27 of the Act on White-Collar Workers

Apart from termination by mutual consent (*einvernehmliche Auflösung*), Austrian law distinguishes between ordinary termination and immediate dismissal for good cause. Causes for dismissal are listed in section 27 of the Act on White-Collar Workers. They include disloyalty in service, inability to perform the agreed upon services, violation of the duty of non-competition, assault and offences against good morals or against the employer and his representatives, or other acts that render the employee unworthy of the employer's trust. Statutory labour law provides more causes for blue-collar workers.

In the case of individual terminations, certain periods of notice *(Kündigungs-fristen)* are mandated. The Act on White-Collar Workers (section 20) provides that the employer must observe a notice period of six weeks ending on the last day of a quarter, unless the employment contract states that the notice period may end on the fifteenth or the last day of the month. The law extends the notice period from six weeks to two months for employees who have been continuously employed for two years. After five years of employment, the notice period is extended to three months, after fifteen years to four months, and after twenty-five years to five months. Collective bargaining agreements may provide for longer notice periods. Shorter notice periods for blue-collar workers exist in collective bargaining agreements. It is permitted to release an employee from work during the notice period, while the employee remains entitled to a full salary.

Under Austrian law, no special form of termination is stipulated. Therefore, an oral termination is valid unless otherwise stipulated in a collective bargaining agreement.

2.1.2 Section 105 of the Labour Constitution Act

Austrian labour law provides general protection against groundless termination of employment, which also involves the works council. If no works council exists even though the plant has at least five employees, the remaining provisions are nevertheless applicable and entitle the employee to contest the termination.

In general, the employer must first notify the works council of the intended termination. The works council may approve, acquiesce or object within a period of five working days. The employer may only proceed after this period has expired or the works council has reacted; otherwise the termination will be void. In the case of approval of the termination by the works council, the employee is only entitled to contest the termination by filing an action based on unlawfulness. In the case of acquiescence, the employee may contest the termination by filing an action based on unlawfulness or unsocial termination. Upon objection, the works council (or – only in the case of inactivity on the part of the works council – the employee) is entitled to file a complaint with the labour court. The labour court may order that the termination be set aside for the following reasons:

- The termination is unlawful (for example, trade union activity, activity in the works council, justified claims against the employer).
- The termination is socially unjustified (infringement of substantial interest of the employee). In this case the employer can present reasons for justification, such as the personal characteristics of the employee or economic reasons that prevent continuing the employment.

If the termination is set aside, the employment relationship will be reinstated. The employee is therefore entitled to full payment and also for back-payment for the duration of the legal procedure. Social security contributions must also be paid for the same period.

2.2   RIGHTS OF THE WORKS COUNCIL

2.2.1   Sections 108 and 109 of the Labour Constitution Act

In general, the works council is entitled to be informed by the employer of all issues concerning the economic situation of the enterprise, and may submit suggestions and proposals to the employer. In the case of major changes, the employer must notify the works council before enforcing any measures. According to the regulations under the Labour Market Policy Act, the works council must be informed of the intention of enforcing measures as early in advance as possible – even before the employer has notified the planned collective redundancy.

According to the Labour Constitution Act, collective redundancies are regarded as 'major changes to the plant' (*Betriebsänderung*), which result in serious disadvantages for a significant proportion of employees or even the entire workforce. Therefore the employer has a duty to supply the works council with relevant information, particularly about all social matters concerned. According to its consultation and co-determination rights, the works council is entitled to call in an expert and to present proposals to the employer in order to prevent, eliminate or mitigate unfavourable consequences for the employees.

If the planned workforce reduction affects a significant proportion of the employees in a plant with more than twenty employees, the works council may demand the conclusion of a social compensation plan or social plan (*Sozialplan*). Social plans should prevent, or at least mitigate, negative effects on the employees. A social compensation plan, according to section 109 of the Labour Constitution Act, qualifies as a plant agreement. A social compensation plan is a compulsory plant agreement (*erzwingbare Betriebsvereinbarung*): If the parties fail to agree upon these matters, any party can call upon a Conciliation Board (*Schlichtungsstelle*) to decide on the issue.

2.2.2   Section 111 of the Labour Constitution Act

Furthermore, in plants with more than 200 employees, the works council may oppose any measure that would have a considerable negative effect on the employees. This means that in the case of the intended closing of an enterprise, such opposition can suspend closing for a period of four weeks but cannot impede it.

In an enterprise with more than 400 employees, the works council also has the possibility to appeal to the National Economic Commission (*Staatliche Wirtschaftskommission*) if national economic interests are at stake. This

Commission will only act as a mediator to facilitate an agreement between the works council and the employer.

2.3 NOTIFICATION TO THE PUBLIC EMPLOYMENT MARKET SERVICE

2.3.1 Section 45a of the Labour Market Policy Act

According to section 45a of the Labour Market Policy Act (*Arbeitsmarktförder-ungsgesetz*), a collective redundancy occurs if the employer plans to reduce the workforce of a plant by a certain number of employees within a thirty-day period.

This regulation requires the employer to notify the local office of the Public Employment Market Service if one of the following terminations is planned:

- at least five employees, in a plant with more than twenty and less than 100 employees;
- at least 5% of the employees, in a plant with more than 100 and less than 600 employees;
- at least thirty employees, in a plant with more than 600 employees; or
- at least five employees of the age of forty or more, in any plant.

The threshold of terminations to qualify as a collective redundancy is significantly lower than that laid down in the relevant EU directive (98/59/EC). The provision on mass lay-offs covers all kinds of termination of employment relationships that result from the employer's initiative (including immediate dismissals, termination by mutual consent and even resignation by the employee if the employer has put pressure on him/her). However, these grounds for termination are not taken into account by the Public Employment Service. The only purpose of section 45a of the Labour Market Policy Act is to provide the Public Employment Market Service (*Arbeitsmarktservice*) with information to arrange appropriate steps. The Public Employment Market Service usually initiates consultation talks with all parties concerned to prevent cases of hardship, in particular for older employees, and to apply appropriate labour market instruments. Mass lay-offs are not, however, subject to the approval of any authority under Austrian law. The only relevant criterion is the time period in which the collective redundancy is carried out.

Notification must be made in writing at least thirty days before the first statement of termination. In the absence of such prior notification, any notice to an employee would be invalid. Also, during the thirty-day period, any statement of termination and any termination by mutual consent must be approved by the Public Employment Service of Austria. Such notifications require detailed information regarding age, gender, professional qualification and responsibility of each of the employees whose termination is intended. If the employer and the works council have concluded a social plan, the Public Employment Service may agree to reduce the thirty-day waiting period. On the other hand, this period may be longer under the provisions laid down in some collective bargaining agreements.

The employer must inform the works council about the notification to the Public Employment Service. This obligation exists independently of that under the Labour Constitution Act.

2.4   COSTS AND RISKS

2.4.1   Social Plans

Most social plans concluded between managements and works councils contain special severance pay regulations that provide for extra payments or lump sum payments, in particular for vulnerable employee groups such as older and disabled people. Social plans may also cover financial arrangements for organizing retraining schemes, compensatory wage adjustments and rules for preferential reemployment of former employees or the right to remain in company-owned apartments.

2.4.2   Severance Payment (Section 23 Act on White-Collar Workers)

If the termination by notice becomes effective, the employee is primarily entitled to a severance payment (*Abfertigung*). The general provisions regarding severance payments also apply to employees whose employment has been terminated in the course of a collective redundancy. At present, there are two different severance payment schemes in force in Austria. The old scheme is generally applicable to employees whose employment with the employer began before 1 January 2003. The new scheme applies to employees who commenced employment after 31 December 2002 or who have agreed to transfer from the old scheme to the new one.

According to the old severance payment scheme, an employee is entitled to severance payment upon termination if the employment has lasted three or more years and is not terminated by the employee, unless for a good cause, or by the employer for a good cause. The amount of the payment is always a multiple of the last average monthly salary and depends on the duration of employment as follows:

Years of Service	Months Worth of Severance Pay
3-4	2
5-9	3
10-14	4
15-19	6
20-24	9
More than 25	12

Under the new scheme, the employer permanently contributes to the severance payment, which is paid to a pension fund on a monthly basis. This contribution amounts to 1.53% of the salary including benefits. Upon termination of the employment, the employee has to claim the payment directly from the pension fund if he has at least three years of service. The employee also has the option to save this entitlement towards a future pension. Unlike the old scheme, the employee does not lose the entitlement if the employee resigns or is dismissed for a justified cause. Thus, no severance payment has to be paid by the employer for the employees falling under the new scheme.

2.4.3   Vacation Compensation

Employees usually have the right to at least twenty-five working days of paid vacation, which may be increased by law or collective bargaining agreements according to years of service as laid down in the Vacation Act (*Urlaubsgesetz*). As there is no obligation on the employee to take vacations during the working year, and it is possible to carry forward untaken vacation for two years, an employee may accumulate a claim to seventy-five working days (or even more). In the case of termination, the employee is entitled to a pro rata payment for accrued vacations.

2.4.4   Payment for Non-competition

Non-competition clauses are valid in Austria if they are explicitly agreed upon, do not exceed one year and do not impede unreasonably the employee's job opportunities (section 36 of the Act on White-Collar Workers). The employer is restricted from enforcing a non-competition clause if the employer caused termination by ordinary termination, by dismissing the employee without good cause or by giving good cause to the employee to terminate. In the first case, the employer may still enforce the non-competition clause by continuing to pay a full salary during the whole period of non-competition. Once stipulated, a unilateral change of a non-competition clause by the employer is not enforceable.

2.4.5   Protected Groups of Employees

Several groups of employees enjoy special protection against ordinary termination and immediate dismissal. They include: members of (as well as candidates for) the works council, pregnant employees and parents on maternity leave, employees on unpaid leave or part-time employment for educational purposes and handicapped employees. Terminations usually require some justified cause and/or the approval of the labour court or an administrative agency. Termination without approval may be null and void.

2.4.6   Notice Periods (Section 20 of the Act on White-Collar Workers)

Costs also arise from the employees' entitlement to their salary during the notice period, as notice periods may cover five or more months.

2.4.7   Further Redundancy Costs and Risks that May Occur

If the employer dismisses an employee without good cause, the employment normally ceases immediately. The employee is thus entitled to full payment, including the payment (*Kündigungsentschädigung*) that would have been due if the employment had been terminated regularly. The employee is also entitled to have the termination set aside under the rules of protection against termination (see 2.1 b.).

Costs may also arise from contractual parachutes, employment law disputes and from additional severance payments that may be agreed to after an individual reinstatement or to settle pending disputes.

Damage to the corporate image and political pressure by members of the Social Partners (*Sozialpartner*) comprise the most significant non-financial risks for strikes and industrial conflicts. These are extremely rare in Austria.

3   ADVICE FOR LEGAL PRACTICE

3.1   TIMING

It goes without saying that redundancy schemes should always be well prepared. Preparation requires sufficient time. If the redundancy scheme is well prepared, the works council will have no opportunity to prevent the measures being taken. One should be aware that the works council has the power to delay redundancies. It is highly recommended to provide the works council and the Public Employment Market Service with information as early as possible.

3.2   COSTS AND RISKS

Apart from the statutory regulations, several collective bargaining agreements provide for measures that serve to moderate the consequences of termination of employment in the course of mass lay-offs. Thus, knowledge of the applicable collective bargaining agreements is key. Furthermore, the notification to the works council should be as detailed as possible. The works council usually claims not to be informed sufficiently. Hence, poor information will extend negotiations. Finally, any breach of the formal requirements of Austrian law can generate costs that could be avoided by proper preparation.

BELGIUM

Hans Arnold

1   OVERVIEW

Redundancy schemes in Belgium are governed by the provisions of the act of 3 July 1978 relating to employment contracts (hereinafter referred to as the 'Employment Act'), and by the Royal Order relating to this act. Some collective labour agreements, concluded under the auspices of the National Labour Council and joint committees, have restricted or modified the exercise of the legal right to terminate employment. Special rules on collective dismissal have been laid down under the Collective Labour Agreement No. 24 of 2 October 1975 and by a Royal Order of 24 May 1976. The law of 26 June 2002 (the Law) regulates the closure of enterprises.

The Generation Pact, enacted by the law of 23 December 2005, promotes an active policy for restructuring and employment, and applies to enterprises faced by collective dismissals.

In considering dismissal under Belgian law, the first important issue to be faced is the distinction between a blue- and a white-collar worker. Notice periods applicable to blue-collar workers are found in the Law as well as in collective bargaining agreements, whereas those for white-collar workers are determined in the Employment Act. In general, the Employment Act provides for ways to terminate an employment contract without the consent of the employee. As a rule, either party to an employment contract is free to terminate the contract at any time, without the need for administrative approval. In the event that a notice period is mandated, certain time restrictions and formalities apply. In the event that no such notice period is mandated, dismissal can take place at any moment and without any formalities. Compensation must be paid in lieu of notice. Thus, in the event that no notice is given, this compensation corresponds to the notice period that should have been given (e.g., notice period three months, compensation three months).

A second distinction must be made between the dismissal of an individual and the multiple dismissal. In principle, no specific procedure need be followed for the dismissal of an individual. The opposite is the case in the event of a multiple dismissal.

Finally, we can conclude that the Belgian legislature initially aimed at providing the employee with strong financial protection against dismissal by his employer (by means of high redundancy payments and unemployment benefits). However, recent legal initiatives aim to modify the existing dismissal system into a more 'reemployment-oriented' system.

2   MAJOR REGULATIONS

2.1   TIMING

2.1.1   Termination by Giving Notice

2.1.1.1   *Duration*

2.1.1.1.1   Blue-Collar Workers (Articles 37 and 59 of
               the Employment Act)

Notice periods applicable to blue-collar workers vary in accordance with the employee's seniority and are determined by reference to the applicable collective bargaining agreement. The latter depends on the employer's activities. Notice periods for blue-collar workers tend to be very short. For example, a blue-collar worker with over twenty years' service is seldom entitled to a notice period that exceeds 112 calendar days.

2.1.1.1.2   White-Collar Workers (Articles 37 and 82 of
               the Employment Act)

Notice periods applicable to white-collar workers depend primarily on the employee's salary. The Law on Employment Contracts provides that if the employee's gross annual remuneration does not exceed 28,093 euros (EUR) (amount as of 2007), the minimum period of notice equals the so-called 'legal minimum', which is equivalent to three months' notice for every five years' seniority. In the event that the employee's annual salary (which includes all benefits to which the employee is entitled at the moment of the dismissal) is higher than the threshold, the notice period is either determined by the parties by mutual agreement or by the labour court. In practice, parties often use the so-called 'Claeys formula' in determining the notice period. This formula determines the notice period on the basis of a person's seniority along with his or her age and salary.

For employees earning at least EUR 56,187 gross per year (amount as of 2007) the employer and employee are authorized to determine the required notice period in the event of the employer terminating the employment contract. This agreement must be concluded no later than the moment the employee begins working for the employer. This notice period must be at least the legal minimum. Given that the result of the Claeys formula can amount to several years' salary for a white-collar worker with substantial seniority and earnings, it is advisable for a company to incorporate such a clause in the employment agreement.

2.1.1.2 *Formalities (Article 37 of the Employment Act)*

Notice must be given by registered mail, which is deemed to be delivered three working days after it has been sent. The notice period will start running from the first Monday of the week (for blue-collar workers) or the first calendar day of the month (for white-collar workers) following the week or month during which notice was given. The notice period can also be specified by bailiff's writ, which has immediate effect. This method is obviously more costly than notification by registered mail and is seldom used in Belgium. It is of paramount importance that the document notifying the employee of the notice period specify the duration of the notice period as well as the starting date. Furthermore, it must be signed and dated by a person who can bind the employer in this respect. Particular to Belgium is the fact that three official languages exist. The document does not have to be written in three languages. In most cases, it is investigated in what language the document should be. In case of doubt, the document is written up in all three languages: Dutch, French, and German.

2.1.2 Termination by Breach of Contract

In the event that in a case of breach of contract no notice period is given, the dismissal may proceed without any formalities; compensation in lieu of notice will, however, be payable.

2.1.3 Collective Dismissal

'Collective' dismissal means any dismissal ordered for one or several reasons not attributable to the individual worker and affecting over a period of sixty days the following numbers of workers:

(a) ten or more workers in undertakings employing between twenty and 100 workers;
(b) at least 10% of the number of workers in undertakings employing an average of between 100 and 300 workers; or
(c) thirty or more workers in undertakings employing an average of at least 300 workers.

In this respect a specific time schedule is to be followed (see below).

2.2   INFORMATION AND CONSULTATION

2.2.1   **Individual Dismissal**

In essence, a formal obligation to give reasons for dismissal does not exist under Belgian law. However, if the contract is terminated for serious cause, the employee must be informed of the reason for dismissal.

Given the fact that the employer's options are either to terminate with notice or to pay compensation in lieu of notice, the employer must be very careful when deciding whether or not to dismiss an employee for serious cause.

Certain strict formalities concerning the communication of the reason for the dismissal must be followed. Firstly, the contract must be terminated no later than the third working day after the day on which the facts justifying the dismissal became known to the person having authority to dismiss. The termination of the contract can be done orally. Secondly, a letter stating the reasons justifying the dismissal must be sent by registered mail to the employee concerned no later than the third working day following the dismissal. Notification by bailiff's writ is also permissible.

In the event of the dismissal of an individual, the employer is not obliged to hear representations from any party. In some cases, however, a hearing with the employee concerned may be recommended (e.g., in the event of dismissal for serious cause) or required (e.g., pursuant to company policy or a collective bargaining agreement).

With respect to unprotected workers, there is no obligation to provide information or hold consultations, nor is there any requirement to enter into an agreement with the bodies representing the staff.

2.2.2   **Collective Dismissal**

In the event of a collective dismissal, the employer must comply with a number of obligations to provide information. The employees must be informed before the decision to act towards a collective dismissal is taken. Information must be furnished to the director of the Regional Employment Office (Article 8, Royal Order of 24 May 1976). Commencing from the moment the employer notifies the director of the Regional Employment office, no dismissals may take place for a thirty-day cooling-off period (Article 9, Royal Order of 24 May 1976).

The employees must be provided with all relevant information. Certain information, such as the reason for the collective dismissal and the number of employees affected, must be given in writing. The employer must deal with the works council or, in the absence thereof, with the Union Representative. In the event that there is no Union Representative, communication should take place with the personnel or their representatives.

A copy of the communication must be sent to the director of the Regional Employment Office.

It should be noted that in the event an operation qualifies as the closing of the business, further information must be provided. It is possible that statutory obligations to provide information pursuant to the laws relating to collective dismissal, and those relating to the closing of businesses may apply simultaneously. The employees must be consulted. The employer, together with its authorized representatives, must examine all possibilities in order to prevent the dismissals or to alleviate the consequences for the employees concerned. Several meetings should be held, at which the employees' representatives should have the opportunity to ask questions, make objections or submit counterproposals. These must be examined by the employer. The law does not provide specific formalities in relation to the aforementioned obligations. Given the fact that the employer must be able to demonstrate that these obligations have been respected, it is highly advisable to draft minutes of the meetings held.

The employer must inform the director of the Regional Employment Office of his intention to proceed with a collective dismissal. This information must be given in writing and sent by registered mail. Certain additional information, such as the activities of the company and information regarding the employees who may be dismissed, must be communicated as well.

A copy of the notification sent to the director of the Regional Employment Office must also be provided to the works council (or other representative body) and be published within the company. In the event that the employer's obligations to provide information and hold consultations are not met (fully), the employer may incur criminal or administrative sanctions. The collective dismissal procedure may be suspended, or the employer may even be required to restart the procedure. In the event that an employee's contract was or is to be terminated by means of a notice period, the notice period may be suspended.

Employees whose contracts were terminated by means of payment of compensation in lieu of notice may have to be reintegrated in the company.

2.3   RISKS

2.3.1   Language Legislation

Depending on the geographical location of the employer, Dutch, French, or German must be used. Each region has its own legislation regarding the language to be used, and, in the event of contravention of the applicable legislation, sanctions vary. The Flemish region features the strictest legislation in this respect. In the event that a language other than Dutch is used, the document concerned will be considered null and void. The Flemish Decree stipulates that the nullity may not harm the rights of the employee. This implies that an employee may choose whether or not to comply with the document concerned, or even with individual parts thereof.

2.3.2   Notice Restrictions

There are two categories of workers who enjoy protection against dismissal: those covered by the general prohibition and those protected for particular reasons.

The most protected categories of workers are employee representatives and non-elected candidate representatives in the Works Council and the Committee for Protection and Prevention at Work. These employees may only be dismissed for economic or technical reasons, as defined by the joint committee of the sector in which the employer is active, or for a serious cause that has been recognized by the court. Strict procedures must be followed. Violation of the applicable law of 1991 may entail a financial burden for the employer of up to eight years' salary per worker.

Certain other workers are protected from dismissal because of their position or circumstances. For example:

- A trade union delegate may only be dismissed on grounds unrelated to the exercise of his or her functions.
- A pregnant woman may not be dismissed from the date on which the employer is informed of her pregnancy until the end of the month following postnatal maternity leave, except for reasons unconnected with her physical state resulting from her pregnancy or confinement (section 40 of the Labour Act of 1971).
- A worker who is called up for service in the armed forces may only be dismissed on grounds unrelated to the worker's fulfilment of his military obligations (Article 38(3) of the Employment Act).
- An industrial doctor may be only be dismissed on grounds related to his or her competence or for reasons which cause no harm to his or her technical or moral independence.
- A worker who has filed a complaint with the Inspectorate of Social Leg- islation, or who has brought an action before the Labour Court with the object of ensuring compliance with the requirement of equal treatment between men and women with respect to conditions of employment, may only be dismissed for reasons unconnected with the complaint or action (Article 136, Act of August 1978).
- A worker holding a political office may not be dismissed, except on grounds unrelated to the fact that the worker holds a political office (Article 5, Act of 19 July 1976).
- A worker on paid study leave may only be dismissed on grounds unrelated to this circumstance (Article 117, Act of 22 January 1985).

2.3.3   Wrongful Dismissal (Article 63 Employment Act)

In the event that a blue-collar worker is dismissed, it is important to ensure that the termination is not considered 'wrongful'. A dismissal is wrongful if it has nothing to do with the behaviour or capabilities of the worker or with the needs of the company, and the employer will be liable for an additional indemnity equal to six months' salary, as provided for by the Employment Act.

2.3.4   Abusive Dismissal

White-collar workers may challenge their dismissal as 'abusive'. However, in most cases it is quite difficult to prove abusive dismissal, and for white-collar workers the burden of proof is on the worker. The judge may grant damages ex aequo et bono.

2.3.5   Reinstatement

There is no entitlement to reinstatement, except for members of the Work Council and the Committee on Occupational Safety and Health, who may request reinstatement if wrongfully dismissed. If the employer refuses to reinstate them, it must pay them special compensation.

2.4   Costs

2.4.1   Calculation of the Dismissal Cost

The following payments are due upon each termination of an employment contract. First, irrespective of the termination modalities (such as notice or compensation in lieu of notice), the employee is always entitled to vacation pay.

Furthermore, it should be determined whether the employee concerned is entitled to a pro rata end-of-year premium. In most cases, this can be determined by consulting the applicable collective bargaining agreement that has been concluded in the joint committee of the sector to which the employer belongs.

The employee is entitled to salary for any bank holidays that occur during a period of thirty days following the termination of the contract, unless the employee has already entered into another employer's service in the meantime.

Other compensation may relate to the employee's function (e.g., a clientele compensation to which a sales representative may be entitled) or his age (see below). Compensation may also be due if a worker is protected against dismissal (see below). In some cases, compensation for unfair dismissal or for abusive dismissal may also have to be paid (see below).

2.4.2   Collective Dismissal

In the event of a collective dismissal, collective dismissal compensation may be payable. This compensation is equal to half of the difference between a net capped salary and the unemployment allowance to which the person is entitled. The compensation is payable for a maximum of four months and is subject to social security contributions. This compensation cannot be cumulated with the closing compensation.

When an operation qualifies as the closing of a company, a lump sum closing indemnity must be paid. The maximum amount is EUR 5,355.60. This amount is indexed on an annual basis. No social security contributions are due on this sum.

2.4.3   Damages in Case of Breach of Contract

In the event that no notice period is given, an indemnity in lieu of notice is due. On this indemnity, social security contributions (around 35% employer's contributions) must be paid.

2.4.4   Social Plan

Collective redundancies are usually covered by a social plan. A social plan can either be agreed upon with the unions or the works council. The plan usually contains formal procedures regarding information and consultation during the process, and social measures such as outplacement and financial compensation.

3   ADVICE FOR LEGAL PRACTICE

3.1   TIMING

It is important to ascertain whether the worker to be dismissed is a white-collar worker or a blue-collar worker, since the respective notice periods vary dramatically. If a probation period is still running, it is advisable to terminate the contract during the probation period since shorter notice periods apply during that time.

3.2   INFORMATION AND CONSULTATION

In the event that an operation qualifies as collective dismissal and/or the closing of business, a strict timetable should be prepared and followed in order to ensure compliance with all applicable laws.

Given the different information and consultation requirements, a step-by-step plan should be prepared regarding collective redundancies. This plan should include the different stages in the information and consultation process.

3.3   RISKS

A decision must be taken whether to give notice or pay compensation in lieu of notice. Notice should be given in line with the legal requirements. During the notice period, the employee is required to continue working. In some cases, this is not desirable from a commercial or human resources point of view. The fact that the legal suspension of an employment contract, such as for illness or holidays, might prolong the notice period, may induce employers to terminate the contract and pay compensation in lieu of notice.

3.4 COSTS

3.4.1 Calculation of Dismissal Cost

When calculating the worth of the notice period, the total salary and associated benefits (such as contributions to the group insurance paid by the employer or private use of company car) must be taken into consideration. Therefore, an exhaustive list of all of the employee's salary components and benefits should be made in order to obtain an accurate result.

Furthermore, it should be investigated whether the employee is protected against dismissal. In most cases, employees may not be dismissed on the grounds on which their protection is based.

It must also be borne in mind that certain categories of workers are entitled to extra payments arising out of their responsibilities or their age. Sales representatives may be entitled to a clientele compensation to cover the loss of clientele. One of the conditions of entitlement to such compensation is the requirement that the representative has in fact introduced new clients to the company. Where the employment contract provides for a non-competition clause, the representative is assumed to have gained clients for the company. Therefore, it is important to verify the contents of the employment contract before proceeding to dismissal.

3.4.2 Cost of Older Employees

Upon dismissal, workers older than forty-five years with at least one year of seniority can claim assistance in finding a new job. Such assistance must be provided by a recognized agency and may cost several thousand euros. Older workers may also be entitled to monthly payments from the employer in addition to their unemployment allowance. The age at which one becomes entitled to the so-called 'bridge pension' scheme varies according to the sector in which the company is active, and should be verified by reference to the applicable collective bargaining agreement. The cost can amount to several hundred euros per month and may continue for a number of years (namely, the period between the expiry of the notice and the date when the employee becomes entitled to a full state pension, normally at age sixty-five).

BULGARIA

Anelia Dinova
Todor Kakchev

1   OVERVIEW

1.1   REGULATIONS

The termination of employment relationships in Bulgaria is regulated primarily
by the Bulgarian Labour Code (LC). The LC was adopted in 1986 and has been
subject to numerous amendments. It is extensive in scope and detail, as a result of
which the area of employment relations in Bulgaria is quite heavily regulated
compared to other sectors of economic activity. In addition, the profound change
in the political regime (1989) and Bulgaria's EU accession (2007) account for the
introduction of new institutions and legislative instruments, such as the Promotion of Employment Act (2001), Collective Labour Disputes Settlement Act
(1990), Information and Consultation with Employees in Multi-national Enterprises, Groups and European Companies Act (2006), which tackle additional
aspects of the employer-employee relationship. Employees, represented by
their trade unions, may seek to conclude collective bargaining agreements,
wherein, inter alia, further conditions related to the termination of employment
relationships are negotiated and introduced, beyond the minimum standards set
by the LC.

©2008 Kluwer Law International B.V., The Netherlands.
Maarten van Kempen, Lisa Patmore, Michael Ryley, and
Robert von Steinau-Steinrück (eds), *Redundancy,* pp. 19-28.

1.2   REDUNDANCY

Bulgarian legislation does not provide a legal definition of 'redundancy'. For present purposes, this term will be construed to encompass cases where the employer has ceased or intends to cease to carry on business for the purpose of which the employees have been employed or where the need for employees to carry out a particular type of work has ceased to exist or has diminished, that is, cases where the dismissal of employees has become necessary as a result of objective reasons related to the economic activity of the employer and is not related to the performance, or the ability to perform, of the employees themselves. The initiative for redundancies, therefore, lies with the employer.

Bulgarian law generally divides employment contracts into fixed-term and indefinite-term contracts. An additional differentiation exists with regard to whether the employment contracts are with or without a probation period. The legal importance of this latter distinction is that the employer may terminate arbitrarily an employment contract with a probation period during the period of the probation without notice and without cause.

For present purposes, redundancies during probation periods will not be discussed, since these do not generally pose legal or economic hurdles.

1.3   CAUSE (ARTICLE 328, PARAGRAPH 1, ITEMS 1-4)

The LC prohibits, in principle, the introduction of arbitrary redundancies by the employer for employees under indefinite employment contracts. Thus, redundancies should always be well-grounded and for cause.

Redundancy causes are explicitly and exhaustively enumerated in the law. These include:

– complete closure of the employer's enterprise;
– partial closure of the employer's enterprise;
– staff reduction based on changes in the Employment Grid;[1]
– decrease in the volume of work; and
– work stoppage for more than fifteen days.

The fact that redundancy is the cause for the termination should always be indicated and substantiated by the employer in its termination notice to the employee; whether or not grounds exist to support the redundancy is the primary focus should an employee who has been made redundant challenge the termination in court.

---

1. The Employment Grid is a statutorily required internal document, maintained by the employer, which outlines the positions – types and work places – in the enterprise and internal co-relations. It is developed by the managing body(ies) of the employer within the framework of the commercial laws.

2   MAJOR LEGAL REGULATIONS

2.1   TIMING

2.1.1   Notice Period (Article 328, paragraph 1 in relation to Article 326, paragraph 2 of the LC)

When it comes to redundancy, the concept of the LC is that such termination of employment always occurs upon prior notice and after expiry of the notice period.

The regular notice period under the LC is thirty days; the notice period under fixed-term employment contracts is three months but may not exceed the remaining term of the contract.

The thirty days statutory notice period may be contractually extended in the individual employment contract to up to three months. Contractual extension to the term of the notice period may also be agreed upon in the Collective Labour Agreement[2] for the employees of an enterprise, or nation-wide for a certain industry. Such agreements apply *ex lege* to the individual employment contracts of the individual employees – members of the trade union or those who have explicitly indicated in writing their will to accede to the Collective Labour Agreement.

As a matter of legal principle, the LC does not define the length of the notice period by reference to the length of service of the respective employee. Thus, in the absence of additional contractual extensions, an employee with less that one year's length of service and an employee with twenty years length of service will be subject to the same thirty day statutory notice period.

From a procedural perspective, any notice of termination must be given in writing individually to the employee(s) concerned; it should be signed by the statutory representative(s) of the employer or other persons explicitly authorized to this effect.[3] The employee should counter-sign the notice in recognition of its receipt.

The notice period starts running from the day following the day on which the termination notice has been received by the employee.

---

2. Collective Labour Agreements between trade unions and employers' representatives in certain industries (for example: mining, metallurgy, and the like) can be negotiated and signed on a national basis, covering all employees who are members of the respective trade union and irrespective of the position of the individual employer. The existence of such nation-wide Collective Labour Agreements do not preclude the ability of the employees in a specific enterprise, represented by their trade union, to enter into an additional enterprise-related Collective Labour Agreement with their respective employers.
3. Statutory representatives of companies in Bulgaria are defined by the Commercial Act. These individuals by law represent and bind a company vis-à-vis third parties, both internally (vis-à-vis employees) and externally. Delegation of authority as regards employment relations is possible by means of corporate law procedures, dependant on the type of company.

2.1.2   Collective Redundancies

In 2006, amendments to the Bulgarian legislation were introduced to reflect the provisions of EU Directive 98/59 on the Approximation of the Laws of the Member States Relating to Collective Redundancies (Directive 98/59). Currently, the Bulgarian statutory definition of collective redundancies matches the legal definition as per Directive 98/59 (§ 1, item 9 of the Additional Provisions of the LC).

A strict procedure as outlined in the LC and the Promotion of Employment Act applies in the case where a redundancy scheme meets the definition of a collective redundancy. It involves (as major steps):

- Provision of formal information in writing by the employer to the employees' representatives and trade unions at the enterprise: Such information should include details of the reasons for the mass lay-off, the scope of its application and the starting date for the redundancies.
- Commencement of consultations between the employer and employee representatives and trade unions at least forty-five days prior to the dismissal starting date (Article 130a, paragraph 1 of the LC): The purpose of these consultations is to determine whether it is possible to avoid, or to reduce the scope of, the redundancies, and/or to reach an agreement on mitigation of the negative impact on employees.
- Filing formal notification by the employer with the Employment Agency[4] at least thirty days prior to the dismissal starting date: The notification must be accompanied by detailed information on the reasons for the collective redundancies, the number of employees to be affected, individual positions and qualifications per employee, the time schedule for performance of the collective redundancies and any selection process that will be used. A copy of the notification package must be delivered to employee representatives and trade unions at the enterprise not later than three days after the package has been filed with the Employment Agency.
- Formation of teams composed by representatives of the employer, the employees and the Employment Agency: The purpose of the teams is to develop measures for post-redundancy education, qualification and re-qualification, identification of vacant job positions and possibilities for the commencement of independent economic activity.

The start date for redundancies cannot be earlier than thirty days after notification to the Employment Agency has been filed.

Most of the requirements related to mass lay-off procedures are not focused on a specific pre-determined result but aim primarily to establish an environment of clear, transparent and publicly accessible rules within which the redundancies will be carried out. Employers are obliged to demonstrate good will, cooperativeness, and readiness to mitigate or minimize the negative impact of the redundancy

---

4. The Bulgarian Employment Agency is a state institution with units throughout the country.

process, while recognizing the inevitability of negative effects on employees as a result of the objective changes in the business and economic environment.

2.2   INFORMATION AND CONSULTATION

2.2.1   Collective Redundancies

See above in section 2.1.2.

2.2.2   Works Councils, Employees' Representatives

Trade unions traditionally play the role of employees' representatives vis-à-vis the employer. The right of employees to form trade union organizations is protected by the Bulgarian Constitution. Trade unions represent the traditional organizational instrument engaged by employees to protect their interests and raise claims before the employer (e.g., demand the execution of or changes to the Collective Bargaining Agreement at the enterprise). In their actions, trade unions represent the respective membership group at an enterprise. There are no restrictions on more than one trade union organization being set up at an enterprise.

Another form of employee representation that does not yet enjoy vast popularity in practice is representation via specifically elected employee representatives. The election takes place at the general assembly of employees at the specific enterprise. In their actions, employee representatives represent the work force as a group (i.e., all employees).

Both the trade unions and the employee representatives are not assigned specific functions in the case of individual dismissals but need to be consulted and informed in the legally prescribed manner when collective redundancies are to be implemented (see above in section 2.1.2) or whenever material changes in the employer's business and/or employment policy are planned.

2.3   RISKS

2.3.1   Selection Criteria (Article 329 of the LC)

The right of selection in the case of redundancy provides the employer with the ability to perform an assessment of its employees and to retain the more qualified and genuinely better performing employees by dismissing the less qualified/worse performers, even in the case where their positions, as per the Employment Grid, are not directly affected by the redundancy scheme.

Following the amendments to the LC in 2001, professional qualities and professional performance by employees have been entrenched by law as the sole criteria to be applied by the employer in the selection process. The so-called 'social criteria'[5] have been repealed; selection based on (but not limited to) gender, religion, nationality – criteria which are or may be deemed to represent direct or indirect discrimination – is also illegal.

The law sets forward the right of selection as the employer's right, not as an obligation. Therefore, the evaluation of employees is usually not an obligatory stage in the redundancy process. Its applicability depends on the specific type of business, the particular employer and the overall structure of the workforce at the enterprise. The right of selection becomes an obligatory stage in the redundancy process, however, in industrial sectors or businesses where a large number of working positions exist within the same or a similar group of work functions, and not all employees from the group are subject to the redundancy (e.g., staff reduction in the position of truck-driver in a cement production enterprise where ten out of twenty drivers are dismissed).

Employers need to pay attention to the procedural and material aspects of implementation of the assessment process when they invoke the right of selection in a redundancy scheme. Existing evaluation processes[6] in which employees have regularly been subject to evaluations and the results have been documented and maintained in the employees' personal files are a stepping stone to facilitating the process. In the absence of such practice (as is often the situation in large Bulgarian enterprises), the exercise of the employer's right of selection within a redundancy scheme should be looked at as a project in itself. Clear, adequate and objective criteria should be introduced for assessment. The entire process from start to finish should be detailed and transparent to the employees. Typically, ad hoc assessment committees or commissions are established to guarantee impartiality, transparency and objectivity in the process. Finally, the results of the assessment should be well documented by the employer.

All of the foregoing is of crucial importance should any of the dismissed employees challenge the dismissal in court. A large body of precedent has been accumulated over the years with respect to the practical implementation of the employer's right of selection, its scope, procedure and the documentation involved in the process.

2.3.2   Notice Restrictions (Article 333 of the LC)

Without prejudice to the availability of the right of selection as outlined above, certain categories of employees enjoy specific protection under Bulgarian law, and additional processes must be carried out prior to their dismissal in a redundancy scheme.

---

5. Considerations related to the individual's social, marital, or other status.
6. The introduction and performance of regular evaluations of employees is not a statutory requirement under Bulgarian law.

The statutory protection of specific categories of employees applies in the case of redundancy due to:

(a) partial closure of the employer's enterprise;
(b) staff reduction based on changes in the Employment Grid; or
(c) a decrease in the volume of work.

The following categories of employees are subject to specific protection in such cases:

(1) mothers of children younger than three years of age;
(2) spouses of men who have started their mandatory military service;
(3) employees who have previously been reassigned work within the enterprise due to medical reasons;
(4) employees who suffer from certain diseases;
(5) employees who have commenced a period of approved leave;
(6) nominated representatives of workers pursuant to the applicable procedures per the LC; and
(7) employees who act as members of negotiation bodies with European Work Councils or representative bodies with a European commercial or cooperative company – during the period of their mandate.

Redundancies that concern an employee who falls into any of these categories are permissible with the prior approval of the Bulgarian Labour Directorate.[7] Additionally, the dismissal of employees who suffer from certain diseases can only be implemented after receipt of an expert opinion by a specialized labour medical commission.

The approval/non-approval of the Labour Directorate is to a great extent a discretionary decision, based on the Labour Directorate's sole judgement on a case-by-case basis.

The annual report of the Labour Directorate for 2005 shows that out of a total of 757 requests, 360 redundancy pre-approvals were given.

The dismissal of employees who act as trade union representatives must have the prior approval of the central management of the respective trade union organization. This protection continues for a period of six months after the expiry of their mandate or release from the position.

Another two categories of employees, pregnant women and employees on maternity leave, are, by law, outside the scope of the application of redundancy schemes in the circumstances set out at the beginning of this section. These employees can only be subjected to redundancy in the case of a complete closure of the employer's enterprise.

It is important to note that the applicability of employee protection is determined on an individual basis at the moment the notice of termination of the employment contract is served on the employee.

---

7. The Bulgarian Central Labour Inspecorate is a state institution with structural units throughout the country.

2.3.3   Protection against Unfair Dismissal

The Bulgarian legislation is very stringent in its requirements related to redundancy implementation. The historical protection of employees in the environment of a state economy accounts for the general pro-employee bias in the interpretation of the law by the Bulgarian courts.

If an employee is successful in challenging a redundancy, this could result in a declaration that the dismissal is illegal. This, in turn, implies mandatory reinstatement of the employee by virtue of a court order and/or payment of compensation as indicated above. Often such developments in court are based solely on formal or procedural violations of the legislation, without evaluation of the economic substance of the case (e.g., the termination documentation is not signed by the statutory, or duly authorized, representative of the employer or the selection criteria are not specifically listed in the redundancy documentation). The court may invalidate the dismissal should it conclude, in its sole discretion, that the redundancy is not justifiable from a factual perspective (e.g., redundancy based on staff reduction would be declared illegal, should it be proven to the court that the employer has formally removed the specific position from its Employment Grid but has vested the same functions into a differently labelled new position).

Thus, the implementation of redundancy schemes is difficult and heavily procedural.

2.3.4   Wrongful Dismissal

Should the redundancy result in termination of the employment contract prior to the expiration of the notice period, the severance pay to the employee must include additional monetary compensation, pro-rated to the reminder of the notice period (Article 220, paragraph 2 of the LC).

2.3.5   Discrimination

Redundancies based on gender, race, nationality, ethnicity, citizenship, origin, religion or faith, education, personal or public position, disabilities, political belief, age, sexual orientation, family status, property status, or other irrelevant factors as may be proclaimed by law or any international treaty to which Bulgaria is a party are explicitly prohibited by the Protection from Discrimination Act.

2.4   Costs

2.4.1   Compensation

The minimum severance pay in the case of redundancy amounts to the one-month gross employment salary under the individual employment contract (Article 222 of the LC). Collective bargaining agreements and/or individual employment contracts may stipulate higher severance pay in the case of redundancy for the respective industry/enterprise/employee. The employee is also entitled to receive monetary compensation for any unused paid annual leave, whether related to the current year or to prior periods.

2.4.2 Damages Unfair Dismissal

The importance of compliance with procedures related to redundancy is most apparent when the monetary consequences of dismissals proclaimed illegal by a court are examined; in such cases, the employee can claim full gross salary severance payment for the entire period that he/she has been unemployed, up to six months (Article 225, paragraph 1 of the LC). Furthermore, if the individual has been employed following a dismissal that has been found illegal by a court, but such employment has involved a lower salary, the individual is entitled to receive the difference in salary for up to a six-month period after his/her dismissal.

3 ADVICE FOR LEGAL PRACTICE

3.1 TIMING

Timely planning and proper implementation of the various notification, consultation and negotiation procedures as well as pro-active and prompt communication with the Employment Agency are essential for the valid initiation and completion of mass lay-offs. The importance of these should not be underestimated by employers.

3.2 INFORMATION AND CONSULTATION

As a matter of practical advice, redundancies should generally be performed in close cooperation between employer's management and HR/legal counsel.

3.3 RISKS

Timely advice must always be sought by employers at the earliest stage when redundancy, or work-force restructurings that are likely to cause redundancy, is contemplated. It is of crucial importance – in terms of time and costs – that the process is analyzed in-depth and mapped in advance, to ensure that the applicable redundancy procedures and – most importantly – the required underlying documentation are properly generated, agreed on, and implemented.

3.4   Costs

Due to the risks associated with the unilateral termination of the employment relationship, which in the worst case scenario may lead to the invalidation of the dismissal, reinstatement of the employee to his/her former position and related severance payments, employers often prefer to achieve a termination of employment by mutual consent. As a result of its contractual nature, i.e., both parties act under the legal presumption of understanding and accepting the consequences of their legal acts, the implementation of this option leaves little scope for successful challenge.

Under the LC, termination by mutual consent is possible also in cases where a severance payment of a minimum of four times the employee's gross monthly salary is paid by the employer.

Although it is usually associated with severance pay to the employee, the termination of the employment relationhip by of mutual consent often saves the employer time and redundancy costs. Therefore, the mutual consent termination is often the preferred option from a risk management perspective.

CYPRUS

Dr Achilles C. Emilianides

1   OVERVIEW

1.1   EMPLOYMENT REGULATIONS IN GENERAL

In Cyprus, employer and employee rights and obligations are governed by statute, and, in the absence of appropriate statutory provisions, the rules and principles of contract law apply. Redundancy schemes such as the Termination of Employment Law no. 24/1967 (TEL), enacted pursuant to Recommendation 119/1963 of the International Labour Organization, are primarily governed by statute. The Collective Dismissals Law no. 28(I)/01 was adopted in 2001 in order to harmonize Cypriot legislation with the Collective Dismissals Directive 98/59/EC. Another instrument, the Industrial Relations Code (IRC) was negotiated and signed by the Government, employers and trade unions in 1977. While the IRC has undoubted practical importance, it is a purely voluntary agreement and is of non-binding legal effect. Adherence is dependent on the goodwill of the parties.

It should be noted that, in Cyprus, the terms of any collective employment relationship are not binding on the parties, and they must be incorporated into the specific individual employment relationship in order for the terms set out therein to apply. In the absence of a specific reference thereto, the terms of the individual employment relationship take precedence over those set out in the collective agreement. Collective employment relationships will only be binding on the parties concerned where the ownership of a business is transferred due to a merger or

©2008 Kluwer Law International B.V., The Netherlands.
Maarten van Kempen, Lisa Patmore, Michael Ryley, and
Robert von Steinau-Steinrück (eds), *Redundancy,* pp. 29-35.

to the legal transfer of ownership. In such cases, the transferee must abide by the collective employment relationship currently in force for one year following the transfer.

1.2   REDUNDANCY

Employees may only be made redundant on one of the grounds set out in section 16 of Law 24/1967, and the burden rests upon the employer to prove that the redundancy conforms with the statutory provisions. If the employer satisfies the burden of proof, the employee is entitled to compensation from the Redundancy Fund. Alternatively, if the dismissal is considered to be unfair, then the employer has to compensate his former employee for unfair dismissal. In any event, individual notice periods and procedural requirements must be followed.

2   MAJOR LEGAL REGULATIONS

2.1   TIMING

2.1.1   Periods of Notice

Before dismissing an employee, the employer is required by law (Article 9 TEL) to give a period of minimum notice. The length of this period depends on the length of time during which the employee was continuously employed by this employer:

– notice of one week is required for continuous employment of 26-51 weeks;
– notice of two weeks for continuous employment of 52-103 weeks;
– notice of four weeks for continuous employment of 104-155 weeks;
– notice of five weeks for continuous employment of 156-207 weeks;
– notice of six weeks for continuous employment of 208-259 weeks;
– notice of seven weeks for continuous employment of 260-311 weeks;
– notice of eight weeks for continuous employment over 312 weeks.

The minimum notice period is extended to thirty days in cases of collective dismissals (see section 2.2.2 below).

2.1.2   Notification to Ministry of Labour

An employer intending to dismiss employees is initially required to notify the Ministry of Labour and Social Security at least one month before the dismissals. The notification should include the number of employees affected, details of the departments in which the affected employees work, the specialization and the names of the employees affected as well as their family obligations, and the reasons for the dismissal. The Ministry may mediate with the employer to attempt an agreement for an alternative solution other than dismissal. If no such solution is found, the employer may proceed with the dismissals. These provisions apply to both individual and collective redundancies.

2.2   INFORMATION AND CONSULTATION

2.2.1   Individual Redundancy

The TEL does not require employers contemplating dismissals to consult with and provide information to employee representatives. However, the IRC requires that the employer notify the specific trade union involved at least two months before the date of the redundancy. Once the notification has taken place, there should be a process of consultation with the unions and the employees as soon as possible. It must be emphasized once again that no legal sanction may be imposed for failure to comply with the aforementioned provisions of the IRC.

2.2.2   Collective Dismissals

Collective Dismissals Law no. 28(I)/01(CDL) provides that an employer contemplating mass redundancies within the meaning of Article 2 of CDL must inform and consult employee representatives in good time; the purposes of the consultation being to come to an agreement on avoiding or limiting the dismissals and to mitigate the effect on the employees affected. The employer must provide the employees' representatives with all available information. If no alternative agreement is reached, then the redundancies proceed as per the notice. Mass redundancies within the meaning of Article 2 of CDL are defined as dismissals of:

- at least ten employees, for employers who employ more than twenty but fewer than 100 employees;
- at least 10% of the number of employees, for employers who employ more than 100, but less than 300 employees; or
- at least thirty employees, for employers who employ more than 300 employees.

2.3   RISKS

2.3.1   Legal Requirements of Redundancy

Redundancies are only justified if based on at least one of the grounds for dismissal set out in TEL. A dismissed employee is entitled to receive payment from the Redundancy Fund if that employee:

(a) was dismissed on one of the grounds for dismissal set out in TEL;
(b) has been employed by the same employer for a continuous period of at least 104 weeks before termination; and
(c) has not reached the age of retirement before the date of termination.

The grounds for dismissal are the following:

- The employer has ceased, or intends to cease, operation of the business where the employee is employed. This provision applies when the employer is subject to bankruptcy or similar proceedings and the business is part of the property which is subject to bankruptcy. It also applies where the employer ceases to operate the business and is not transferring ownership of the business. It does not apply, however, where the employer has ceased, or intends to cease, to operate the business, due to a transfer of the business in its entirety or in part.
- The employer has ceased, or intends to cease, to operate the business at the location where the employee is employed. The Industrial Disputes Court has judicial discretion to decide in what circumstances it is reasonable for the employee to continue to be employed, despite the change in the location of the employment. The decision whether continuation of employment would be reasonable should take into account the personal circumstances of the employee, the costs and risks involved and the degree of the change of location. If the location of business changes substantially, the court will normally accept that there is a justified ground for dismissal.
- Modernization, mechanization, or any other change in the method of production or organization that necessitates a reduction in the number of employees or a change in the products, the method of production or the expertise required by the employees. The employers have the discretion to choose the methods of production or organization that would lead to a better overall efficiency for their business, so long as the change of method is substantive and has become necessary due to technological, market or other similar developments. Such a change of method is justified grounds for dismissal, so long as it relates to the proper functioning of the business, and it also objectively necessitates a reduction in the number of employees. The desire of the employer to hire new employees (possibly younger or with lower pay) in place of the existing employees does not amount to a change in the method of production or organization and does not justify dismissal. Similarly, the dismissal of an employee in order to transfer his responsibilities to another existing employee does not amount to a change of organization and does not constitute justified grounds for dismissal.
- The disbanding of a specific department (but not of a specific position), so long as the department in question is not being transferred to another legal entity as a result of a merger or of a legal transfer. The disbanding of a department due to a change of organization, or because the business has changed the ambit of its activities, would be considered to be justified grounds for dismissal.
- Reduction in the turnover of the business, difficulties in placing products in the market, credit difficulties, lack of orders or lack of raw materials. It should be noted, however, that an employee may only be made redundant

due to a permanent and not a temporary reduction in the turnover of the business; thus it must be a situation where the end of this state of affairs cannot be foreseen. A temporary drop in the turnover in a seasonal business, or one due to a temporary recess in the activities of the business, is not justified grounds for dismissal. It should be noted further that the fact that there are losses, or that the employer had set higher aims for his business with respect to profits or turnover, or that the employee is on a high salary, do not constitute a drop in turnover and are not justified grounds for dismissal. Similarly, a drop in the volume of work done by the employee, as opposed to a drop in business, does not constitute justified grounds for dismissal.

Employees may only be made redundant based on the above grounds. Dismissals not made on these grounds may be considered to be unfair, and the employer may be liable to compensate the employee financially.

2.3.2 Selection Criteria

Before resorting to making employees redundant, the employer should consider other less drastic solutions. If dismissals are unavoidable, however, these should be made on a last in, first out basis, with the longest serving employees being dismissed last. This principle may not apply where the business is being modernized, where there is any other change in the method of production or organization or if the oldest serving employees do not have the necessary qualifications or cannot adapt to the changes. Similarly, the aforementioned principle may not apply when there are other considerations, such as health problems, financial or personal issues or limited possibilities for relocation. Where the employer wishes to hire new employees of the same specialization within a period of eight months after a dismissal, he has the obligation to give priority to his former employees.

2.3.3 Notice Restrictions

Where an employee notifies the employer of a pregnancy or of an approved adoption, that employee may not be made redundant at any time prior to the end of three months after returning from maternity leave. The employer may, however, dismiss a pregnant employee if she is guilty of serious misconduct, if the business has ceased to function or if the contract of employment has expired.

2.3.4 Wrongful Dismissal

Notice must always be given in writing. Should an employer fail to give the required notice, the employee shall be entitled to receive payment in lieu of notice. The employer may choose to pay the employee in lieu of the notice period, in which case the employee is required to accept the payment.

2.3.5   **Application to the Redundancy Fund and Action
                    in the Industrial Disputes Court**

Upon dismissal, the employee may apply for compensation from the Redundancy
Fund. The Redundancy Fund is a public law legal entity established by the
Council of Ministers, and is funded by contributions from employers. The
employer must complete an application form, setting out his reasons for terminating the employment. If the Fund accepts that the employer had grounds
to dismiss the employee, he will be recognized as being redundant. If, however,
the application is rejected, the employee may file an action in the Industrial
Disputes Court claiming compensation from the Fund and also from the former
employer for unfair dismissal. If the Industrial Disputes Court decides that there
were no grounds for dismissal, the employer has to pay compensation to the
former employee.

The onus is on the employer to prove, on the balance of probabilities, that he
had legal grounds to dismiss the employee; if he discharges his burden, the
employee is entitled to receive compensation from the Redundancy Fund. If,
however, he fails to discharge this burden, he will have to compensate the employee for unfair dismissal. It should be noted, however, that the employee may be
compensated either by the Fund or by the employer, but not by both. Should the
Industrial Disputes Court come to the conclusion that the dismissal was orches-
trated by the employer and the employee in connivance against the Redundancy
Fund, the employee might lose his right to receive any compensation at all. The
hiring of replacement employees by the employer is not in itself evidence of the
fact that there were no legal grounds for dismissal.

In the following circumstances, the employee might not be entitled to receive
compensation from the Redundancy Fund:

- The employer offered an alternative suitable position or location of employment to the employee before the termination of the employment contract
  and the employee unreasonably rejected the offer. In this context, suitable
  means that the terms of employment, the salary and other benefits should be
  similar to those of the previous employment contract. Similarly, whether or
  not the employee's rejection was unreasonable is a subjective question and
  depends on his personal circumstances.
- The employment contract was terminated due to a change of employers and
  was immediately renewed by the new employer. The employee will be
  entitled to receive compensation from the Redundancy Fund in situations
  in which he satisfies the Industrial Disputes Court that he has reasonable
  grounds for not accepting the new employer's offer of employment.
- The employer is a company, and the employee is transferred to another
  affiliated company that is either a parent company or a subsidiary, or both
  belong to the same group of companies.

2.3.6 Unfair Dismissal

The court will not only examine whether the dismissal was legally justified, but also whether it was made in good faith. Thus, the court may examine whether the employer reasonably examined other options, and whether the dismissal was indeed the last resort. Although the court will usually be satisfied should the employer convince it that there were legal grounds for the dismissal, a finding of bad faith on the part of the employer might lead them to the opposite conclusion.

2.4 COMPENSATION

The amount paid in compensation depends primarily on the length of employment. An employee is entitled to two weeks' salary in respect of each year of the first four years of continuous employment, to two-and-a-half weeks' salary for each year between the fifth and the tenth year of continuous employment, to three weeks' salary for each year between the eleventh and the fifteenth year of continuous employment, to three-and-a-half weeks' salary for each year between the sixteenth and the twentieth year of continuous employment, and to four weeks' salary for each year between the twenty-first and the twenty-fifth year of continuous employment of the employee. If any remaining period of continuous employment does not amount to fifty-two weeks, then a remaining period of twenty-six or more weeks shall amount to one full year of continuous employment for the purposes of awarding compensation. Any agreement between an employer and an employee to the effect that the latter will not claim any redundancy payment in return for any benefit provided by the employer is void and has no legal effect. The amount of compensation awarded by the Fund equals the amount of compensation that would have been awarded by the employer. The maximum amount of compensation that may be awarded by the Fund for termination of employment due to redundancy amounts to 24.50 British pounds sterling (GBP).

3 ADVICE FOR LEGAL PRACTICE

Redundancy schemes operate on the basis that the employer had legal grounds for making the employee redundant. Should this not be the case, the Industrial Disputes Court will rule that the dismissal was unfair, and the employer will be ordered to compensate his former employee. Redundancy schemes should always function based on the aforementioned procedural requirements, namely the minimum notice period requirements and the notification to the Ministry of Labour. Employers should also be able to prove to the Court that they acted in good faith and that they did consider less drastic options before taking the decision to dismiss the employee concerned.

CZECH REPUBLIC

Tereza Kadlecová
Eva Svobodová

1   OVERVIEW

In the Czech Republic the following statutes regulate the legal relationship between the employer and employee:

- Act No. 262/2006 Coll., the Labour Code, as amended (Labour Code);
- Act No. 435/2004 Coll., on employment, as amended (Employment Act); and
- Act No. 251/2005 Coll., on inspection of work, as amended (Inspection of Work Act).

The basic premise as set out in the Labour Code is that 'what is not expressly forbidden is permitted', so parties to an employment contract have a significant amount of freedom in their negotiations as to the contents of the contract. There are mandatory provisions however, and these regulate matters such as the termination of employment and collective redundancies.

Section 52 of the Labour Code specifies the grounds for the dismissal of an employee:

- The employer ceases to exist as such.
- The employer relocates.
- The employee becomes redundant as a result of a decision of the employer.
- The employee cannot fulfill his duties due to health problems.

  – The employee does not meet the requirements prescribed by legal regulations
    or does not meet the requirements for the proper performance of such work.
  – The employee breaches his/her obligations arising from legal regulations.

The first three grounds are known as the 'organizational grounds', and they are
the grounds on which employers usually rely when dismissing an employee. The
following are examples of dismissals on organizational grounds: redundancies
brought about by the employer's decision to change the direction in which the
business is heading, to upgrade technical equipment, to increase efficiency by
reducing his workforce or to affect any other organizational change.

  The employer has the duty to notify the trade union in advance of giving an
employee a notice of termination or before terminating an employment relationship (section 61 of the Labour Code), and in the event of a collective dismissal he
has to inform the trade union or the works council (section 62 of the Labour Code).

2   MAIN REQUIREMENTS AND CONSIDERATIONS

2.1   TIMING

2.1.1   Notice Periods

Employers are required, under section 51 of the Labour Code, to give a minimum
of two months notice to employees before making them redundant. The period
begins to run on the first day of the calendar month after the giving of the notice.

  The notice must be in writing, and special delivery requirements apply; it must
be given by the employer directly to the employee. If it is not duly delivered, or if
the notice does not contain the essentials stipulated by the Labour Code, the
employee may challenge the validity of the notice.

  The employment contract may set out a longer notice period by agreement
between the parties. If this is the case, the same period applies whether the employer
is dismissing the employee or the employee is submitting his resignation.

2.1.2   Collective Redundancies

Collective redundancies are governed by section 62 of the Labour Code. A collective
redundancy is defined as 'the termination of employment relationships for organizational reasons'. Section 52(a)-(c) defines the term 'organizational reasons' as:

  (a) the insolvency of the employing company or part of it;
  (b) the relocation of the employing company or part of it; or
  (c) a change in the employing company's entrepreneurial goals or technical
      equipment, a reduction in the number of employees in order to increase
      efficiency or to affect any other organizational change.

Grounds (a) to (c) constitute what are known as the 'Organizational Reasons'.

The rules on collective redundancies apply when the number of dismissals in a period of thirty days exceeds a specified threshold:

– ten employees, if the company employs 20-100 employees;
– 10% of employees, if the employer employs 101-300 employees; or
– thirty employees, if the employer employs more than 300 employees.

In considering whether the threshold has been met, any redundancy within a thirty day period in which there have already been five other redundancies being affected for organizational reasons will be taken into account if it is taking place as a result of an agreement between employer and employee.

Every employee being dismissed in a collective redundancy must be told of the employer's intention to institute these dismissals at least thirty calendar days before the actual notice is served.

2.2   INFORMATION AND CONSULTATION

The employer must provide every employee with information concerning labour relations and must ensure that employees are consulted about such information (section 13 (1) let. d of the Labour Code). The employer also has to notify the trade union before issuing a notice of termination or before terminating an employment with immediate effect (section 61 of the Labour Code). In the event of its having to affect collective dismissals, the employer has to report the matter to the trade union or the works council (section 62 of the Labour Code).

2.2.1   Collective Consultation

Where the employer proposes to affect collective redundancies, and the employer is a member of a recognised trade union or works council, it must inform and consult the representatives of the trade union or works council. Under the Czech Labour Code, employees may be represented either by a works council or by a trade union but not by both. A trade union is a legal entity consisting of at least three employees, and it has the legal capability to enter into collective agreements on behalf of the employees. Works councils do not have a legal personality, and they only serve as a channel of communication and mediation between the employer and its employees. They do not have control rights over their members as a trade union does. If there is no works council or trade union, then the employer must inform and consult all of the affected employees instead.

The employer must notify the representatives of the affected employees, or, if there are no such representatives, the affected employees themselves, in writing, of its intention to affect collective redundancies at least thirty days before a notice of termination is served on the employees.

At a minimum, the notice must contain the following information:

– confirmation of the proposal to collectively dismiss certain employees;
– the reasons for the proposals;

- the number and occupational groups of employees whom it is proposed to dismiss;
- the total number of employees employed by the employer who fall within the affected occupational groups;
- the timescale of the proposed redundancies;
- the proposed method of selecting the employees who may be dismissed; and
- the proposed severance payment to be paid to the redundant employees.

The employer must also serve a similar notice on the Labour Authority, and in addition to the information contained in the notice to the employees, it must set out the details of when the information and consultation process with the representatives began or will begin (section 62 (4) of the Labour Code). A copy of this notice must also be given to the employees' representatives.

At the same time the employer should commence a consultation process with the representatives, during which they should discuss possible ways of avoiding or reducing the number of redundancies or at least of mitigating the detrimental consequences of the collective redundancies. This will involve the parties looking at the possibility of redeploying employees into alternative roles or of moving their place of employment to different locations.

The Labour Code only requires that the consultation process be carried out with a view of reaching agreement. There is no duty to actually come to an agreement.

On completion of the consultation process, the employer must deliver a written report to the Labour Authority comprising:

- its decision to affect collective redundancies;
- the result of the consultation with the representatives;
- information as to the total number of employees employed by him; and
- the number and occupational groups of the employees affected by the collective redundancies.

A copy of this notice must be made available to the employees' representatives (section 62(5) of the Labour Code). The employer is also obliged to inform the affected employees that the required notice has been given to the Labour Authority.

The employment of those workers who are to be made redundant may not come to an end before the end of thirty days after the delivery of the notification to the Labour Authority. This is the case unless the employee confirms that he has no objection to having his employment terminated before the expiry of the required thirty days.

Where the employees have no representatives, all of the aforementioned processes are carried out directly with the employees.

2.3   Risks

The grounds on which a Czech employer may terminate an employee's employment contract are very limited. See section 52 of the Labour Code (discussed above).

2.3.1 Protected Categories of Employees

The Labour Code provides certain specific groups of employees with protection against dismissal, and in most circumstances the employer may not dismiss an employee who is:

- temporarily unable to work due to illness or injury;
- due to exercise a public office and therefore fully released from his/her job;
- pregnant, on maternity leave, or on parental leave; or
- contracted to work the night shift but temporarily unable to work such a shift.

An exception to the above is where the employer, or the department in which the employee works, is due to close down or to relocate.

2.3.2 Selection Criteria

The courts have held that the employer has the right to choose which of his employees to make redundant. This right may be restricted by collective agreement. Evidently, the laws against discrimination all apply, and the employer may not select employees on grounds that might be considered to be discriminatory.

2.3.3 Unlawful Dismissal

Where an invalid notice of dismissal is served on an employee, or where his employment is terminated without the required notice having been served, the employee may notify the employer in writing that he wants to be reinstated. When this happens, and the employee has requested reinstatement without undue delay, the employment relationship continues. In these circumstances, the employee may claim compensatory wages from the date that the employer was notified of his desire to be reinstated until the earlier of the date the employer starts to assign work to the employee or the date when the employee's employment is validly terminated.

If the employee does not inform the employer, in writing, without undue delay, that he wants to be reinstated, the employment is validly terminated at the end of notice period. Where the employment was terminated immediately and with no notice, the employment will have ended on the date that the employment was terminated, but the employee will be entitled to his average monthly earnings for what would have been the notice period.

Either the employer or the employee may ask the courts to determine whether the termination was valid, provided that the application to the court is made no later than two months from the date of termination.

2.3.4 Discrimination

The employer must treat all employees equally, and the discrimination laws are fully applicable.

2.4   Costs

2.4.1   Severance Payments

If an employee's employment is terminated for organizational reasons, the employee is entitled to severance pay amounting to at least three times his average monthly earnings, calculated on the basis of rules set out in the Labour Code. The severance payment must be paid by the employer to the employee on the next pay day following the termination of the employment relationship.

If the employee's employment is terminated by mutual consent for organizational reasons, the employee is also entitled to a severance payment, as set out in the preceding paragraph.

2.4.2   Damages

The employer is liable to his employee for damages caused to him in the performance of his normal work as a result of the employer's breach of a statutory duty or as a result of the employer's intentional conduct against good morals.

2.4.3   Administrative Offence (Sections 21 et seq. of the Act on Inspection of Work)

The employer commits an administrative offence and may be fined if found to be in breach of the following:

- provisions of labour law (sections 62, 277, 279, 280, 287 of the Labour Code) regarding cooperation with the trade union or works council (fine up to 200,000 Czech korunas (CZK); c. EUR 7,150);
- provisions of the Labour Code regarding termination of the employment relationship (fine up to CZK 300,000; c. EUR 10,700); or
- the principle of equal treatment (fine up to CZK 400,000; c. EUR 14,300).

In such cases the Work Inspectorate may impose on the employer fines in the amounts set out above.

If the documents have not been properly prepared or delivered to the trade union, works council or the affected employees, as appropriate, or where there has been a procedural breach, high cost penalties may be imposed on the employer, and he may be banned from making any dismissals for a specified period of time.

3   PRACTICAL ADVICE

The following may also occur if there is found to be a failure in the employer's compliance with the requisite procedures.

- The employment may be held to have been invalidly terminated.
- The employer may face a possible claim for damages.

- The employer may be fined by the state.
- The employer's reputation and goodwill may be harmed.
- Employees may lose confidence in the employer.

The employer should also ensure that:

- There are valid grounds for dismissal.
- The decision to affect organizational changes is made before serving notice.
- The grounds for termination are clearly set out in the notice.
- The notice is delivered to the employee, ideally in person in the presence of witnesses.

DENMARK

Ewa Ljung Rasmussen

1   OVERVIEW

In Denmark, employment law is divided into collective employment law (regulating collective agreements) and individual employment law (the rules surrounding an individual's employment contract).

Danish employees are divided into two categories: workers and salaried employees. The Salaried Employees Act (*Funktionærloven*) regulates the content of employment contracts, and contains rules of employment for salaried employees regarding termination of employment, severance pay and protection against unfair dismissal. Blue-collar workers, on the other hand, have no statutes stipulating the general content of their employment contracts or standard working conditions, save for a few categories of workers such as agricultural and domestic workers and seafarers. Unless a collective agreement or specific statutes cover the worker, the parties are free to decide the content of the employment contract. Moreover, for blue-collar workers, there are no general legal requirements regarding termination of the employment contract.

In the context of redundancy, the most important statutes are the Collective Dismissals Act (*Lov om kollektive afskedigelser*) and the Information and Consultation Act (*Informations og Samrådsloven*). These statutes contain certain consultation and information requirements that come into play upon undertaking redundancies. There are also a number of generally applicable statutes that may render a dismissal unlawful if they are made for a particular reason, such as the Act

©2008 Kluwer Law International B.V., The Netherlands.
Maarten van Kempen, Lisa Patmore, Michael Ryley, and
Robert von Steinau-Steinrück (eds), *Redundancy*, pp. 45-53.

on Equal Treatment for Men and Women in the Labour Market (*Ligebehandling-sloven*). Moreover, contravention of such generally applicable statutes can result in an obligation to pay compensation to the dismissed employee.

Finally, when making salaried employees redundant, the employer must take into consideration the rules relating to notice periods and compensation payments in cases of unfair dismissals, and to mandatory redundancy payments as set forth in the Salaried Employees Act.

2   MAJOR LEGAL REGULATIONS

2.1   TIMING

2.1.1   Periods of Notice

2.1.1.1   Salaried Employees

When terminating a non-fixed term employment contract, notice must be given in accordance with section 2 of the Salaried Employees Act. Only in the event of a material breach by one of the parties can the contract be terminated without notice.

During the first six months of employment, a salaried employee is entitled to one month's notice expiring at the end of the calendar month in which notice is given. After six months' service the notice period is extended to three months for every three years of employment, up to a maximum of six months for nine years of service. From an employer's point of view, it is important that notice of termination be given before the start of the next three-year cycle.

During an agreed-upon probationary period of not more than three months, only fourteen days' notice must be given.

These notice periods may be extended by the individual employment contract or collective agreement.

2.1.1.2   Workers

With regard to workers, most collective agreements contain rules specifying the amount of notice that must be given. The specific rules regarding notice vary, depending on the collective agreement in question, but usually a worker with one year's service is entitled to notice of fourteen to twenty-one days, depending on length of service and the age of the worker. Collective agreements usually provide for longer notice periods for shop and safety stewards.

However, unless there is a collective agreement or an individual employment contract stipulating a certain period of notice, the worker is, in principle, not entitled to any notice whatsoever. Nevertheless, case law suggests that workers should be given the right to reasonable notice.

2.1.2 **Timelines for Notification, Information, Consultation and Negotiation**

2.1.2.1 *Individual Redundancy*

In the event of an individual being made redundant, there are no specific legal requirements for the employer to inform or consult with the works council or union representatives. The only requirement is that the applicable notice period must be given. But if a relevant collective agreement so provides, an employer may be under duty to inform and consult with the council or union.

While there is no specific duty in connection with redundancies, it should be noted that there is a general obligation in the Information and Consultation Act of 2005 for companies with thirty-five employees or more to inform and consult their employees through their representatives regarding conditions that are important to their employment. The extent of the obligation, especially with regard to the question of whether the Act confers individual rights upon the employees, remains to be decided by the courts.

2.1.2.2 *Collective Redundancy*

In case of collective redundancy, there is a duty to inform and consult contained in the Collective Dismissals Act. The provisions of this Act apply when:

- companies employing 20-99 employees plan to make at least ten employees redundant within thirty days;
- companies employing 100-299 workers plan to make at least 10% of the employees redundant within thirty days; or
- companies employing 300 or more workers plan to make at least thirty employees redundant within thirty days.

Where collective redundancies are announced, negotiations between the company and the employees (or their representatives) must take place as early as possible, with a view either to totally avoiding redundancies or to limiting them as much as possible.

The company must give written notice to the employees or their representatives containing all necessary information, which at a minimum sets out:

- the reasons for the redundancies;
- the number and occupation of employees affected;
- the number and occupational groups of employees employed by the company;
- the selection criteria for deciding who should be made redundant;
- information about any redundancy payments provided by individual or collective agreements; and
- the proposed time frame.

Such notice should be given in enough time for the information to be used as the basis for negotiations. Even though the Act does not stipulate a time frame in which notice must be given, it is clear that the information should be given within a reasonable amount of time before negotiations are due to take place. At the same time, a copy of the notice must be sent to the Labour Market Council (*Arbejdsmarkedsrådet*). This is the 'first notice' to the Council.

If the company, after negotiations with the employees or their representatives, chooses to go ahead with the proposed redundancies, it must notify the Labour Market Council, which may decide to take measures to assist the workers concerned. The Act does not stipulate when this 'second notice' should be sent, but in practice it is usually done shortly after the first meeting with the employees or their representatives. In the event that 50% of the employees in a company with more than 100 employees are to be affected by the redundancy, the notice may not be sent earlier than twenty-one days after the negotiations have been initiated, unless otherwise stipulated in a collective agreement. The employees are also entitled to receive a copy of this notice. Individual dismissal notices may be given only after the 'second notice' has been sent to the Labour Market Council.

None of the proposed redundancies can take effect until thirty days have elapsed after the 'second notice' (or eight weeks in cases where 50% of the employees in a company with more than 100 employees will be affected), unless otherwise agreed to in a collective agreement.

No later than ten days after the 'second notice' has been sent, the company must notify the Labour Market Council of the names of the affected employees. This constitutes 'third notice' to the Council. Again, the employees concerned must be notified at the same time.

The employer has an obligation to notify the Council as soon as possible with regard to the final result of the negotiations. This is the 'fourth notice' to the Council. In practice, this notice is often sent in connection with the 'third notice' mentioned above.

The rules of the Collective Dismissals Act may be superseded by a provision in the collective agreement, provided that the employee is given equal or better protection under such agreement. A collective agreement may also contain information and consultation requirements that apply to collective redundancy. If acting for an employee or group of employees, and in the event that there are only limited numbers of employees dismissed or redundancies are to be made over a long period of time, it is wise to ensure that such requirements are included when negotiating a collective agreement, as these are not provided by the Collective Dismissals Act.

2.2   INFORMATION AND CONSULTATION

2.2.1   Works Councils and European Works Councils

In Denmark, works councils (*Samarbejdsudvalg*) are not regulated by law. Workplace employee representation in the public sector is, however, regulated by the

Cooperation Agreement (*Samarbejdsaftalen*) and by the Danish Employers' Confederation (*Dansk Arbejdsgiverforening*, DA) and the Danish Confederation of Trade Unions (*Landsorganisationen i Danmark*, LO). Under the terms of the Co-operation Agreement, employees in public sector companies with more than thirty-five employees can request the right to form a works council.

The works council has the right to be informed and consulted as stipulated in the relevant agreement.

According to the Act on European Works Councils (*Lov om europæiske samarbejdsudvalg*), employees in a company with at least one thousand employees in the Member States of the EU and the EEA, or with at least 150 employees in a minimum of two Member States, can request permission to form a European Works Council.

It should be noted that employee representatives in the private sector are often regulated by the terms of collective agreements.

2.2.2 Collective Dismissals Act

The employer is under duty to consider the possibility of transferring employees to other positions in his company prior to making any redundancies.

If this is not a viable option, however, the criteria for the selection of employees to be made redundant must be objective. As a general rule, it is acceptable to consider a combination of factors, such as: length of service, age, qualifications, flexibility, absences due to illness, prior disciplinary warnings and the total cost of paying and retraining the employee in question, if retained.

Even if the criteria used are not objective, there are no special sanctions specified in the Collective Dismissals Act. Potentially, however, compensation may be awarded under other provisions of Danish law, if the selection criteria are unfair, or as a result of the provisions set out in an individual and/or collective agreement.

With regard to the right of the employees to participate in the actual redundancy process, it should be noted that the Act provides that the extent of such participation and input into the ultimate determination is limited. The employer is, however, obligated to initiate negotiations with the employees and to make an effort to continue the employment relationship where viable. Furthermore, the employees are entitled to put forward comments to the Labour Market Council in relation to the second and fourth notices mentioned above.

2.2.3 Information and Consultation Act

The aim of this piece of legislation is to establish a dialogue between the employer and the employees through the employee representatives. The employer can only refuse to provide information if the provision of that information would seriously harm the activities of the company. The Act does not apply if the employees already have a right to be informed and consulted under a collective agreement.

The provisions of the Information and Consultation Act are supplementary to the provisions of the Collective Dismissals Act.

2.3   COSTS AND RISKS

2.3.1   Periods of Notice and Redundancy Payment

2.3.1.1   Salaried Employees

A salaried employee has the right to receive full pay during the notice period. In addition, the employee has the right to receive a mandatory redundancy payment under section 2(a) of the Salaried Employees Act of one, two, or three months' salary, where he has been employed by the company for twelve, fifteen, or eighteen consecutive years respectively. The rule does not apply if the employee is entitled to a pension from the employer under a pension scheme that the employee entered into before he reached the age of fifty or a pension scheme through the National Pension Scheme.

There is no additional redundancy payment provided for in the Collective Dismissals Act.

There may be a provision that provides for increased redundancy payments in an individual employment contract or in a collective agreement.

2.3.1.2   Workers

A worker has the right to receive full pay during the notice period. In addition, the individual employment contract or collective agreement may stipulate that a worker is entitled to a certain redundancy payment. It is most likely that such an agreement will be in place in business sectors affected by industrial change. The Collective Dismissals Act does not make any provision for workers to receive redundancy payments.

There may be provisions entitling workers to increased redundancy payments in individual employment contracts.

2.3.2   Protection against Unfair Dismissal

2.3.2.1   Salaried Employees

According to section 2(b) of the Salaried Employees Act, if the employer fails to show reasonable grounds justifying the redundancy, the employer may be obliged to pay compensation to any employee who is made redundant after having been employed for a continuous period of at least one year. The amount of compensation depends upon the employee's length of service and age, along with other relevant circumstances, but cannot be more than half the employee's salary for his notice period.

If an employee is thirty years old or older when he is given his dismissal notice, he may be entitled to compensation amounting to three months' salary. An employee with ten years of service may be awarded compensation of up to a maximum of four months' salary, and an employee with fifteen years of service may be awarded a maximum of six months' salary.

Where salaried employees are unfairly dismissed, collective agreements may provide for increased compensation to be paid by employers.

2.3.2.2 Workers

Workers are not protected against unfair dismissal and do not have the right to compensation. However, in accordance with the Main Agreement (*Hovedaftalen*) entered into between the Danish Employers' Confederation and the Danish Confederation of Trade Unions, if an employee is dismissed without reasonable grounds, the dismissal can be overruled and the employee reinstated as well as awarded compensation. The amount of compensation is dependant upon the employee's length of service and other relevant facts of the case.

2.3.2.3 Transfer of Undertakings

If a company plans to make one or more employees redundant in connection with a transfer of undertaking, the transfer itself cannot, according to the Transfer of Undertakings Act, be regarded as reasonable grounds for termination. The Act applies both to salaried employees and workers.

2.3.3 Protected Employees

Many collective agreements include special restrictions concerning the dismissal of shop stewards. Shop stewards are normally entitled to a longer notice period, and their employment can only be terminated if absolutely necessary.

In accordance with the Information and Consultation Act, safety stewards, board level employee representatives and employee representatives enjoy the same protection as shop stewards.

According to the Act on Equal Treatment of Men and Women in the Labour Market, an employee who is pregnant or on maternity/paternity leave or who has asked for time off in connection with pregnancy or childbirth is entitled to compensation if made redundant. The defences that may be open to the employer are that the dismissal was for objective reasons and/or that the selection of the employee in question was made solely based on operational criteria. The burden of proof in these cases rests on the employer and is very difficult to prove.

The amount of compensation payable is established according to the employee's length of service and other relevant facts in the case. Case law demonstrates that compensation of six to twelve months' salary is often awarded. However, the Act does not set a limit on the amount of compensation. An employee may demand reinstatement, but this rarely happens.

2.3.4   Fines and Penalties

In the event that the employer fails to comply with the rules of the Information and Consultation Act and/or the Transfer of Undertakings Act, the employer may be fined.

In the event that the employer fails to comply with the rules regarding information and consultation under the Collective Dismissals Act, employees who have been made redundant may be entitled to compensation of up to thirty days' salary (section 11). Eight weeks' salary may be awarded as compensation in cases where 50% of the employees in a company with more than 100 employees are affected, unless otherwise agreed upon in a collective agreement. In this case, however, any salary paid during the notice period will be set off against the compensation.

In case of a breach of the Collective Dismissals Act, the employer may also be fined. However, recent case law suggests this is an unlikely outcome.

Further penalties and compensation may be stipulated in any relevant collective agreement.

3   ADVICE FOR LEGAL PRACTICE

3.1   Timing

Redundancy schemes should be prepared well in advance to ensure that the employer take measures to meet all deadlines, both statutory and non-statutory, and so that any delaying tactics from the employees or the employee representatives, and/or any other unforeseen obstacles to the redundancy procedure, can be avoided or mitigated.

It should be noted that negotiations cannot begin before the employer has provided the employees or the employee representatives with the information to which they are entitled in accordance with the Collective Dismissals Act.

The employer should also take into account any extended notice period to which protected employees may be entitled, or that are stipulated in the individual's employment contract.

3.2   Information and Consultation

If the outcome of the negotiations with the employees or the employee representatives is that the employer will carry on with the redundancy plan, the employer should draw up detailed minutes of all the meetings.

Individual notices of dismissal should be delivered personally to each of the affected employees. In the case of absent employees, the dismissal notice should be sent by registered mail, and the employer should request a proof of delivery note.

3.3   COSTS AND RISKS

There are no significant cost implications in the case of breach of the information and consultation procedures. However, there are non-financial risks to consider, such as damage to the company's reputation and the working relationship with the trade unions and the employees.

With regard to the selection process, the employer should carefully consider whether it is necessary to select any protected employees for redundancy, since there is a risk that considerable amounts in compensation would have to be paid to such employees if the dismissal is held to be unlawful.

ESTONIA

Maksim Greinoman
Daisy Tauk

1   OVERVIEW

1.1   INTRODUCTION

Redundancy schemes in Estonia are subject to two main pieces of employment law legislation – the Employment Contract Act (ECA) and the Unemployment Insurance Act (UIA).

An analysis of Estonian employment law in general, and redundancy regulations in particular, should begin with a brief discourse on modern Estonian history. After regaining its independence in 1991, Estonia found itself with a largely plan-based economy and predominantly state-owned businesses, most with large debts. The ECA, enacted in 1993 in order to replace the communist-era Employment Code, was aimed at striking a compromise between the interests of employees unable to find another job and the interests of employers often unable to pay salaries.

Although adjustments to the law and harmonization with the law of the European communities resulted in certain modifications, Estonian employment law still includes post-communist features. In particular, the law provides generous employee protection, leaving very few issues for resolution in a collective bargaining format. In addition, Estonian employment law confers on the Employment Disputes

Commission and the court the power to reinstate an employee to his or her former position, even if this is against the wishes of another party to the employment contract.

The following discussion aims to present a brief overview of the statute and case law as of June 2007 and to outline the main features of Estonian redundancy law, enabling a comparison with laws in other European jurisdictions.

1.2   REDUNDANCY

Estonian individual employment law offers considerable protection to employees. An employer is only entitled to terminate an employment contract (whether a fixed-term contract or not) if explicitly permitted to do so by statute.

Estonian employment law provides for only three business situations in which employees may be dismissed when their jobs become unnecessary, i.e., redundant:

- business liquidation;
- employer insolvency; and
- employee lay-offs.

1.2.1   Business Liquidation

An employer is entitled to terminate an employment contract upon liquidation of the enterprise, agency or another organization, under ECA Article 86(1).

In the case of a company, partnership or co-operative, liquidation is the process of selling assets and satisfying debts. This process usually begins with a resolution of shareholders, partners or members that precedes the winding up of the company, partnership, or co-operative. Estonian law does not provide for liquidation proceedings of a sole entrepreneur/trader, and no legislation provides guidance on when such an individual may terminate employment contracts under this provision. Once the company shareholders, partners or members of a co-operative pass a resolution to start liquidation proceedings, the employer is entitled to rely upon the provisions of redundancy under the ECA.

Since it is rare for an employer to discontinue a loss-making business without trying to sell the business as a going concern, termination of employment contracts on this ground is not common. A recent change in the law, which came into force on 1 January 2007, introduced the same redundancy payments for all three types of redundancy. There is no reason to prefer this ground for termination to others, but it is worth bearing in mind that an employer must prove that genuine liquidation proceedings are under way in order to rely on it.

1.2.2   Employer Insolvency

In contrast to employee termination as a result of liquidation proceedings, insolvency as a formal statutory reason for termination is much more straightforward. An employer who is declared insolvent or whose insolvency is terminated by abatement, i.e., an employer who is found unable to pay his debts and lacks assets to payeven the costs of the insolvency proceedings, may terminate employment contracts without notice (ECA Article 87(4)).

Interestingly, the National Court has adopted a formalistic approach in this area. In Decision No. 3-2-1-126-02, the court held that if the insolvency proceedings end without the winding-up of the company, for example, because an appellate court has invalidated the decision of the court of first instance, this does not affect the previous termination of an employment contract. However, redundant employees may demand to be re-hired for any positions that become vacant within six months.

In Estonian insolvency law, employee claims do not have any preferential ranking (e.g., there is no ring-fenced fund for them); therefore, employees are at obvious risk of not having their claims satisfied. For this reason, certain limited protection is available through the compulsory unemployment insurance programme.

1.2.3 Employee Lay-Offs

Employee lay-offs are defined as the termination of employment contracts following a decrease in work volume, reorganization of production and/or work or reinstatement of an employee to a previous position that requires the termination of the current work (ECA Article 98(1)). The existence of such circumstances is a matter of fact, and the National Court has provided little guidance on this except to point out that the reasons for lay-offs are economic circumstances that result in an insufficient amount of work (National Court Decision No. 3-2-1-18-00).

1.3   COLLECTIVE REDUNDANCIES

Estonian law provides specific protection for employees in the case of mass termination of employment, following the implementation of the January 2002 EC Directive 98/59. In order to determine whether a collective termination/ redundancy has taken place, employers need to count the number of employment contracts terminated during a month. The number of terminations needed to trigger a collective redundancy depends on the size of the employer. An employer with:

- up to nineteen employees needs to dismiss five or more employees;
- 20-99 employees needs to dismisses ten or more employees;
- 100-299 employees needs to dismiss 10% of the employees;
- more than 300 employees needs to make thirty or more dismissals (ECA Article 89[1]).

Interestingly, collective redundancy proceedings do not affect the obligation of the employer to comply with and follow individual redundancy proceedings as described below. Therefore, both procedures can run simultaneously.

2   MAJOR REGULATIONS

2.1   TIMING

2.1.1   Notice Periods

Notice periods depend on the employer's grounds for redundancy and are as follows:

- In the case of company liquidation, termination is subject to a two-month notice period (ECA Article 87(1)1).
- In the case of insolvency, the employer may terminate employment contracts without notice (ECA Article 87(4)).
- In the case of lay-offs, different notice periods apply (ECA Article 87(1)3), which are based on the length of time that an employee has been working for a specific employer. If the period of employment has been for:
  - less than five years, the notice period is two months;
  - at least five years but less than ten, the notice period is three months;
  - ten years or longer, the notice period is four months.

A contract is terminated by a written irrevocable and unconditional notice, and it is the employer's obligation to formalize the termination of the employment contract (ECA Articles 72, 73).

2.1.2   Collective Redundancies

An employer may only start collective termination of contracts thirty days after consent has been given by a labour inspector, provided that the employees' representative did not extend the consultation period for an additional thirty days (ECA Article 89^3(5), (6)). (For further information see below in section 2.2.1).

2.2   INFORMATION AND CONSULTATION

2.2.1   Collective Redundancies

Prior to collective termination of employment contracts, an employer must consult with an employee representative with the aim of reaching an agreement on the following issues:

- avoiding termination of employment contracts or reducing the number of terminations;
- measures to alleviate the consequences of the terminations and ways to support affected employees in their search for work, re-training or in-service training (ECA Article 89^2(1)).

To that end, an employer must, in real time, provide the employee representatives – or if such representatives are not appointed, then relevant employees – with all necessary information concerning the intended collective termination of employment contracts. The bare minimum required by an employer is to communicate, in writing:

- the reasons for collective termination of employment contracts;
- the names of the employees affected (including their selection criteria);
- the total number of employees in the undertaking; the period of time during which the intended termination of employment contracts will take place; and
- the basis for the calculation and payment of benefits to employees (ECA Article $89^2(2)$).

Consultation, as such, may be limited to a one-time communication as described above with no obligation on the part of the employer to arrange any meetings. However, employees may propose measures on how to avoid termination of contracts, and an employer is obliged to review them. An employer must have a good reason not to follow such proposals (ECA Article $89^2(3)$); however, there is no case law on whether a court is entitled to examine grounds for refusal from a business point of view. There is no further obligation by an employer to engage in further communication.

Finally, consent of a labour inspector must be obtained (ECA Article $89^3(1)$). The decision must be made in one week (ECA Article 146). The labour inspector checks whether the formal procedure has been followed (ECA Article $89^3(4)$), but he is unlikely to interfere in any business-based judgment that led to the lay-off decision.

2.3   RISKS

2.3.1   Selection Criteria

2.3.1.1   Lay-Offs

In deciding which employees are to be laid off, the employer must strictly observe the preference rankings given by ECA Article 99. The top ranking employees are the employee representatives, who have a preferential right to remain at work. They are followed by employees for whom this is their principal job. Of the persons employed in a principal job, first preference is given to those with higher performance ratings. Criteria for comparing performance ratings are not stipulated, but, if challenged, the employer must be able to show that it has been fair.

In the case of equal performance results, preference is given to any of the following employees:

- those who have contracted an occupational disease or suffered a work-related injury at the hands of the employer;

- those with seniority;
- those with dependants; or
- those who are developing their professional skills and expertise in an educational institution providing vocational training (ECA Article 99(3)).

The language of the law cited above is far from specific, and it is up to an employer to prove under this provision that the selection of employees to be laid off is fair.

The courts may determine whether the employer observed the preferential procedure, with the burden of proof on the employer (Decision No. 3-2-1-22-01). The statutory selection procedure may not be substituted by a contest or competition (Decision No. 3-2-1-103-06).

Furthermore, after an employer has identified the employees to be laid off, they must be offered another vacant position, if one exists. It is important to note that an employer is under an obligation to offer not just a comparative position, but all positions where the employee may perform his/her tasks (Decision No. 3-2-1-103-06). The statutory requirement even covers positions that stipulate considerably lower qualification requirements than those which the employee possesses and, therefore, even those positions that the employee is highly likely to reject. Obviously an employee is not required by law to take such a position, and in this case, the employer may proceed with the lay-off. However, failure by the employer to observe this requirement is deemed to be a material violation of the lay-off procedure.

Violation of the above provisions will result in the decision being unlawful, which entitles the affected employee to the remedies as described in section 2.3.3.3.

It should be noted that the above selection criteria do not apply to other redundancy grounds, and in some cases, the employer may be flexible. However, it is worth bearing in mind that an employer who does take such a flexible approach may run the risk of accidentally treating employees unfairly.

2.3.2   Notice Restrictions

There are restrictions on laying off the following categories of employees:

- the ill;
- those on holiday;
- pregnant women or those with a child under the age of three;
- striking employees; and
- those performing duties in the interests of employees (ECA Articles 91(1), 92(1)).

These are the only limitations under the statute.

Laying off such persons is unlawful and entitles the employees to remedies. Termination of an employment contract due to insolvency or business liquidation is permitted, but termination of pregnant employees or those with children under the age of three requires the consent of a labour inspector (ECA Articles 91(2), 92(2)).

2.3.3   Disputes

Disputes associated with redundancy are governed by the same procedures as other employment disputes.

2.3.3.1   *Illicit Dismissal*

Estonian employment dispute legislation requires that the notice period be strictly observed, since termination of employment by either party before the notice period ends will result in the defaulting party having to pay the other compensation equal to an average day's salary for each remaining day of the notice period (ECA Article 84).

An employee is entitled to challenge termination of his/her employment contract on this basis by alleging that the statutory prerequisites are not fulfilled.

As long as there are actual grounds for termination of the employment, and the procedural requirements are observed, an error in identifying the exact legal grounds for termination is potentially excusable (National Court Decision No. 3-2-1-106-97).

Nevertheless, because there has been a considerable amount of litigation on this issue, it is strongly recommended that an employer state the relevant legal grounds and cite the appropriate legal provision when terminating a contract. It is of critical importance to note that response to the redundancy notice does alter it and, as explained by National Court Decision No. 3-2-1-134-96, the fact that the employee consented to the employer's decision to be laid off does not mean that the legal basis of the termination of the employment contract has changed to termination by mutual consent of the parties. Rather, it means that in the view of the employee, the employer has acted correctly in laying him/her off.

The evidence demonstrates that the second noticeable legal challenge is a simultaneous application of several grounds for the termination of an employment contract. This may occur, for example, when, an employment contract is terminated due to lay-offs as well as the employee's incapacity to work. To date, this issue remains unresolved by the National Court, since employers tend to rely on just one provision that they find suitable. Nevertheless, the option of relying on several provisions of the ECA may be recommended in certain cases.

2.3.3.2   *Jurisdiction*

Disputes arising from redundancy cases are subject to the jurisdiction of the court and the Labour Dispute Commission, if the latter has jurisdiction over the dispute. An employee is free to select whether to apply to the commission or to the court. However, since the commission normally delivers its decision within one month, and the application does not incur state fees (Individual Employment Disputes Act (IEDA) Articles 9(1), 16(1)), the commission is usually the preferred option.

The Labour Dispute Commission is entitled to review disputes where the value of the claim is no more than 50,000 Estonian kroons (EEK) (approximately

4,200 United States dollars (USD)). Decisions of the Labour Dispute Commission are legally enforceable (Enforcement Procedure Code Article 2(1)7).

Individual employment disputes are subject to the jurisdiction of the court where an employer is registered, the place of work or the place of the employee's own residence (Civil Procedure Code Articles 79(1) and 92).

2.3.3.3   *Remedies following Unfair Dismissal*

In the case of an unlawful termination, the Labour Disputes Commission and the court may grant the following remedies:

- declare that the termination of the employment contract was unlawful and reinstate the employee to his/her former position, change the date of termination or change the legal grounds for termination (IEDA Article 29);
- order the employer to pay the average salary for the period when the employee could not perform his/her duties because of the employer's breach of the employment contract or, if the employee does not want to be reinstated into his/her former position, then he/she may be paid compensation of up to six months' salary (IEDA Article 30(1), (2));
- order the employer to transfer the employee back to his/her position or reinstate past conditions of employment (IEDA Article 31(3)).

In addition, any order to carry out the above applies to the employer's obligation to pay the employee (where appropriate) for any breach of the notice period.

If, on the day of the hearing, the employee has not found another job, the employee is normally awarded compensation of two to four months' salary. If an employee has found a new job, compensation will generally be paid only for the period of unemployment.

2.3.4   **Performance after Termination Date**

If employment continued after the termination date of the employment contract, the termination is invalid and it is the obligation of both parties to continue the employment contract (ECA Article 83(3)).

2.3.5   **Discrimination**

Estonian law prohibits discrimination. This includes where an employer orders employees to discriminate against other employees, directly or indirectly (ECA Article 10(2), (3), 10^2). Although the burden falls on the employer to show no discrimination took place (ECA, Article 144^1(1)), the existing law actually discourages employees from relying on the anti-discrimination provisions. First, violation of the lay-off procedure is more obvious, and, second, the only remedy for breach of this prohibition is compensation for damages, including moral damages. Taking into account the civil law system, such damages are likely to be lower that those normally awarded for an unlawful lay-off.

However, a breach of Estonian anti-discrimination legislation may be more risky for the employer in the context of redundancy because, as stated above, the statutory criteria for termination of employment contracts in these cases is missing.

2.4 COSTS

2.4.1 Statutory Compensation

Employees who have been continuously employed by the employer for up to five years are entitled to two months' average salary as a statutory compensation payment. For employees who have been employed between five and ten years, this amount increases to three months' salary and employees who have worked for the same employer for ten years or more are entitled to four months' salary (Article 90(1) of the ECA).

The statutory compensation may not be decreased, but the parties are free to agree upon higher compensation through either an individual or collective employment agreement.

2.4.1.1 Insolvency

In cases where the employer becomes insolvent, or insolvency proceedings are terminated due to the lack of any noticeable property, i.e., where the employer has no money with which to pay the employee(s), compensation is paid by the Estonian Unemployment Insurance Fund (UIA). This includes the total compensation for the termination of the employment contract and any other amounts due under the employment contract, not exceeding the employee's three-month salary or three-month Estonian average salary, whichever is lower (UIA Articles 19, 20).

UIA is a legal entity, established under public law (UIA Article 1(2)). Insurance payments are collected by compulsory payments charged to both employers and employees by the Estonian taxation authorities.

2.4.1.2 The Unemployment Insurance Fund (UIA)

In the case of collective redundancies, compensation is partially paid by the UIA. The contribution payable by the UIA varies according to period of employment. Employees working for less than five years are entitled to one month's average salary. Employees employed between five and ten years are entitled to 1.5 months' average salary and employees employed for ten years or more are entitled to two months' salary (ECA Article 16(1)). The amounts paid by the fund are not recoverable from the employer.

2.4.2   Compensation Plans

Although compensation plans are allowed, they are rarely offered in Estonia, except to senior management.

3   ADVICE FOR LEGAL PRACTICE

3.1   Timing, Risks, and Costs

Redundancy provisions under Estonian law are fairly technical. From an employee's point of view, a range of possibilities exist enabling employees to dispute the termination of their contract and obtain remedies as appropriate. From the employer's point of view, complying with the correct procedure may considerably decrease the costs of the redundancy process. Managing redundancy requires careful advance planning, and it is advisable, if possible, to keep all three redundancy options open.

3.2   Risks

Employers should be aware that, in the context of redundancy claims, the Estonian Labour Commissions are notorious for favouring employees. The statistics illustrate this fact. In the first three months of 2007, of the total number of cases reviewed by the Labour Disputes Commissions, 59% of employee claims were satisfied in full and 19% were satisfied partially.[1]

---

1. Labour Commission statistics for the first quarter of 2007, available online at <www.ti.ee/public/files/2007/1_KV/2007_1_%20kv_X.pdf>.

FINLAND

Riitta Sedig
Pavel Koivistoinen
Petteri Viljakainen

1   OVERVIEW

1.1   FINNISH LABOUR LAW

An assessment of redundancy schemes in Finland requires consideration of Finnish labour law, collective agreements and employment contracts. The areas of Finnish labour law that impact on redundancy schemes include employment contracts law, co-operation law, collective agreements law, occupational health and safety law and social security law.

The most important statute regulating redundancy matters in Finland is the Employment Contracts Act (TSL), which stipulates the ways in which an employment relationship may be terminated, acceptable grounds for termination, the termination procedure, applicable notice periods, an employer's obligation to offer other work, re-employment obligations and liability for damages.

In the event of collective redundancy, the procedure for terminating an employment contract is also regulated by the Act on Co-operation within Undertakings (YTL), which came into operation on 1 July 2007. This act, as well as the obligation for an employer to comply with the mandatory obligation procedure provisions (Co-operation Procedure), applies only to companies that regularly employ at least twenty employees (YTL, § 2.1).

Maarten van Kempen, Lisa Patmore, Michael Ryley, and
Robert von Steinau-Steinrück (eds), *Redundancy*, pp. 65-75.

Collective agreements may record the agreement of employer and employee associations with regard to certain redundancy matters, even if the agreement provisions conflict with the provisions of the Employment Contracts Act. A collective agreement is not only binding on its signatory parties and their members; it may also have general applicability, binding non-member employers working in the respective branch (although non-member employees will not be bound).

1.2   METHODS OF TERMINATING AN EMPLOYMENT CONTRACT

1.2.1   Contract for an Indefinite Period

The baseline for Finnish labour law is an employment contract concluded for an indefinite period. There are several ways in which such a contract can be terminated, including:

- termination upon notice;
- rescinding the employment contract;
- deeming the employment contract to be dissolved;
- an agreement between the parties to terminate; and
- the lapse of an employment relationship.

1.2.2   Termination upon Notice

The right to give notice of termination applies in relation to employment contracts of an indefinite term. Fixed term employment contracts cannot be terminated upon notice, unless the parties have specifically agreed to this at the time the employment contract was formed or if the employer goes bankrupt or is reorganized. Both the employee and the employer can give notice to terminate the employment contract, but only the employer must have legal grounds for doing so. Termination upon notice is discussed further below in section 1.3.

1.2.3   Rescission

An employer may rescind an employment contract only for an 'extremely weighty reason'. Such a reason may be deemed to exist in the event that an employee breaches or fails to carry out his/her duties to such an extent that it would be unreasonable to expect the employer to continue the employment relationship even for the notice period (TSL, 8:1.1).

1.2.4   Deemed Dissolution

If either party to an employment contract has been absent from the workplace for at least seven days without notifying the other party of a valid reason for the absence, the other party is entitled to deem the employment contract dissolved from the date on which the absence began.

1.2.5   Termination by Agreement

The parties can agree to terminate the employment contract simply by stating that the employment relationship ends. The parties may freely choose the termination date and they do not need to observe a notice period. Whereas an employee is usually entitled to receive unemployment benefits seven days after termination of the employment contract, if the parties have agreed to terminate the employment contract, the entitlement only begins ninety days after termination.

1.3   LEGAL GROUNDS FOR GIVING NOTICE OF TERMINATION

1.3.1   Introduction

In accordance with the Employment Contracts Act, an employer may give notice to terminate an employment contract only for a 'proper and weighty' reason (TSL, 7:1). There are two types of acceptable grounds for giving notice: grounds related to an employee's person and financial and production-related grounds.

1.3.2   Grounds Related to an Employee's Person (TSL, 7:2)

An example of a proper and weighty reason for giving notice on grounds related to the employee's person is if the employee committed a serious breach or neglect of his/her obligations, or if a significant change occurred in an employee's circumstances that prevented him/her from coping with his/her duties.

1.3.3   Financial and Production-Related Grounds (TSL, 7:3)

An employer may give notice to terminate an employee's contract of employment if the work to be offered has diminished substantially and permanently for financial or production-related reasons or because the employer's operations have been restructured. If the amount of work the employer is able to offer decreases, it is entitled to adjust the number of its employees and their working hours in order to correspond to the employer's changed needs. Giving notice of termination, making lay-offs or changing full-time employment contracts into part-time work can accomplish this end. However, an employer cannot give notice to terminate an employee's contract of employment if there is an opportunity to reassign the employee or retrain the employee for other work within the company.

There are no acceptable reasons for giving an employee notice on financial and production-related grounds if:

- either before or after the employer has given notice of termination, it has employed a new employee for similar duties, even though the employer's operating conditions have not changed during that period; or
- the restructuring of the employer's operations has not caused any reduction in the amount of work available.

1.3.4   Special Situations

In some cases, an employee has special job security, meaning that he or she cannot be given notice of termination on the usual grounds. The types of employees who have special job security of varying degrees include pregnant employees, employees on family leave, employees who serve in the capacity of employees' representatives, employees carrying out military or non-military service and employees working in an assigned business.

2   MAJOR LEGAL REGULATIONS OF TERMINATION UPON NOTICE

2.1   TIMING

2.1.1   Pre-notice Hearing in the Case of Individual Dismissals

If the employer plans to make redundancies by giving notice of termination on grounds related to an employee's person, it must provide the employee with an opportunity to give his/her opinion on the grounds for termination before the employment contract terminates (TSL, 9:2). Failure to provide the employee with this opportunity will not affect the validity of the termination but may affect the amount of compensation awarded to the employee if the termination is held to be unlawful. In practice, employers usually comply with this obligation.

2.1.2   Pre-notice Negotiations in the Event of Collective Redundancy

In accordance with the Act on Co-operation within Undertakings, an employer must observe the co-operation procedure before making decisions on measures that may lead to it giving notice of termination to employees, making lay-offs or reducing employees' working time on financial or production-related grounds. An employer starts negotiations to reduce the workforce by providing employee representatives with a written proposal for negotiations at least five days before the negotiations begin. The content of the information an employer must provide is set forth in section 2.3 below.

     If an employer is planning to give notice to an employee or employees, then it must, at the start of the negotiations, also provide a plan for promoting the future employment of the employees; see the discussion in section 2.5.3 below.

     Unless the parties agree otherwise, the Act on Co-operation within Undertakings states that the co-operation negotiations must last for at least fourteen days if less than ten employees are to be made redundant and at least six weeks if ten or more employees are being made redundant.

     If an employer has intentionally or negligently failed to comply with the Co-operation Procedure, compensation may be awarded to an employee who has suffered as a result of the employer's failure to negotiate. However, the termination of the employment contract is still effective, even if an employer has not followed the Co-operation Procedure.

Within a reasonable time after the co-operation negotiations, an employer must provide the employee representatives with an overview of the decisions that it contemplates making on the basis of the co-operation negotiations. The required content of the overview of the employer's decisions is set forth below in 2.3.1.

2.1.3 Pre-notice Procedure in Financial and Production-Related Cases where the Co-operation Procedure Is Inapplicable

In certain situations, such as an employer's bankruptcy, death and reorganization, the notice requirements are less stringent.

If an employer does not have to follow the Co-operation Procedure, it must still provide employees with an explanation of the grounds for, and the alternatives to, the redundancies that it plans to make on financial or production-related grounds. It should do so as soon as possible and before giving notice of termination of the employment contracts (TSL, 9:3). In this situation, an employer does not have any obligation to negotiate. The termination is effective even if the employer fails to provide an employee with an explanation as outlined above. However, neglecting this notification obligation may affect the amount of compensation that is awarded to an employee if the termination is later found to be unlawful.

2.2 NOTICE PERIODS

2.2.1 Introduction

Either party wishing to terminate an employment contract by giving notice or by rescinding the contract must provide notice to the other party (TSL, 9:4). Therefore, providing the other party with notice of termination is considered an essential requirement of validly terminating an employment contract, either upon notice or by rescission.

2.2.2 Termination upon Rescission

If an employment contract is terminated by rescission, the employment relationship ends when the other party receives the notice.

2.2.3 Termination upon Notice

If an employment contract is terminated upon notice, the notice period starts from the date that the notice is given. Notice of termination shall be delivered to the other party in person. If this is not possible, it may be delivered by letter or electronically.

At the latest, the notice is deemed to have been received on the seventh day after the notice was sent.

The length of the notice period depends on the length of the employment relationship and, in the absence of agreement in the employment contract or applicable collective agreement, is determined by the Employment Contracts Act (TSL, 6:2-3). The agreed notice period may not be longer than six months. The employer may agree to a notice period that is longer than the one agreed to by the employee, but not vice versa.

If the Employment Contracts Act determines the notice period, the length of the period is calculated by reference to the uninterrupted duration of the employment relationship. Absences due to reasons such as lay-off, family leave, military service, or study leave do not interrupt the duration of the employment relationship. Such periods count towards the employee's length of service, unless an applicable collective agreement stipulates otherwise. Under the Employment Contracts Act, an employer must provide the following notice of termination to an employee (TSL, 6:3.1):

- fourteen days, if the employment relationship has continued for up to one year;
- one month, if the employment relationship has continued for more than one year but not more than four years;
- two months, if the employment relationship has continued for more than four years but not more than eight years;
- four months, if the employment relationship has continued for more than eight years but not more than twelve years; or
- six months, if the employment relationship has continued for more than twelve years.

An employee must provide the following notice of termination to an employer (TSL, 6:3.2):

- fourteen days, if the employment relationship has continued for not more than five years; or
- one month, if the employment relationship has continued for more than five years.

2.3   INFORMATION AND CONSULTATION

2.3.1   Collective Redundancy

As discussed in section 2.1.2 above, if an employer plans business measures that are likely to result in redundancies, then it must discuss the grounds for, the influences behind and the alternatives to these measures with the employees' representatives as part of the co-operation procedure negotiations. Five days before the negotiations, the employer must give the employees' representatives the following information:

- the grounds for the planned measures;
- a preliminary estimate of the number of employees who will be given notice of termination or will be laid off or suffer a reduction in working hours;
- an explanation of the grounds on which the employees subject to redundancy measures were selected; and
- an estimate of the timeframe during which the measures are to be implemented.

The employer must also discuss the plan for promoting the future employment of its employees. The reason for this discussion is to limit the number of employees made redundant and to reduce the negative consequences that the dismissed employees will face (see the discussion in section 2.5.3 below).

Within a reasonable time after the co-operation negotiations, an employer must provide the employee representatives with an overview of the decisions that it contemplates making on the basis of these negotiations. Depending on the negotiated matters, the overview must at a minimum contain the following information:

- the number of employees from each group of personnel that are to be given notice of termination, laid off or whose working hours are to be reduced;
- the duration of lay-offs; and
- the timeframe during which the employer plans to implement any redundancies.

2.4 RISKS

2.4.1 Selection Criteria

Procedures relating to the selection criteria for dismissal are ordinarily only required in connection with decreasing the number of blue-collar employees. The order of dismissal is not prescribed by any act, but organizations representing employers and employees conclude agreements on the selection criteria for the order in which employees are to be dismissed. The terms and conditions of these agreements are usually complied with, as a failure to do so results in fines and higher damages in the event that the redundancy is held to be unlawful.

The contents of the agreements on decreasing the workforce are similar in almost every case. In accordance with the decreasing orders, the skilled and professional employees that are significant to the functioning of the company and those employees that have lost part of their working capacity during the term of their employment must be dismissed last. In addition, the employees' length of service and the burden of maintenance liabilities must be taken into account when planning the decreasing order.

2.4.2 Re-hiring Employees

An employer who is considering hiring new employees has an obligation to offer new work to any employees whom it has laid off, employees working on a part-time basis and employees given notice on financial and production-related grounds (in that order), providing that the new work is the same as, or similar to, the work that was or is performed by those employees. The obligation to offer work to employees given notice on financial and production-related grounds is effective for nine months after their contract of employment is terminated. The redundant employee shall be given priority amongst job applicants even if external applicants are more qualified. However, the employee does not have to be re-employed on his/her old terms and conditions of employment.

In contrast, fixed-term employees have no right to new employment contracts after their original contracts expire.

2.4.3   Notice Restrictions and Special Protected Employees

As described above in section 1.3.4, certain employees enjoy special protection against dismissals. For example, an employer is only entitled to terminate the employment contract of a shop steward elected on the basis of a collective agreement or of an elected representative on the basis of grounds relating to the employee's person providing it obtains the agreement of a majority of the employees whom the shop steward or the elected representative represent.

There are only limited circumstances where an employer is entitled to terminate the employment contract of a shop steward or an elected representative on financial and production-related grounds, namely, in the event of a reorganization procedure or in connection with the bankruptcy or death of an employer. Even then, certain conditions apply:

- The work of the shop steward or elected representative must have completely ceased.
- The employer is unable to provide the shop steward or elected representative with work matching his/her professional skill (or alternative suitable work) and is unable to train him/her for alternative work.

Safety representatives enjoy the same protection.

An employer must not terminate an employment contract on the basis of an employee's pregnancy or because an employee is exercising his or her right to family leave. An employee must provide the employer with evidence that she is pregnant if the employer so requests.

If an employer terminates the employment contract of a pregnant employee or an employee on family leave, the termination shall be deemed to have been made because of the employee's pregnancy or family leave unless the employer can prove that there was some other valid reason.

An employer shall only be entitled to terminate the employment contract of an employee on maternity, special maternity, paternity, parental care, or child care leave on financial and production-related grounds if its operations cease completely.

2.4.4 Wrongful Dismissal

An employer who terminates an employment contract without observing the appropriate notice period is liable to pay the employee compensation representing full pay for a period equivalent to the notice period. Full pay includes, for example, payment in lieu of vacation that would have accrued during the notice period. An employee who has not observed the notice period is liable to pay the employer an amount equivalent to his pay for the notice period. If the notice period has been observed in part only, the liability is limited to the equivalent of the pay due for the non-observed part of the notice period.

2.4.5 Unlawful Dismissal

ILO Convention No. 158 (1982), by which Finland is bound, imposes the basic presumption that employees cannot be dismissed without a valid reason.

The Employment Contracts Act states that if an employer intentionally or through negligence commits a breach of the obligations arising from the employment contract or this Act, it shall be liable for any resulting loss caused to the employee. Liability for termination of the employment contract in breach of this rule is determined under Chapter 12, section 2 of the Act. This rule only applies to employers.

The Employment Contracts Act states that if an employee intentionally or through negligence commits a breach of the obligations arising from the employment contract or this Act, the employee shall be liable for any resulting loss caused to the employer in accordance with the grounds laid down in the Compensation for Damages Act.

In practice, the most common disputes arise from different opinions on the legality of the ground on which the employer justifies the dismissal.

2.4.6 Discrimination

The Employment Contracts Act requires equal treatment and prohibits discrimination against any employee. An employer must not discriminate (without justification) against employees on the basis of the employee's age, health, disability, national or ethnic origin, nationality, sexual orientation, language, religion, opinion, belief, family ties, trade union activity, political activity or any other comparable circumstance. Provisions on the prohibition of discrimination based on gender are outlined in the Act on Equality between Women and Men (609/1986). The definition of discrimination and burden of proof in cases concerning discrimination are outlined in the Non-discrimination Act (21/2004).

An employer must not, without a proper and justifiable reason, apply less favourable employment terms to fixed-term and part-time employees merely because of the duration of their employment contract or working hours, respectively.

An employer must also treat employees equally unless there is an acceptable reason for doing otherwise that derives from the duties and position of the employees.

An employer must not discriminate when recruiting employees. An employer who breaches the anti-discrimination rules may suffer fines and pay higher compensation awards to employees in the event that they are deemed to have been unfairly dismissed.

2.5   Costs

2.5.1   Damages in the Case of Unlawful Dismissal

If termination of an employment relationship is considered unlawful, the employer is liable to compensate the employee up to twenty-four months' pay, or thirty months' pay in the case of employees' representatives. The amount of compensation is influenced by a number of factors, such as the duration of unemployment and lost income, the employee's length of service, the employee's age and chances of obtaining new employment, the employer's action upon terminating the employment relationship, the employee's conduct that led to the termination and the employer's and employee's circumstances in general. There is no specific calculation method employed, and, therefore, compensation is determined by the court on a case-by-case basis. The court assesses compensation if it finds that a dismissal was unlawful. The average compensation varies between four and eight months' salary.

Even if an employer is found to have unfairly dismissed an employee, it is not obliged to reinstate the employee. The only exception is the employer's obligation to offer work to employees who have been given notice on financial and production-related grounds of employment, which, as mentioned above, is effective for nine months after the termination of their contract of employment. If an employer does not fulfil his obligation to offer work, he may be liable to pay compensation, due to his default, but nevertheless, he will not be obliged to reinstate the employee.

2.5.2   Damages for Neglect of Co-operation Procedure (YTL, § 62)

An employee may be awarded compensation if his/her employer has intentionally or negligently breached the co-operation procedure and the employee has been given notice of termination, laid off, or the employee's working hours have been reduced. Compensation may be awarded irrespective of the legality of the redundancies or of the connection between the employer's failure and the redundancies. Compensation for the employer's failure to follow the co-operation procedure is awarded to compensate the employee for any mental suffering, and it does not reduce any compensation that the employee might be entitled to due to the illegality of the redundancies. The maximum amount of compensation is EUR 30,000.

2.5.3   Social Plan

In providing notice to terminate an employee's contract of employment on financial and production-related grounds, an employer must comply with several other obligations in relation to promoting future employment. The rules relating to social plan have recently been transferred from the Act on Co-operation within Undertakings to the Employment Contracts Act.

An employer dismissing an employee must, as soon as possible prior to terminating a contract of employment on financial and production-related grounds or in connection with a reorganization procedure, provide the employee with an explanation of the grounds of termination, the alternatives to termination and the employment services that are available. If the employment contract is terminated on the basis on the bankruptcy or death of the employer, the bankrupt's or deceased's estate must provide an explanation of the grounds for termination to the employees as soon as possible. The Act on the Public Employment Service obligates the employment authorities to plan the necessary employment services in cooperation with the employer and representatives of the employees.

An employer who terminates an employee's contract of employment on financial or production-related grounds must inform the employment office of the termination without delay if, prior to the expiry of the notice period, the relevant employee has at least three years' service with the same or different employers. The same obligation applies to an employer in relation to an employee who, upon the termination of employment, has been in fixed-term employment for at least three consecutive years or has been employed on a fixed-term basis for at least thirty-six months of the previous forty-two months.

An employer shall, with the consent of the employee, attach any information available it has on the employee's education, work tasks and work experience to the notice to the employment office.

An employer is also obligated to inform the employee of his/her rights to the employment programme referred to in the Act on the Public Employment Service and the employment programme supplement referred to in the Unemployment Security Act (1290/2002).

3   ADVICE FOR LEGAL PRACTICE

The Finnish rules covering labour relations are rather specific, and the majority of them are mandatory. As a result, a local labour law expert should be consulted on any labour relations issue. It is important that contracts of employment are correctly worded and constructed, and that the correct formalities and procedures are followed. For example, the Act on Co-operation within Undertakings must be considered in connection with nearly every change to an employee's employment. In addition, although the main rules regarding grounds for dismissal are statutory, the expertise of local labour lawyers is needed to evaluate the legality of the proposed ground. The need for expert labour law counsel cannot be overemphasized, as labour law disputes can be expensive and time consuming and may attract undesirable publicity.

FRANCE

Roselyn Sands
Etienne Pujol
Laurent-Paul Tour

1   OVERVIEW

Under French law, a dismissal must either be based on personal grounds (i.e., specific to the individual employee concerned, such as negligence or misconduct) or economic grounds (i.e., unconnected to the individual concerned).

A dismissal for economic reasons can be individual or collective. The procedures vary, depending on the number of workers to be dismissed and the size of the company. For the purpose of the present article, 'redundancy' is defined as the collective economic dismissal of ten or more employees[1] within a thirty-day period.[2]

---

1. The same statutory employer obligations apply in any one of the following situations:

    – the dismissal of ten or more employees for economic reasons over a period of thirty days (in which case a job saving plan (*plan de sauvegarde de l'emploi*) must be implemented);
    – in companies with a headcount of fifty or more employees, the dismissal of ten or more employees for economic reasons over three consecutive months without reaching the limit of ten or more employees dismissed for economic reasons over a period of thirty days, in which case any further dismissal is subject to these rules;
    – companies that dismiss eighteen or more employees during a given calendar year without implementing a job saving plan (*plan de sauvegarde de l'emploi*) must implement such a scheme for any dismissals for economic reasons within the first three months of the subsequent calendar year.

©2008 Kluwer Law International B.V., The Netherlands.
Maarten van Kempen, Lisa Patmore, Michael Ryley, and
Robert von Steinau-Steinrück (eds), *Redundancy,* pp. 77-87.

Any redundancy requires compliance with rules relating to the economic situation of the company, the employer's duty to prevent redundancy, its obligation to try to relocate the employees, the determination of the order and priority for redundancies, and the priority of rehiring.

For redundancy schemes, the works council and the *Direction Départementale du Travail et de l'Emploi* (the Labour Inspector, hereinafter referred to as DDTE) play an important role. The employer must comply with information and consultation procedures that relate to the works council.

2   MAJOR LEGAL REGULATIONS

2.1   Dismissals for Economic Reasons

2.1.1   Definition

Pursuant to the Labour Code (Article L.1233-3), the dismissal of an employee for 'economic reasons' is:

> for one or more non-personal reasons and which result from the shutting down or transformation of a job position, or a substantive amendment to the contract of employment . . . , which in turn result from, inter alia, economic difficulties or technological developments.

Thus, according to the Labour Code, it is possible to make employees redundant[3] in order to maintain the competitiveness of the company in one of two situations:

- the introduction of new technologies; or
- the existence of economic difficulties.

Case law has strictly interpreted the latter to mean that the company must suffer serious economic difficulties.[4] It is not sufficient that the company merely wants to improve profits.

---

2. The Labour Code envisages that an employer may attempt to circumvent the rules and regulations with respect to redundancy by timing the dismissals so that the requisite number of dismissals does not occur within a thirty-day period of time. To avoid this, Article L. 1233-26 provides that, if an employer dismisses more than ten employees during three consecutive months for economic reasons, each additional economic dismissal during the following three months is treated as if it had occurred within the same thirty-day period.
3. Or to impose the modification of an essential contract term of employment, such as a reduction of hours, salary, or a termination of employment.
4. Economic difficulties must meet, at the very least, the following criteria:
    - exist on the date of termination of the employment contract (i.e., it is not possible to lay off employees in anticipation of possible future difficulties) and
    - be objective in nature and sufficiently serious in order to be verifiable by the courts: in practice, this corresponds to problems such as long-term financial difficulties (e.g., several years of losses and no foreseeable recovery) as opposed to a temporary downturn in activity.

Pursuant to French case law precedent, it is also possible to justify a redundancy scheme by the necessity to maintain the competitiveness of the company.[5] However, this measure may only be invoked if the redundancy scheme is the only way to ensure the company's survival in a particular sector or line of business.

2.1.2 Scope

If the company has only one plant, the economic difficulties will be assessed with respect to the company alone and the line of business in which it operates. However, if the company is part of a group, the economic difficulties must be assessed according to the following criteria:

- the company (i.e., not just the specific plant where lay-offs are contemplated);
- the line of business in which the company operates;
- the group to which the company belongs; and
- the line of business in which the group operates.

The principles set out above apply to all dismissals for economic reasons, regardless of the number of employees involved. However, in the event of redundancy schemes, specific legal obligations must be fulfilled, as detailed below.

2.2 INFORMATION AND CONSULTATION PROCEDURES

2.2.1 Preliminary Requirements

2.2.1.1 Employer's Duty to Prevent Redundancy

French employers have an obligation to help their employees adapt as their jobs evolve and to provide them with the appropriate training.

They are required to anticipate the evolution of jobs and skills prior to, and in order to avoid, any redundancy. The law encourages discussion within companies to encourage employers to act preemptively to conclude specific agreements that would prevent redundancy. For this purpose, small and medium-sized companies may benefit from public support for the implementation of a proactive plan in respect of jobs and skills (*plan de gestion prévisionnelle de l'emploi et des compétences*).

Even in the absence of case law regarding this issue, it is important that companies comply with these provisions. Indeed, there is a risk that employees will successfully challenge their redundancy by demonstrating that the employer did not comply with its prior obligation to anticipate their job's evolution and adapt the job accordingly.

---

5. It is possible for an employer to dismiss employees in order to maintain competitiveness if the employer foresees economic difficulties linked to technological developments.

2.2.1.2   Relocation Obligation

The main risk in terms of redundancy schemes relates to the employer's obligation
to search for available redeployment positions before making employees redundant. This risk is increased in companies belonging to an international group,
where the search for available positions must be made within the entire group.

Practically speaking, the search for available positions (letters being sent to all
companies within the group) will have to be made at an early stage of the redundancy process, that is, as soon as the works council is informed.

In the event of legal action initiated by terminated employees before the
Labour Courts, if the employer cannot demonstrate the effectiveness of its search
for available redeployment positions within the group, the redundancy will be
deemed as without cause. Such a finding will entitle redundant employees to
damages, the amount of which will depend on the employees' length of service,
age, and the harm suffered by the employee due to his/her dismissal.

2.2.2   Redundancy Procedure

In the event of a redundancy procedure, the employer is not required to convene
and hold an individual meeting with the employee, as in the case of a dismissal for
personal reasons, unless the company does not have employee representatives.

The redundancy procedure generally requires the employer to advise the
employees of their rights to reemployment within the company or group of companies, should suitable positions become available during the upcoming year.

The employer must formally propose to the employee the legal redeployment
scheme(s) applicable to the company, which mainly aim at offering professional
training and support in the employee's search for another job after the termination
of his/her employment contract.

In addition, the employer must meet with the employees' representatives and
present a detailed document explaining the redundancy scheme, including:

– the reasons for the redundancy;
– the number of employees to be made redundant;
– the timing; and
– the selection criteria, assessed by professional category, used to identify
  employees to be made redundant.

Unless otherwise provided by the applicable industry-wide collective bargaining
agreement, these criteria are:

– the length of service of the employee;
– the dependants of the employee;
– the difficulty the employee will face in searching for reemployment
  (because of handicap or age, for example); and
– professional skills.

These factors must all be weighed and considered; no one factor alone can determine the decision.

The redundancy may be implemented by the employer only after the proper informing of and consultation with the works council, under two separate procedures: the 'Book IV' procedure, focusing on the economic justification for the restructuring and redundancies; and the 'Book III' procedure, focusing on the job saving plan, which must demonstrate the measures the employer commits to put in place to avoid the redundancies or to minimize the negative consequences of those redundancies that cannot be avoided.

The Book IV and Book III procedures may take between two and six months to complete.

Please note that 'Book IV' and 'Book III' relate to chapters of the former Labour Code, which has been renumbered as of 1 May 2008. However, although chapters III and IV no longer exist in the Labour Code, the expressions continue to be used in common practice.

2.2.2.1   *Outline of the Book IV Procedure*

Employers must inform and consult the works council prior to making any decision that may, inter alia, have an impact on the size and structure of the workforce.

The Book IV procedure entails a notice of meeting with the accompanying explanatory documents, a first meeting for discussion, and a second meeting[6] at which the view of the works council is obtained.

The works council must be informed and consulted with while the measures are still in the planning stages. The employees' representatives must be consulted on the proposed reorganization, that is, they must vote on the project. Such a vote, whether positive or negative, is not binding upon the employer, who is free to carry out the redundancy procedure after a negative vote. However, the redundancy process may not be implemented in the absence of a vote of approval from the works council.

2.2.2.2   *Outline of the Book III Procedure*

The centrepiece of the Book III procedure is the negotiation of the job saving plan. This plan is a crucial step in the redundancy information/consultation process.

If the plan is incomplete or insufficient, it may be declared null and void. In practical terms, this means that the entire process must be started again, and no employee can be made redundant until the process is completed. If the employer fails to restart the process, the termination of employment contracts would be considered null and void and the employees reinstated.[7] As with the Book IV

---

6. The works council may decide to be assisted by a certified public accountant, to be paid for by the company. In that case, the timetable is extended (at least three weeks) due to a third meeting with the works council.
7. The Law of 18 January 2005 provides that the judge may order the employee's reinstatement, 'unless it is impossible, in particular due to the closing of the site or the establishment or the absence of any available positions allowing the reinstatement'.

procedure, the Book III procedure entails a notice of first meeting with the accompanying explanatory documents, a first meeting for discussion, and a second meeting where the view of the works council is obtained. The works council can also demand the intervention of an expert, in which case a third meeting takes place.

The DDTE monitors all activity with respect to redundancy and receives minutes of the meetings between the employer and the works council. The DDTE must be informed of the proposed redundancy, and must be provided with the same information and documentation as the works council. If the DDTE finds an irregularity in the procedures followed or decisions made, it notifies the employer in writing and proposes changes that should be implemented. The employer must respond to the DDTE's comments and cannot notify the employees of the redundancy until the DDTE's concerns are addressed satisfactorily.

2.2.3   'Method Agreements'

The announcement of a closure or a restructuring plan is, to some extent, a dramatic event; employees need time to realize that even if this closure is, at this stage, still a project, there is little chance of convincing the employer not to proceed.

Pursuant to the Law of 3 January 2003, confirmed by the Law of 18 January 2005, the applicable procedure for redundancy procedures may be partly defined, at an industry group or company level, by collective bargaining agreements, named 'method agreements' (*accords de méthode*). Based on the new legal provisions, method agreements may define the following:

- the rules according to which the works council is convened and informed with respect to the economic and financial situation of the company, and according to which it can propose alternative solutions aimed at avoiding the economic plan underlying the collective redundancy;
- the organization of professional and/or geographical mobilization activities; and
- the rules governing the conclusion of a collective bargaining agreement regarding the job saving plan and the anticipated contents of such a plan.

2.3   COST AND PENALTIES

2.3.1   Legally Required Costs

In addition to any severance payment provided for in the job saving plan, redundant employees are entitled to statutory redundancy indemnities under the French Labour Code and/or the applicable collective bargaining agreement (whichever is most favourable).

As regards the cost of redundancy under French law, employees are entitled, upon the termination of their employment contracts, to the following categories of payment:

– Notice period or compensation in lieu of such – This is generally, three months for executives, two months for supervisors and one month for blue collar workers.
– Compensation in lieu of paid holidays for any accrued holiday not yet taken at the date of the termination of the contract – This includes holiday accrued during the notice period which amounts to 10% of the corresponding notice period indemnity.
– Severance payment: The minimum statutory severance payment in the event of redundancy (*indemnité de licenciement*) is provided for by the French Labour Code. In the event of redundancy, the indemnity is equivalent to one-fifth of the employee's monthly salary per year of service.[8]
– Any individual contractual termination entitlements: This includes, for example, golden parachutes.

2.3.2   Job Saving Plan Costs

2.3.2.1   *Supplemental Termination Indemnity*

A supplemental termination indemnity is often included in the job saving plan in order to obtain the cooperation of the works council and/or to compensate for the damages suffered because of the redundancy. This indemnity is not a legal requirement. It can be proposed to employees who decide to leave the company on a voluntary basis. The amount of this supplemental indemnity depends on the negotiation with the works council and may vary based on different criteria such as the length of service of the employee, age, and personal situation.

2.3.2.2   *Redeployment Leave Costs*

In companies of 1,000 or more employees or in companies that are part of a group employing 1,000 or more employees, a proposal must be made to the employees to participate in redeployment leave (*Congé de Reclassement*) of four to nine months beginning during the notice period, the cost of which is borne by the company. During the period that corresponds to the notice period, the employee receives his/her full remuneration.

---

8. With an additional entitlement of two-fifteenths of the employee's monthly salary per year of service if the employee has been with the company for ten years or more.

For the period of redeployment leave that exceeds the notice period, the employer must grant the employee 65% of his/her last average gross remuneration (based on the last twelve months' remuneration).

In companies or groups with less than one thousand employees, the employee must receive a proposal for a 'personalized redeployment agreement' (*Convention de Reclassement Personnalisé*). Should the employee agree to sign such agreement, his/her employment contract would be considered terminated by mutual agreement.

2.3.3   Additional Termination Costs

2.3.3.1   Litigation Costs

The employee may seek damages from the employer before the Labour Court on the grounds that his/her redundancy is not based on a valid economic grounds. If the claim is successful, the employee will be entitled to damages.

If the employee's years of service are more than two years, and if the overall number of employees is eleven or more, the Labour Court may propose reinstatement of the employee. If the employee and/or the employer refuse the reinstatement proposal, the judge may award to the employee damages, which may not be less than the equivalent of six months' salary.

It should be noted, however, that presumed damages equal to six months' salary is merely a minimum, and the Labour Courts often award more significant damages to employees, depending on their length of service, age and personal situation.

2.3.3.2   Assedic Reimbursement Costs

French law also provides that the court must, in such a case, order the employer to reimburse the French Unemployment Fund (*Assedic*) the amount of unemployment compensation that the government has paid to the employee between the date of the redundancy and the date of judgment, capped at six months' compensation at the capped rate of four times the 2008 Social Security Ceiling (i.e., 4 × EUR 33,276 = EUR 133,104).

2.3.3.3   Miscellaneous Costs

Employees' lawsuits may lead to extra legal litigation fees. Other costs include the payment of potential non-compete clauses.

2.3.4   Principal Penalties

If the rights of employee representative bodies are obstructed, the legal representative of the company may be held liable under criminal law (with a maximum imprisonment of one year and/or a maximum fine of EUR 3,750 and a maximum imprisonment of two years and/or a maximum fine of EUR 7,500 in the event of a repeat offence).

If a job saving plan is held to be null and void by the courts, the resulting redundancies are annulled and the employees are entitled to be reinstated by the company. Should they refuse the benefit of this measure, the French Labour Code provides that such employees are entitled to a minimum indemnity of twelve months' salary.

Even where the validity of the job saving plan is not called into question, employees may seek compensation on the grounds that their dismissal was not based on a *genuine* and *serious* cause, as explained in section 2.3.3.1 above.

The Law of 18 January 2005 provides for restrictive deadlines for legal actions, aimed at challenging the regularity of the collective redundancy procedure as applied to ten employees or more over a thirty-day period. These limits tend to be more protective of the employer than were the previously applicable legal provisions.

3   RECOMMENDATIONS

It is not possible to provide an exhaustive list of risks (and corresponding delays) to which a company may be exposed while implementing a redundancy process. Employees' representatives or staff can initiate a large range of procedures that have the objective or effect of delaying the termination process. These delaying tactics mean that the number of possible court cases cannot be exhaustively listed due to the creative minds of litigators or trade unions; in addition, other unpredictable situations may suddenly arise to delay the entire process.

3.1   TIMING IS CRITICAL

3.1.1   Anticipate the Length of the Procedure

The entire process, that is, the Books IV and III informing and consultation procedures, may take from two to six months if carried out successively, depending on the relations with the works council and the DDTE.

If sufficient time is available, the employer may investigate other possible options and have open discussions with the works council on these investigations. In such a case, the first informing of the works council may take place at a very early stage, before the Books IV and III procedures have been initiated.

It is essential to establish a precise calendar of all information and consultation procedures to be carried out. That calendar should be sufficiently flexible to accommodate potential delays.

3.1.2   Anticipate Delays

Many delaying tactics can be used[9] to slow down the redundancy procedure, if not to stop it entirely. It is difficult to predict how long the delay is likely to last, as

---

9. Strikes of employees in redundancy situations are not uncommon.

this will depend on the good/bad faith of the employees' representatives and on the support they receive from staff. In similar cases, two to four-week delays are common, not including the time entailed if litigation is instituted.

Since the redundancy process may not be implemented in the absence of a vote from the works council,[10] one of the delaying tactics commonly used by the employees' representatives is to delay their vote until additional information has been provided; this delays the entire process.

In the event that no vote is recorded, the employer will have to take legal action and petition a judge to acknowledge that all proper information was duly given to the employees' representatives and that the company should be permitted to carry on the implementation of the redundancy procedure.

Additional delays can occur in the attempt to reach an agreement with the works council or the trade-union representatives, when the job saving plan is negotiated measure-by-measure; these negotiations are time consuming and generate expenses. This is the main reason why so much time is lost; the Books IV and III procedures often take longer than expected due to these protracted negotiations.

3.2   ADEQUATE JOB SAVING PLAN

Even though the Labour Code does not compel the works council to agree to the job saving plan, and does give the right to the employer to decide on its contents unilaterally regardless of the works council outcome, the importance of the job saving plan is so crucial that an agreement with the works council, and, if possible, with the trade-union representatives, would secure this plan against court actions initiated by employees' representatives or employees themselves.

Indeed, the consequence of a court action may be critical; the judge can cancel the job saving plan, resulting in cancellation of the redundancies. The employees are then deemed to be still employed, and the employer can either: restart the whole procedure (which will take three to six months, if not longer) and provide for a better job saving plan, or settle with each employee on an amount of damages (in addition to the severance pay and the job saving plan if already implemented) in order to obtain from the employees a waiver of their rights to sue the employer in court.

However, avoiding disputes over the job saving plan is even more essential in order to have a chance to close a company or to reduce the size of a workforce without engendering undue hostility or bad publicity.

3.3   SOCIAL AND POLITICAL CONTEXT IN FRANCE

Employers should bear in mind that numerous announcements of the closure of plants and job saving plans have made public opinion very sensitive to such

---

10. This is why particular care will have to be brought to the drafting of the information documents to be remitted to the members of the works council. However, this will not prevent such members asking for additional information, whether in good or bad faith.

circumstances. Hence, increased scrutiny from the DDTE[11] is to be expected when the information is made public and the consultation process carried out.[12]

In addition, if the city where the site to be closed has experienced the closure of another significant industrial facility, this situation will lead both local elected officials[13] and the DDTE to pay additional attention to compliance with the redundancy procedure, the effectiveness of the redeployment efforts, and the content of the job saving plan to be negotiated with the employees' representatives.

In the light of these constraints, it is advisable to make early, unofficial, and confidential contacts with the local DDTE, the mayor of the city and the *Préfet* of the *département*, before any compulsory contacts, in order to explain the economic difficulties suffered and the financial efforts carried out by the group as regards the job saving plan.

---

11. The content of the job saving plan will come under close scrutiny from the DDTE, which may propose amendments to the job saving plan throughout the procedure and until the last meeting with the works council. The employer must provide a detailed answer to all suggestions before being able to terminate employees.
12. The DDTE assesses the sufficiency of the content of the job saving plan. Should this content be deemed insufficient, the job saving plan should be redrafted; otherwise, the employer would be exposed to the judge's veto (within eight days from the end of the first works council meeting, or the second meeting if a chartered accountant has been appointed).
13. This remark is particularly relevant in the event of forthcoming national or local elections.

GERMANY

Robert von Steinau-Steinrück
Alexander von Vogel

1   OVERVIEW

Redundancy schemes in Germany must deal with various employment law considerations. Separate legislation governs an individual's employment relationship to collective bodies representing the interests of employees, for example, works councils.

The most important piece of legislation governing an individual's employment is the Protection against Unfair Dismissals Act (*Kündigungsschutzgesetz*). This statute is applicable to all establishments with more than ten employees. As a general rule, termination of employment is only valid if based on grounds permitted by law. If such is not the case, the termination is deemed to be unfair, and, as a consequence, the employment relationship continues. The aim of the Protection against Unfair Dismissals Act is to perpetuate the existence of employment relationships. However, in practice, most claims end in termination with severance payment being made (*Abfindung*).

In addition to the requirements of foregoing act, on making an individual redundant a notice period must be observed.

In the event of a collective redundancy, there are important codetermination and information requirements that must be fulfilled as part of the redundancy scheme. In establishments with more than twenty employees, reconciliation of interests (*Interessenausgleich*) must also be attempted, and a social plan (*Sozial-plan*), typically with severance payments, must be negotiated.

2   MAJOR LEGAL REGULATIONS

2.1   TIMING

**2.1.1   Periods of Notice (§ 622 Code of
              Civil Law (BGB))**

When it comes to termination, German law distinguishes between ordinary termi-nation and immediate termination for cause. Generally, reducing, restructuring, or even closing down operations is not considered enough to give an employer the right to terminate employment for cause.

The standard notice period is four weeks, or twenty-eight days, with notice taking effect on the fifteenth or at the end of the calendar month. During the first six months of employment, however, the employer and the employee may mutu-ally agree to shorten the notice period. The statutory minimum notice period varies, depending on length of service, from one month after two years of service to a maximum of seven months after twenty years of service.

These minimum notice periods may only be modified in certain circum-stances. They may be extended by an employment contract, or extended or short-ened by a collective bargaining agreement. However, as a general rule, the shortening of an individual's notice period is not valid.

A written, signed notice of termination must be delivered for the termination to be effective. The day on which the dismissal notice is delivered is not part of the notice period.

**2.1.2   Hearing of the Works Council (§ 102 Works
              Constitution Act (BetrVG))**

If the employees of a company with five or more employees request permission to establish a works council (*Betriebsräte*), that is, a committee of employee repre-sentatives), then the company cannot object. Members of the works council are elected for four years and need not be members of a union.

If a works council exists, it must hold a hearing before every dismissal, in fulfilment of § 102 of the Works Constitution Act (*Betriebsverfassungsgesetz*) (BetrVG). The hearing, however, does not signify the commencement of the dis-missal notice period. In the case of an ordinary dismissal, the works council has a period of one week within which to state its objections in writing. In the case of a dismissal for cause, the works council has three days to state its objections, subject to this period being extended by agreement. The works council may, however, make a final statement before the time period elapses.

2.1.3 Codetermination Rights of the Works Council (§§ 111-113 BetrVG)

In the event of mass redundancies or major restructuring, the employer and the works council, in certain circumstances, must negotiate a reconciliation of interests (*interessenausgleich*) and a social plan *(sozialplan)*, setting out how the employer will compensate employees for the social and financial disadvantages suffered as a result of redundancy.

Where an employer intends to close down part of a business, this is classed as an 'operational change' (*betriebsänderung*) under § 111 sentence 3 no. 1 BetrVG. The employer is obliged to notify the works council in good time of a planned 'operational change'. The notice must be given when planning is far enough advanced for a final decision to be made. The works council has the right to codetermine whether and how redundancies shall be made. The notice is deemed to be late if a final decision has already been made.

2.1.4 Collective Redundancies (§§ 17-22 KSchG)

Depending on the size of the business and the number of employees to be dismissed within a certain period of time, advance notice of the redundancies to the local labour office may be required. Once notified, the redundancies may only take effect after one month (§ 18 KSchG), but employers should take into consideration that the labour office has the power to extend this period to two months if the problems caused by the redundancies are not likely to be solved within the initial period. Once the notice period has ended, the dismissals must take place within the ninety-day 'free period', as set out in § 18, paragraph 4 KSchG. If this is not possible, then, under the circumstances set out in § 17, paragraph 1 KSchG, a new notice may have to be filed. These circumstances are that the employer must notify the Agency for Employment within thirty calendar days prior to dismissing:

- more than five employees in establishments that regularly employ more than twenty and fewer than sixty employees,
- 10% of the regularly employed employees or more than twenty-five employees in establishments with at least sixty and fewer than 500, and
- at least thirty employees in establishments which regularly employ at least 500 employees.

These dismissals shall be equivalent to other terminations of the employment relationship brought about by the employer (§ 17, paragraph 1 KSchG).

The employer must also make appropriate disclosures to the works council in writing and in good time; these disclosures must include the reason for the redundancies and the number and occupational groups of the affected employees. If the works council does not respond to this disclosure, the notice is only effective if the employer can prove that it informed the works council at least two weeks prior to submitting the notice.

2.2   INFORMATION AND CONSULTATION

2.2.1   Hearing of the Works Council (§ 102 BetrVG)

The information given in the notice to the works council must include the personal details of the worker affected, the reason and grounds for dismissal, and the notice period. The information provided must be precise. If a formal or material error is found in the hearing of the works council, the letter of notice is deemed to be invalid. It is therefore very important that all requirements of the works council hearing are met.

The employer must describe the circumstances pertaining to the dismissal in such a way that the works council will be able to assess the validity of the dismissal and grounds given, take a position and raise substantive objections without needing to research the circumstances further. In stating these grounds, however, the employer is only obliged to offer those details that he considers relevant to the dismissal. Grounds for dismissal that existed and were known to the employer at the time of the hearing but were not made known to the works council may not be introduced into any subsequent court proceedings. Thus, as a rule, the employer is not obliged to reveal to the works council all the grounds for dismissal, but only those on which it actually intends to base the dismissal.

A dismissal will only be in violation of § 102 BetrVG if the employer fails to inform the works council of the grounds on which it is relying. If there are mitigating circumstances in the employee's favour, the employer must so inform the works council.

The works council is free to consent to the dismissal or to express doubts or objections to the same. If the works council fails to make any response within the specified time period, it will be deemed to have given its consent. If the works council objects to an ordinary dismissal, it must communicate its objection to the employer in writing within one week, citing its grounds (§ 102, paragraph 2 sentence 1 BetrVG). If the works council objects to a dismissal for cause, it shall communicate its objection to the employer immediately, but at the latest within three days, giving its reasons in writing (§ 102, paragraph 2 sentence 3 BetrVG).

If, pursuant to § 102, paragraph 3 BetrVG, the works council raises a valid objection to a dismissal, the employee will have the right to remain in employment after the expiry of the notice period. Thus, the employer must continue to pay the employee throughout any legal proceedings, irrespective of their final outcome.

However, the consent of the works council is not a prerequisite for the validity of a dismissal, unless a valid agreement to this effect exists between the employer and the works council.

If, pursuant to § 102 BetrVG, an error in a works council hearing occurs, it is necessary to establish who is responsible for the error. If the error is the employer's fault then the dismissal will be invalid. A legal error of this kind cannot be corrected later. In contrast, errors that are the works council's fault (e.g., failure to convene a works council meeting in accordance with regulations) will not affect the dismissal's validity.

While there are no formal requirements for the hearing, it is advisable to record the hearing in writing so that, if necessary, the minutes can be used as evidence later. The notice must be given to the chairperson of the works council (§ 26, paragraph 2 sentence 2 BetrVG).

2.2.2 Codetermination Rights of the Works Council (§§ 111-113 BetrVG)

§ 111 sentence 1 of the Works Constitution Act stipulates that the works council must be consulted with regard to the planned closure of a business, and that the conflicting interests of the employees and the company must be balanced against each other in a reconciliation of interests (*interessenausgleich*) and a social plan (*sozialplan*).

The consultation phase follows on immediately from the point of giving notice. The employer must fully exhaust all attempts at reaching an agreement with the works council.

In practice, it is difficult to estimate with any accuracy how long the consultation exercise will last. It may take anywhere from a few weeks to several months. The Works Constitution Act does not set out a timescale during which consultation must take place.

With regard to the social plan, the works council has a genuine right of codetermination. It has the right to conclude the social plan. The purpose of the social plan is to create a reasonable settlement for those employees who will lose their jobs. Therefore the social plan usually includes the provision of redundancy payments for these employees.

The works council has a right to injunctive relief if the employer does not comply with the consultation procedure. The employer may also, in this case, be forced to make severance payments as compensation to affected employees (§ 113 BetrVG), and may be fined an administrative penalty of up to EUR 10,000, under § 121 BetrVG.

2.2.3 Collective Redundancies (§ 17-22 KSchG)

§ 17, paragraph 1 numbers 1-3 KSchG obliges all employers to notify the labour office of redundancies affecting more than a specified number of employees, dependent on the size of the establishment. Failure by the employer to submit this notice pursuant to § 17 KSchG will result in all dismissals made pursuant to the redundancy scheme being deemed invalid.

The main objective of these notice requirements is to enable the local labour office to make arrangements to avoid or mitigate the effects of sudden unemployment in the community. The notice must contain all relevant information concerning the proposed dismissals, such as the number of employees employed, the number of employees to be laid off, the period over which the dismissals are to be effected, the circumstances necessitating such dismissals, and the line(s) of business affected. The notice must also include a statement by the works council (*Betriebsrat*).

2.3   Cost and Risks

2.3.1   Protection against Unfair Dismissals Act (*Kündigungs-schutzgesetz*)

If an employer fails to give adequate reasons justifying dismissal, then the termination will be considered null and void, and an employee can insist on full reinstatement with back pay. In general, German labour courts are not entitled – even at the employee's request – to reach a decision to terminate employment and impose severance pay, nor may the labour courts award punitive damages. However, a labour court will always attempt – and is in fact required by law – to encourage the parties to enter into a settlement agreement.

In addition to the employment legislation discussed above, the Protection against Unfair Dismissals Act (*Kündigungsschutzgesetz*) also applies to establishments with more than ten employees.

According to the Protection against Unfair Dismissal Act, any dismissal notice given to an employee who has served the company for more than six months is valid only if the termination is 'socially justified'. A dismissal will be socially justified if there are personal reasons relating to the individual to be dismissed (*personen- oder verhaltensbedingte Kündigung*) or if there are business reasons (*betriebsbedingte Kündigung*). Personal reasons may be based on the conduct, performance, or health of the employee. Typical business reasons include the restructuring or the closing down of a business.

In addition, where notice is given for business reasons, particularly in the case of the closing down of a business department, the selection of each individual employee to be dismissed must be deemed 'socially just' as compared to those employees who are not to be dismissed. In making this social selection (*Sozialauswahl*), the employer must make its selection between employees holding similar or comparable positions within the same operation. The selection must be based on social criteria rather than on grounds of performance. The social criteria to be taken into account are length of service, age, marital status, and the number of dependants of the employee.

The employer carries the burden of proving that the dismissal is supported by business reasons and that the selection of the employee dismissed is based on social criteria. If the court finds that the dismissal notice is valid, the employment is considered effectively terminated at the end of the applicable notice period.

Additional employment protection exists for works council members, disabled employees, pregnant employees, employees undertaking military service, apprentice employees, and employees on educational leave. These employees may not be dismissed except for cause. Any such dismissal requires the prior consent of the relevant competent authority.

2.3.2   Periods of Notice (§ 622 BGB)

Whether or not employees are required to work during their notice period, they are entitled to be paid during such period. Accordingly, the cost of paying employees during their notice periods must be taken into account when planning redundancy schemes.

2.3.3   Hearing of the Works Council (§ 102 BetrVG)

If there are any errors in the hearing of the works council owing to the fault of the employer, the termination of employment is deemed to be invalid.

2.3.4   Codetermination Rights of the Works Council (§§ 111-113 BetrVG)

The consultation phase follows on immediately after the giving of notice. To avoid delaying tactics being used by the works council, the employer should prepare the notice carefully. The works council can then be given dates for consultation on relatively short notice. The employer must fully exhaust all attempts at reaching an agreement with the works council.

In practice, however, it is difficult to estimate with any accuracy how much time the consultation exercise will take. It may last somewhere between a few weeks and several months.

The details of the social plan depend on several criteria: the average length of service of the employees, the average income, notice periods and whether there are any employees who are specially protected against termination. The amount of redundancy payments set out in the social plan will depend on the disadvantage suffered by the employees and how much the employer can afford to pay. Case law demonstrates that an employer may take into account the potential savings resulting from the closing-down of the plant. This will also depend on the length of the negotiations with the works council, since notice can only be given after a reconciliation of interests has been reached or sufficiently attempted.

Finally, additional costs may arise from additional severance payments to those in the social plan, which may have to be agreed to in order to settle claims.

In most social plans, and also in claims, a formula is used to calculate the severance payment. The simplest possible formula is the following:

$$\text{monthly salary} \times \text{years of employment}$$

The above formula will very often be altered to the following:

$$\text{monthly salary} \times \text{years of employment} \times 50\text{-}75\%$$

2.3.5   Collective Redundancies (§§ 17-22 KSchG)

All formal requirements for collective redundancy must be met because – as with the hearing of the works council – any material error in procedure can have serious consequences, namely the notice being deemed to be invalid.

3   ADVICE FOR LEGAL PRACTICE

3.1   TIMING

The most important advice with regard to timing is, of course, that redundancy schemes should always be well prepared. If the redundancy scheme is well prepared, the works council will have no means to prevent measures from being taken but may be still able to delay implementation. Such delaying tactics will hit the employer harder if it is under time pressure to carry out the redundancies. In such cases, the employer may be forced to concede considerable ground regarding the amount of severance payments it has to make in order to implement the redundancy scheme.

3.2   INFORMATION AND CONSULTATION

To avoid delaying tactics by the works council in the negotiations regarding the reconciliation of interests and the social plan, the notice should be prepared very carefully. Usually the works council will claim that it has not been given sufficient information and, consequently, that the notice period has not yet expired and the consultation phase has not yet begun. Thus, preparing a comprehensive notice will preclude the works council from making such assertions. Before beginning negotiations the works council should be given several possible dates for negotiation.

3.3   COST AND RISKS

As a general rule, the better the preparation, the lower the costs and risks tend to be. In particular, breaches of procedure can be avoided if there has been sufficient preparation. Such breaches can be very costly, since in many cases the consequence is that the dismissal will be declared invalid and the procedure will have to be repeated.

GREECE

Ioannis Meimeteas

1 OVERVIEW

For an enterprise to implement redundancies of a limited or extensive nature and restructure its labour force under Greek labour law, provisions applicable to each individual employment relationship (i.e., specific termination procedure), as well as redundancy provisions of a collective nature (i.e., information and consultation rights of employees' representatives in the event of collective redundancies) should be respected.

1.1 EMPLOYMENT CONTRACTS OF DEFINITE DURATION VERSUS INDEFINITE DURATION

Under Greek labour law, employment relationships are characterized as being of definite duration or indefinite duration. This distinction is important as the reasons, procedures and validity of termination are different for the two types of contract.

1.1.1 Employment Contracts of Definite Duration

As a general rule, for definite duration relationships, premature termination by either party is permitted only for serious cause. If the reason for the premature termination is a breach by the other party, full damages may be claimed. On the other hand, if the employer terminates the agreement because his personal economic situation or that of the enterprise has changed, the court may impose upon him the payment of reasonable termination indemnity (673, 674 Greek Civil Code).

1.1.2   Employment Contracts of Indefinite Duration

In contrast, either party theoretically may terminate indefinite duration relationships at any time and without cause. For such a termination certain requirements are imposed, as well as a termination indemnity. The dismissal should take place in writing, and the employer should provide the termination indemnity even if the dismissal is the employee's fault (e.g., breach of duty, disobedience, repeated absences). The employer is released from its obligation to pay termination indemnity in certain specifically determined cases, for example, if the employee commits a work-related crime. The amount of the indemnity depends on the kind of termination, with notice or immediate. In a termination with notice, the compensation is half of the compensation owed for an immediate termination without notice. In the latter instance, the amount is directly related to the number of prior years' service with the specific employer, and employees are entitled to one month's salary up to a maximum of twenty-four months of salary.

With the provisions of Law No. 1767/1988, works councils were introduced into the Greek legal system and were granted certain information and consultation rights. A more detailed information and consultation structure is provided in Law No. 1387/1983, as amended, for cases of collective redundancies. For a detailed discussion of collective redundancies, see sections 2.1.3, 2.2, and 2.3 below.

2   MAJOR LEGAL REGULATIONS

2.1   TIMING

2.1.1   Period of Notice: Amount of Termination Indemnity

According to Greek labour law, notice does not constitute a condition for the validity of the termination procedure, but it is a factor for determining the amount of termination indemnity. There is no obligation for the employer to justify the decision to terminate. The fact that the termination takes place after the notice period provided by law will only decrease the payable amount, but not the grounds for such a termination.

In the case of immediate termination, according to Articles 1 and 3 of Law No. 2112/1920, the indemnity due is calculated with reference to the employee's prior years of service with the specific employer, namely:

Years of Prior Service	Compensation Amount	Prior Notice
2 months-1 year	1 month's salary	1 month
1 year-4 years	2 months' salary	2 months
4 years-6 years	3 months' salary	3 months
6 years-8 years	4 months' salary	4 months
8 years-10 years	5 months' salary	5 months
10 years completed	6 months' salary	6 months

For every extra completed year of service after ten years, the compensation will be increased by one month's salary and the prior notice due the employee will be increased by one month.

Upon giving the minimum notice required by law, the employer shall pay the employee one half of the lawful termination indemnity as stated above (Article 4 of Law No. 3198/1955). As long as the notice period is observed, the termination provided (compensation amount calculated in monthly salaries based on the number of years' prior service with the same employer) will be reduced by half. The employer can choose whether to terminate the employment agreement immediately and pay the entire amount provided for by law, or give the employee notice and keep him/her on the payroll for the provided period to allow time to find a new job, and then, upon termination, pay one half of the termination indemnity. On the other hand, the employee has the obligation to give notice equal to half of the notice required by the employer, up to a maximum of three months (Article 4 of Law No. 2112/1920).

The employer has an additional notification obligation to the Labour Force Employment Organization (OAED) within the period of eight days following termination (Article 9 of Law No. 3198/1955). If the employer does not proceed with the notification, administrative fines may be imposed, but the validity of the termination of the employment agreement remains intact.

2.1.2   Procedure before the Works Councils

The employees of each enterprise with a labour force of at least fifty persons have the right to elect and constitute into a body a works council for their representation. In enterprises where no trade union is formed, the minimum labour force required to entitle them to a works council may be reduced to twenty persons (Article 1 of Law No. 1767/1988).

The employer is obliged to inform the members of the works council about planned changes in the structure of the enterprise's labour force, including reductions and increases in the number of employees, prior to the implementation of such plans (Article 13(d) of Law No. 1767/1988).

If the employer fails to comply with its obligation to inform employees' representatives, fines may be imposed that can amount to sums of up to EUR 300,000 per violation (Article 16, paragraph 8 of Law No. 1264/1982).

2.1.3   Collective Redundancies

According to Law No. 1387/1983, when an enterprise is contemplating collective redundancies, the employer is obliged, before taking any action, to consult with the employees' representatives in an effort to avoid the dismissals, reduce the number of employees affected or minimize the consequences.

The applicable legislation sets the parameters for determining which redundancies are considered collective (Article 1, paragraph 2 of Law No. 1387/1983). The dismissals must take place over a period of thirty days. The parameters are as follows:

– dismissing at least four employees in establishments normally employing more than twenty and less than 200 people;
– dismissing between 2% and 3% of the employees in establishments normally employing more than fifty people, with the percentage determined for every six-month period according to the Labour Market conditions with a ministerial decision emanating from the Minister of Labour (currently, the applicable percentage is 2%, up to a maximum of thirty employees per month).

A recent amendment to the law (Law No. 3488/2006) relating to the aforementioned limits now includes all kinds of termination of employment relationships in which the termination is initiated by the employer through no fault of the employee, and the total number of terminations within the enterprise for a given month is at least five.

The consultation period lasts twenty days from the date the employer notifies the employees' representatives. The results of the consultation procedure are recorded in minutes and provided to the Prefecture and the Ministry of Labour.

If the parties come to an agreement, the employer can proceed with the collective redundancies according to the agreement after a period of ten days. If an agreement is not achieved within ten days from receipt of the aforementioned minutes, the Prefecture or the Ministry of Labour may:

– extend the consultations for an additional twenty days;
– allow all or part of the dismissals; or
– prohibit all or part of the dismissals.

In the event the parties fail to reach an agreement, the final decision of the Minister of Labour will be based on the circumstances of the case and the prevailing general market conditions (Article 5, paragraph 3 of Law No. 1387/1983).

2.2   INFORMATION AND CONSULTATION

2.2.1   Collective Redundancies

The information and consultation rights of employees' representatives are specifically regulated for collective redundancies. According to Article 4 of Law No. 1387/1983, the employees' representatives for this procedure are considered the legal representatives of an enterprise's trade union with members amounting to at least 70% of the total workforce and the majority of the affected/dismissed employees. If more than one trade union is in place in the enterprise and none of them reach the required 70% criterion, the representatives should be appointed by joint declaration of trade unions representing 70% of the total work force and the majority of the affected/dismissed employees. If there is no trade union or the trade union does not satisfy the above criteria, the employees may elect a committee, through an assembly and secret ballot, for this purpose.

The timing of the procedure and the involved parties are described above in section 2.1.3. As far as the information to be provided to the employees' representatives, the employer should include all necessary information for them to form an opinion, and more specifically provide details in writing concerning:

(1) the reasons for the redundancies;
(2) the number and categories of employees to be made redundant;
(3) the number and categories of employees normally employed;
(4) the period over which the redundancies are to be effected; and
(5) the criteria proposed for the selection of the employees to be made redundant.

(Article 3 paragraph 2(b) of Law No. 1387/1983)

Copies of this information should be submitted to the Prefecture and the Labour Inspection Authority as an aid in their participation in the procedure.

2.3   COSTS AND RISKS

2.3.1   Protection against Dismissal

For certain categories of employees, the employer's right to proceed to termination is restricted. In particular, dismissal protection is extended to the following categories of employees:

- employees on annual leave;
- employees performing their military service;
- pregnant women, during their pregnancy and for one year after delivery; and
- duly appointed employees' representatives.

Employees falling into one of the above categories can be dismissed only for certain causes, and only in accordance with certain procedures specifically provided by law.

Recently, under the provisions of Law 3488/2006 (Article 9) on equal treatment for men and women in the workplace, it has also been established that termination is forbidden:

- for reasons of sexual or family status discrimination;
- for reasons of revenge by the employer connected with sexual or any other type of harassment; and
- as an employer's reaction to a complaint within the undertaking or to any legal proceedings aimed at enforcing compliance with the principle of equal treatment.

2.3.2   Protection against Abusive Dismissal

The termination of an employment agreement of indefinite duration will be invalid if it is not made in writing (in a document referred to as the 'termination document'), or if the employer does not pay the termination indemnity provided by law (Law No. 2112/1920 and Law No. 3198/1955).

Furthermore, the employer's right to terminate the employment agreement must be exercised in accordance with the principle of good faith (Article 281 of the Greek Civil Code), that is to say, the employer should be able to justify the termination of the employment agreement in the event of a court dispute.

As for judicial control of the right to dismiss, two categories of reasons for termination have been accepted as not involving an abuse of rights:

- reasons relating to the employee (inadequacy, breach of duties); and
- reasons referring to the needs and interests of the firm (economic difficulties, diminishing activity, introduction of new working methods or new technology or changes in organization).

A termination is valid when the three conditions of written notice, offer of compensation and fair use of the right of termination have been met. If the court rescinds the dismissal, the employer must reinstate the dismissed employee.

2.3.3   Collective Redundancies

If the employer fails to comply with the specified procedure, the collective redundancies are null and void (Article 6 paragraph 1 of Law No. 1387/1983).

It should be noted that the categories of protected employees enumerated in section 2.3.1 above are also entitled to protection from collective redundancies. In addition to the above, the employer should also respect the social criteria in deciding which employees will be terminated (i.e., marital status, number of children, years of service prior to retirement).

Even where collective redundancies are accepted or approved by the responsible authorities, the employer should pay the legal termination indemnity as provided by law (see above under section 2.1.1) and terminate the employment relationship in writing (Article 6, paragraph 2 of Law No. 1387/1983). The employer is not obliged to make any additional payments to governmental or tax authorities, provided that all outstanding social security contributions are settled.

As the government, through the Minister of Labour, has the final word on whether to permit or reject the collective redundancies, the economic and political effect on the area where the enterprise is active must be considered, together with the overall effect on the unemployment rate. Furthermore, employees' representatives are very reluctant to reach an agreement on collective redundancies, and can exercise pressure on the employer indirectly through the government to protect the employees.

3   ADVICE FOR LEGAL PRACTICE

3.1   TIMING

The employer should observe the information and consultation timetable and be prepared for long and demanding negotiations in which the state will also be involved. The best advice for an efficient implementation of collective redundancy is detailed preparation of the restructuring in order to gain the consent or even the tolerance of the employees. Otherwise, there is significant risk that the process will become overly time consuming and have a negative impact on the employer's interests.

3.2   INFORMATION AND CONSULTATION

The information and consultation procedure must be followed for the collective redundancy to be valid. The fact that the procedure takes place under the supervision of the Ministry of Labour makes the whole process especially demanding. To avoid rejection of the proposed restructuring, the employer should carefully prepare his approach, both to employees' representatives and to supervisory authorities, and be able to justify the necessity of the restructuring for the enterprise's viability in Greece.

3.3   COSTS AND RISK

The cost of the process and the associated risks vary in relation to the extent of the employer's preparations for the proposed changes in labour force structure. Implementing collective redundancies without respecting the procedures provided by law will result in the terminations being null and void, and their validity challenged in the Greek courts. The employees may request reinstatement to their positions with significant financial consequences for the employer's enterprise, in addition to long and costly litigation.

HUNGARY

Dr Imre Krisch
Dr Norá Kürti

1   OVERVIEW

Act No. 22 of 1992 of the Hungarian Labour Code ('LC') governs Hungarian
employment law in the private sector. This chapter covers the rules on redundancy
concerning the private sector. It does not extend to the rules applicable to public-
service employees and civil servants.

2   MAJOR LEGAL REGULATIONS

The LC differentiates between automatic termination of employment and termination of employment by the intention of the parties. In the case of termination
by the intention of the parties, the methods of termination differ according to the
period of the employment relationship.

2.1   FIXED-TERM EMPLOYMENT TERMINATION

This may be carried out by mutual consent of the employer and the employee; by
extraordinary termination on either side; or with immediate effect during the trial
period.

©2008 Kluwer Law International B.V., The Netherlands.
Maarten van Kempen, Lisa Patmore, Michael Ryley, and
Robert von Steinau-Steinrück (eds), *Redundancy,* pp. 105-110.

Furthermore, the employer is entitled to terminate the fixed-term employment with immediate effect when it pays the employee one year's average salary, or his/her average salary for the period remaining if such period is less than one year.

2.2   INDEFINITE EMPLOYMENT TERMINATION

This may be carried out by mutual consent of the employer and the employee; by ordinary termination on either side; by extraordinary termination on either side; or with immediate effect during the trial period.

3   TIMING

3.1   NOTICE PERIODS (§ 92 LC)

The notice period depends on the method of termination. In the case of termination by mutual consent, employment may be terminated at any time without restriction during the employment period. According to the LC, there is no notice period; employment may be terminated immediately or at a later date depending on the intention of the parties. In such cases, the termination restrictions do not apply.

Should employment be terminated by ordinary dismissal, the notice period is set as a minimum of thirty days and a maximum of one year. The notice period is extended based on the length of service.

In cases of extraordinary termination, no notice period applies.

3.2   TIMING OF THE TERMINATION

The right of ordinary dismissal can be exercised without any time limit during employment. However, regard must be had to the restrictions on ordinary termination. The employee cannot be ordinarily dismissed, for instance, during:

- periods of incapacity to work due to illness, not to exceed one year following expiration of the sick-leave period; or
- pregnancy, for three months after giving birth, or during maternity leave.

An extraordinary dismissal can only be carried out within fifteen days of learning of the grounds (the 'subjective' deadline), or within one year of the grounds for dismissal arising, or in the case of criminal offences, within the limitation period (the 'objective' deadline).

If employment is to be terminated without notice during the trial period, this can only be effected on the last day of the trial period.

4   INFORMATION AND CONSULTATION

4.1   INFORMING THE EMPLOYEE BEFORE DELIVERING THE TERMINATION LETTER

Prior to termination by the employer on the grounds of the employee's performance or conduct, the employee shall be given the opportunity to present his/her defence to the complaints raised against him/her, unless it cannot be expected of the employer to give such opportunity in view of the circumstances.

4.2   INFORMATION RIGHTS OF THE WORKS COUNCIL (WORKERS' REPRESENTATIVES) AND THE EMPLOYMENT CENTRE IN CASES OF MASS REDUNDANCIES (§ 94/A LC)

4.2.1   Step 1

The employer's briefing to be sent to the employment centre must state:

- intention to carry out the mass redundancy;
- reasons for the proposed redundancy;
- the number of employees to be made redundant listed by category;
- the number of employees employed during the preceding six-month period;
- the period over which the proposed redundancy is to be executed;
- criteria for the selection of the affected employees; and
- conditions for eligibility and the method of calculating redundancy payments other than those arising from national legislation and/or collective agreement.

4.2.2   Step 2

Notification to be given to the workers' representatives must state:

- the reasons for proposed redundancy;
- the number of employees to be made redundant, broken down by category; and
- the number of employees employed during the preceding six-month period.

4.2.3   Step 3

4.2.3.1   *Information to Be Disclosed and Content of the Consultation*

Information to be disclosed includes:

- the period over which the proposed redundancies are to be executed;
- criteria for the selection of the affected employees; and

 – conditions for eligibility and the method of calculating redundancy payments other than those arising from national legislation and/or collective agreement.

Elements of the consultation to be discussed include:

 – possible ways to avoid collective redundancies;
 – principles of the redundancies;
 – means of minimizing the consequences; and
 – reduction of the number of employees affected.

The employer is not obliged to conclude an agreement with the works council. However, it is obliged to comply with the above deadlines regarding information and consultation obligations. Accordingly, in the event that no agreement is reached by the end of the consultation, the employer is entitled to decide on the redundancy even without employee consent. Should the employer and the workers' representatives reach an agreement in the course of the consultation, it must be documented in writing and a copy sent to the competent employment centre by the employer.

4.2.4   Step 4

This step consists of the employer notifying the competent employment centre of the agreement. If an agreement is reached in the course of the consultation, it shall be documented in writing, and a copy sent to the competent employment centre by the employer.

4.2.5   Step 5

This step consists of the employer notifying the competent employment centre of the decision, in writing, at least thirty days prior to the ordinary dismissal.

4.2.6   Step 6

After notifying the employment centre, but at least thirty days prior to the ordinary dismissal, the employer shall inform the employees affected by the mass redundancy in writing. A copy of this document shall be sent to the workers' representatives and to the competent employment centre.

5   COST AND RISKS

5.1   LEGAL CONSEQUENCES OF UNLAWFUL TERMINATION (§ 100 LC)

Should the labour court establish that the employer has terminated employment contrary to the LC, then, upon request of the employee:

 – the employer shall continue to employ the employee in his/her original position; or

– the employment shall be regarded as terminated on the date when the court's decision becomes final and binding and the employer shall pay to the employee compensation of a minimum of two and a maximum of twelve months' average salary.

In any of the cases above, the employer shall pay the employee the amount of his/her lost wages and any other compensation in respect of the period until the date on which the court decision becomes final and binding.

If his/her employment was not terminated by ordinary dismissal, an employee shall be eligible for the average earnings payable for the notice period and severance pay due in the event of ordinary dismissal.

5.2   NOTICE PERIODS AND SEVERANCE PAY (§§ 92 AND 95 LC)

Costs arise from the notice periods, particularly since some employees may have long notice periods. Employees are entitled to their salary during the notice period, regardless of whether they have to work during this time or not. For these reasons, notice periods must be taken into account when planning redundancy schemes.

The employer is obligated to make severance payments if the employee has been employed by the company for a minimum of three years. The severance payment is only due if the employment was terminated by ordinary termination and in cases of winding up by the employer. The severance payment can be an average salary for between one month and six months, depending on the employee's length of service.

Should the employer terminate the employment by ordinary dismissal, it shall release the employee from his/her working obligations for at least half of the notice period. For this period, the employer is obligated to pay the employee's average salary. The employee is entitled to receive his/her basic salary for the period which he/she spends at work (50% of the notice period).

6   REASONS FOR TERMINATION

The grounds for extraordinary termination are where the employee has:

– wilfully or by gross negligence committed a serious violation of any substantive obligations arising from his/her employment; or
– otherwise acted in a way that makes it impossible for the employer to maintain the employment relationship.

According to the LC, an employee may be ordinarily dismissed by the employer only for reasons in connection with:

– the employee's competence;
– the employee's behaviour in relation to his/her employment; or
– the employer's operations.

No grounds are necessary for termination during the trial period or for termination by mutual consent.

7   MASS REDUNDANCIES: CONSEQUENCES OF
                     THE BREACH OF PROVISION 94/A LC

Any dismissal executed in violation of the applicable provisions of the LC or in breach of the agreement reached by consultation between the employer and the workers' representatives shall be deemed unlawful.

If an employer violates the rights of the works council or the trade union in its procedures, these bodies may seek a remedy in court. The court deals with and resolves such cases within eight days.

8   ADVICE FOR LEGAL PRACTICE

8.1   Timing

The termination will qualify as unlawful where the employer terminates employment by ordinary dismissal during a restricted period or neglects to carry out an extraordinary dismissal during the permitted period.

8.2   Information and Consultation

In general, neither the trade unions nor works councils have rights to influence the redundancy scheme. Within most employment organizations in Hungary, there is no trade union or works council.

8.3   Cost and Risks

Since employees are exempt from paying stamp duty when bringing a case before the labour court at the beginning of the procedure, employees tend to file a lawsuit against their employer if they consider the termination to be unlawful.

It is the employer's duty to establish that the reason provided is sound and true. To avoid the spectre of legal proceedings, employers usually try to terminate the employment relationship by mutual consent, even if this involves a higher payment obligation.

Employers often try to avoid being caught by the mass redundancy laws due to their time-consuming nature.

IRELAND

Kevin Langford

1   OVERVIEW

1.1   REDUNDANCIES IN GENERAL

The law of redundancies is mainly set out in the Redundancy Payments Acts 1967
and 2007 (Redundancy Payments Acts), the Protection of Employment Acts
1977 and 2007 ('the Protection of Employment Acts'), the Unfair Dismissals
Acts 1977 and 2007 (Unfair Dismissals Acts) and in the Common Law.

The Redundancy Payments Acts provide for a payment to be made to qualifying employees on being made redundant. The Protection of Employment Acts
apply to collective redundancies; the Unfair Dismissals Acts and the Common
Law impose obligations regarding the way redundancies are carried out.

The Redundancy Payments Acts define 'redundancy' as follows:

> An employee shall be taken to have been dismissed by reason of redundancy
> if, for one or more reasons not related to the employee concerned, the dis-
> missal is attributable wholly or mainly to:
>
> (a) the fact that the employer has ceased or intends to cease to carry on the
>   business for the purpose of which the employee was employed by him, or
>   has ceased or intends to cease, to carry on that business in the place where
>   the employee was so employed;

©2008 Kluwer Law International B.V., The Netherlands.
Maarten van Kempen, Lisa Patmore, Michael Ryley, and
Robert von Steinau-Steinrück (eds), *Redundancy,* pp. 111-119.

(b) the fact that the requirements of that business for employees to carry out work of a particular kind in the place where he was so employed have ceased or diminished or are expected to cease or diminish;

(c) the fact that the employer has decided to carry on the business with fewer or no employees whether by requiring the work for which the employee has been employed (or had been doing before his dismissal) to be done by other employees or otherwise;

(d) the fact that the employer has decided that the work for which the employee had been employed (or had been doing before his dismissal) should, from then on, be done in a different manner for which the employee is not sufficiently qualified or trained; or

(e) the fact that the employer has decided that the work for which the employee had been employed (or had been doing before his dismissal) should, from then on, be done by a person who is also capable of doing other work for which the employee is not sufficiently qualified or trained.

An employee shall not be taken to be dismissed by reason of redundancy if:

(a) the dismissal is one of a number of dismissals that, together, constitute collective redundancies;

(b) the dismissals concerned were effected on a compulsory basis;

(c) the dismissed employees were, or are to be, replaced at the same location or elsewhere in the State (except where the employer has an existing operation with established terms and conditions), by:

    (i) other persons who are, or are to be, directly employed by the employer; or

    (ii) other persons whose services are, or are to be, provided to that employer in pursuance of other arrangements.

(d) those other persons perform, or are to perform, essentially the same functions as the dismissed employees; and

(e) the terms and conditions of employment of those other persons are, or are to be, materially inferior to those of the dismissed employees.

This definition of redundancy relates to a situation where an employer makes employees redundant in order to replace them with lower-cost workers. Under the Protection of Employment (Exceptional Collective Redundancies and Related Matters) Act 2007, a Labour Court may hold such dismissals to be 'exceptional collective redundancies' for a transitional period of three years from 8 May 2007. (There is provision in the Act for extension of this three-year transitional period.)

In order for collective redundancies to be classifiable as exceptional collective redundancies, the proposal to create such redundancies has to be referred to the Redundancy Panel by the employer or the employee representatives. The Redundancy Panel consists of an independent chairperson, and a member of each of the main employee and employer bodies. Ultimately, the matter may be referred to the Labour Court for an opinion as to whether the proposed collective redundancies are exceptional collective redundancies.

1.2   Collective Redundancies

The Protection of Employment Acts 1977 and 2007 define 'collective redundancies' as dismissals effected by an employer for one or more reasons not related to the individual concerned where in any period of thirty consecutive days the number of such dismissals is:

(a) at least five in an establishment normally employing more than twenty and less than fifty employees;

(b) at least ten in an establishment normally employing at least fifty but less than 100 employees;

(c) at least 10% of the number of employees in an establishment normally employing at least 100 but less than 300 employees; and

(d) at least thirty in an establishment normally employing 300 or more employees.

The term 'establishment' means an employer or a company or a subsidiary company or a company within a group of companies having the independent jurisdiction to effect redundancies.

2   MAJOR LEGAL REGULATIONS

2.1   Timing

2.1.1   **Notice**

Each employee who is to be made redundant must be given proper notice of redundancy. Notice of redundancy must be given in writing. Proper notice is the greater of contractual notice, statutory notice or, in the absence of a contractual term as to notice, reasonable notice.

Entitlement to statutory notice is based on length of service as follows:

– Thirteen weeks to two years' service: one week's notice.
– Two to five years' service: two weeks' notice.
– Five to ten years' service: four weeks' notice.
– Ten to fifteen years' service: six weeks' notice.
– Fifteen or more years' service: eight weeks' notice.

'Reasonable notice' is a common law concept. What constitutes reasonable notice generally depends on the particular employee's status. For senior employees in particular, where there is no written contract of employment, consideration must be given to what constitutes an appropriate period of notice. 'Reasonable notice' for a management employee will be different from that of an entry-level employee.

Concurrently with statutory/contractual notice, where an employee has at least two years' continuous service, it is necessary to serve him/her with completed part A of notice of redundancy form RP50 at least two weeks prior to the date of termination of employment. Upon the date of termination, the employee must sign the RP50 form and receive his/her statutory redundancy payment.

2.1.2   Collective Redundancies

In the case of collective redundancies, the employer must inform and consult with the employees' representatives. The information and consultation process must start as soon as possible but at least thirty days before the first notice of dismissal is given. No dismissal may be implemented nor any notice of termination issued within the thirty-day period.

Even where redundancies do not constitute collective redundancies within the meaning of the Protection of Employment Acts, where employees are being selected for redundancy from a group of employees, the employer must take reasonable time to meet with those employees who are potentially affected and with their representatives in order to inform them of the proposed redundancies and to allow them to express their views.

2.1.3   Notification to the Minister for Enterprise, Trade, and Employment

An employer who proposes to create collective redundancies must inform the Minister for Enterprise, Trade, and Employment at the earliest opportunity and, in any event, at least thirty days before the first dismissal takes effect.

2.2   INFORMATION AND CONSULTATION

2.2.1   Collective Redundancies

Where an employer proposes to implement collective redundancies, it must put in place an arrangement to provide for the appointment of representatives for the affected employees. The employer must then inform and consult with those representatives. The employees may choose not to appoint representatives and instead to be consulted directly. For consultation process purposes, the employer must supply the employees or their representatives with all relevant information relating to the proposed redundancies including:

- the reasons for the proposed redundancies;
- the number and description or categories of employees whom it is proposed to make redundant;
- the number of employees and description or categories normally employed;
- the period during which it is proposed to effect the proposed redundancies;
- the criteria proposed for the selection of the workers to be made redundant; and
- the method for calculating any redundancy payments other than statutory redundancy payments.

The employer must consult in good faith with employees or their representatives on:

- the possibility of avoiding the proposed redundancies, reducing the number of employees affected by them or mitigating their circumstances by recourse to social measures such as, for example, help to redeploy or retrain employees made redundant. On these matters, the employer must not merely consult with the employee representatives but must also negotiate with them; and
- the criteria for deciding which employees will be made redundant.

2.2.2 Notification to the Minister for Enterprise, Trade, and Employment

An employer who proposes to create collective redundancies must provide prescribed information, including the information provided to employees or their representatives, in writing to the Minister for Enterprise, Trade, and Employment. The employer must provide a copy of the notification sent to the Minister to the employees or to their representatives.

2.3 RISKS

2.3.1 Redundancy Legislation

An employee who claims to be entitled to a statutory redundancy payment may bring a claim before the Employment Appeals Tribunal.

An employer that fails to comply with its obligations to inform and consult under the Protection of Employment Acts will be guilty of an offence and may be liable to a fine of up to EUR 5,000. Where collective redundancies are effected by an employer before the expiry of the thirty-day consultation and notification period, the employer will be guilty of an offence and may be liable to a fine of up to EUR 250,000.

2.3.2 Industrial Relations Acts 1946 and 2004

Where there is a dispute as to the redundancy process and/or redundancy payments, the employer and/or the affected employees or their trade union may refer the dispute to the State's industrial relations bodies under the Industrial Relations Acts 1946 and 2004. These bodies are the Labour Relations Commission, which includes the Rights Commissioner service, and the Labour Court.

Industrial relations in Ireland are of a voluntary nature and consequently decisions of the Rights Commissioner and Labour Court are generally not enforceable. However, in certain circumstances one or both parties have to abide by the determination of the Rights Commissioner or of the Labour Court. Where one of the parties appeals to the Labour Court against the decision of a Rights Commissioner, the Labour Court's determination will be binding on the parties. Where employees refer a dispute directly to the Labour Court, the Labour Court will consider the matter on condition that the employees agree in advance to abide by the Court's decision.

A decision of the Labour Court may be enforceable where its intervention in the dispute is by virtue of the provisions of the Industrial Relations (Amendment) Act 2001 as amended by the Industrial Relations (Miscellaneous Provisions) Act 2004. Under these Acts, the Labour Court may issue an enforceable determination where the employer has refused to engage in collective bargaining negotiations and the internal dispute-resolution procedures normally used by the parties concerned have failed to resolve the dispute. The determination may be enforced by the Circuit Court and an appeal on a point of law may be to the High Court.

2.3.3   Injunction

An employee who is to be made redundant may apply to the High Court for an interlocutory/preliminary injunction. If granted, the effect of the injunction would be to restrain the employer from dismissing the employee until the matter has been fully heard by the High Court. To obtain an injunction, the employee must establish that there is a fair question to be tried at a full hearing; that the balance of convenience favours the granting of the injunction; and that damages would not adequately compensate the employee.

An application for an injunction may be brought on the basis that the contract of employment was not validly terminated (e.g., no proper notice was given); that the person who decided to dismiss lacked the authority to do so; or that the dismissal procedure was unfair or otherwise not in accordance with statutory requirements. The interlocutory/preliminary injunction application is heard by the High Court at short notice based on affidavits rather than on oral evidence.

2.3.4   Unfair Dismissal

An employee who has been made redundant may claim that he was unfairly dismissed contrary to the Unfair Dismissals Acts. This claim may be brought before a Rights Commissioner or directly to the Employment Appeals Tribunal. The Tribunal is composed of a nominee of employers' organizations, a nominee of the Irish Congress of Trade Unions and a chairman who must also be a lawyer.

Under the Unfair Dismissals Acts, a dismissal is deemed to be unfair unless the employer can establish its fairness. Redundancy is a defence to unfair dismissal provided that the employer can establish to the satisfaction of the Tribunal/Rights Commissioner that there is a genuine redundancy situation and that the selection of the person to be made redundant was fair.

The Acts provide that if an employee is dismissed but the circumstances apply equally to another employee and either:

- the selection of the employee for redundancy was for one of the automatically unfair reasons for dismissal, e.g., pregnancy; or

– the employee was selected in contravention of a procedure agreed with a trade
union and there were no special reasons for departure from the procedure,

the dismissal shall be deemed to be an unfair dismissal.

If an employer fails to establish to the satisfaction of the Tribunal that an
employee has been fairly dismissed, the Tribunal can make certain orders in favour
of the dismissed employee. It can award either compensation representing the
actual or prospective loss suffered by the employee (capped at two years' remuneration), reinstatement, or re-engagement.

Where an employee has been dismissed as one of a number of exceptional
collective redundancies, the cap on compensation is four years' remuneration for
an employee who had fewer than twenty years' service on the date of the dismissal
and five years' remuneration for an employee who had more than twenty years'
service. An appeal lies from the decision of the Rights Commissioner to the Tribunal, from the Tribunal to the Circuit Court and from the Circuit Court to the
High Court.

2.3.5 Wrongful Dismissal

As an alternative to a claim for unfair dismissal, an employee who was made
redundant may bring a claim of wrongful dismissal to the Circuit Court or High
Court. A claim of wrongful dismissal is a claim that the employer failed to give
the employee the required period of notice. If successful, the Court may award
damages representing what the employee would have earned during the period of
notice.

2.3.6 Discriminatory Dismissal

An employee who was made redundant may bring a claim of discriminatory dismissal under the Employment Equality Acts 1998 and 2004 ('the Employment
Equality Acts'). Under the Employment Equality Acts, an employer may not discriminate against an employee on the grounds of gender, marital status, family
status, race, colour, national or ethnic origins, age, sexual orientation, religion, and
disability or membership in the Traveller community. If successful, the Tribunal
has a variety of orders that it can make, including an award of damages as compensation for the effect of the discrimination (capped at two years' remuneration),
reinstatement, or re-engagement.

2.3.7 Selection Criteria

Irish law does not set out the criteria by which the employer selects which employees to make redundant. Rather, the employer has a general duty to act reasonably
and the selection criteria must be fair. What constitutes fair selection criteria
depends on the circumstances surrounding the redundancy plan. Many employers
use the 'last in, first out' rule often referred to as 'LIFO'.

2.3.8   Notice Restrictions

While an employee is on protective leave (e.g., maternity leave), any purported termination of employment is void. Notice of termination may only be issued to the employee at the end of the period of protective leave.

2.4   COSTS

2.4.1   Statutory Redundancy Payments

Under the Redundancy Payments Acts, employees with more than two years' continuous employment with the same employer may be entitled to a statutory redundancy payment. Employment is taken as being continuous unless it is terminated by dismissal or by the employee's voluntary resignation.

The statutory payment is intended to compensate the redundant employee for loss of security, seniority and other benefits which he/she had in the employment. The payment is calculated as follows:

- two weeks' pay for each year of reckonable service with the employer from the date on which the employee attained sixteen years of age; plus
- one week's pay.

For the purposes of this calculation, a week's pay is capped at EUR 600. The following absences, if they occur during the three years before the date of termination of employment, are not allowable as reckonable service:

- Absence for more than fifty-two consecutive weeks by reason of an occupational accident or disease.
- Absence for more than twenty-six consecutive weeks by reason of any other illness.
- Absence by reason of lay-off by the employer.
- Absence by reason of a strike in the business or industry in which the employee concerned is employed.

A statutory redundancy payment is tax-free. An employer is entitled to a rebate of 60% of the statutory lump sum provided that due notice of dismissal is given to the employee and the statutory forms are used.

An employee is not entitled to a statutory redundancy payment if the employer offered suitable alternative employment which he/she unreasonably refused. The reasonableness of the employee's refusal, however, is usually determined from the employee's point of view, so that in practice, it is generally difficult for an employer to rely on this provision.

2.4.2   Ex Gratia Termination Payments

In addition to statutory redundancy payments, employees in Ireland usually receive enhanced termination payments, the amount of which depend on the industry and the sectoral norms, customs and practices. Ex gratia payments are typically based on a formula related to a number of weeks' pay for each year of the employee's service. Ex gratia redundancy payments are taxable, though they qualify for special tax treatment and may be exempt or qualify for some tax relief.

3   ADVICE FOR LEGAL PRACTITIONERS

3.1   TIMING

Check each employee's contract of employment as well as the staff handbook and any collective agreements that may be in force in order to ensure that employees receive their full notice entitlement. Salary may be paid in lieu of notice if provided for in the employee's contract of employment or if otherwise agreed between the parties.

As noted in section 2.1.1 above, make sure to serve the notice of redundancy form RP50 on employees who have at least two years' continuous service.

3.2   INFORMATION AND CONSULTATION

If the redundancy is one of a number of collective redundancies, ensure that the notification and consultation obligations set out in the Protection of Employment Acts have been complied with. It may be necessary to carry out a redundancy selection exercise based on certain criteria, with the employees potentially affected being given the opportunity to have an input in the selection process.

3.3   RISKS

To reduce the risk of claims by employees or ex-employees affected by a redundancy plan:

- prior to taking any steps towards implementing redundancies, the employer should be satisfied that a genuine redundancy situation exists for those positions being made redundant and that those positions being made redundant are fairly selected;
- the employer should require each employee who opts to take an ex gratia redundancy payment to sign an acceptance form confirming that the payment is in full and final settlement of all claims that the employee may have against the employer.

3.4   COSTS

In addition to statutory redundancy payments, employees and their representatives (e.g., trade unions) will typically seek to negotiate enhanced termination payments which will give rise to an increased cost to the employer. This needs to be factored into an employer's planning or budgeting for the cost of implementing redundancies.

ITALY

Maria Teresa Iannella
Stefania Radoccia

1   OVERVIEW: LAW NO. 223/91 ON COLLECTIVE
DISMISSAL

Collective dismissals and individual dismissals differ:

- based on the number of employees dismissed; and
- based on the reasons for the dismissal itself.

Collective dismissals are permissible in the case of a downturn or change in the activities or work of the company (in the case of companies with more than fifteen employees). However, the employer must justify the reasons for the collective dismissal and must notify the trade-union organizations accordingly.

Law 223 of 1991 governs the procedure, formal tasks, preconditions and consultation with trade unions if a company decides to initiate collective dismissals. Rules regarding collective dismissals may also be set out in collective or interconfederational agreements.

To alleviate the negative effects of collective dismissal, a body called the Wage Guarantee Fund (*Cassa Integrazione Guadagni*) was created to protect employees' wages in the event of a company experiencing a crisis or undergoing restructuring.

©2008 Kluwer Law International B.V., The Netherlands.
Maarten van Kempen, Lisa Patmore, Michael Ryley, and
Robert von Steinau-Steinrück (eds), *Redundancy,* pp. 121-126.

Moreover, Law No. 223/91 introduced important information and consultation requirements that have to be observed in a redundancy scheme, and, if a collective agreement is achieved, a social welfare plan that typically involves the payment of a lump sum to the dismissed employees.

2   REDUNDANCY PROCEDURES: LEGAL
             REQUIREMENTS

Law No. 223/91 provides that a company employing more than fifteen employees and planning to dismiss at least five employees in a period of 120 days as a consequence of the decrease in the availability of work, or as a consequence of the reorganization of the business or the available work, or of the total closure of the enterprise, has to apply a particular redundancy procedure.

2.1   NOTIFICATION AND INFORMATION

The employer is required to notify the employees about the decision to make a collective dismissal through:

- the unions at the site (*Rappresentanze sindacali aziendali* – RSA) and the relevant associations in respect of the category of employees (which are signatories to any national collective labour agreement in force); or, in the absence of RSA at the site;
- the largest unions/associations affiliated with the most representative national confederations in Italy.

The Notice of Redundancy must provide the following information:

- The reasons for the employer's decision.
- The technical, organizational, and productive reasons that do not allow the employer to take different measures in order to remedy the current situation and to avoid, totally or partially, the collective dismissal.
- The number, positions, and professional profiles of the employees to be dismissed and of the personnel to be retained.
- The time frame of the redundancy scheme.
- Any measures to alleviate the possible social consequences of the redundancies.
- The calculation basis for offering incentives for voluntary resignation.

The Notice must contain a copy of the receipt of the payment to the National Agency of Social Insurance (hereinafter, INPS) of a fixed 'contribution', the so-called *contributo d'ingresso* (see section 2.4 below).

A copy of the Notice and of the receipt shall be sent to the appropriate Provincial Labour Office.

2.2   CONSULTATIONS

The representatives of the unions and the employers' association have seven days to ask for a joint examination concerning the redundancy, the reasons which have determined the redundancy, and the possibilities of a different utilization of the personnel so as to avoid redundancies.

The consultation is to be completed within forty-five days. The procedure may or may not result in an agreement; in any event, the results of the joint consultation are to be communicated to the Provincial Labour Office.

In case of disagreement, the Provincial Labour Office may call back the parties for a further examination of the situation and a further attempt to reach an agreement. This second consultation is to be completed within thirty days.

Altogether, the procedure takes seventy-five days, during which the employees continue to remain in their jobs and receive their salaries.

2.3   DISMISSAL

If an agreement is reached or, even in the absence of an agreement, once the procedure is completed, the employer can dismiss the employees by giving them the contractual notice of termination. However, each employee is to be notified of the dismissal not later than 120 days from the end of the consultation procedure.

Unless the dismissal involves all the employees, the criteria for the selection of the redundant employees are usually agreed upon and recorded in the agreement reached with the unions (if any).

In all cases, however, the selection criteria are to be communicated to the Provincial Labour Office, the Regional Employment Commission and the unions, together with a list of the names and data concerning the dismissed employees.

If an agreement between the parties is not reached, Law No. 223/91 provides for statutory criteria for the selection of employees to be dismissed as follows:

- organizational, technical, and productive criteria;
- employee's seniority;
- number of members of the employee's family.

These criteria can be adjusted to correspond with the organizational and technical needs of the employer.

The notice of dismissal is to be given to the employees (within the above-mentioned term of 120 days) in writing; otherwise the dismissal is void.

A list of the employees dismissed is to be given to the Provincial Labour Office, the Regional Employment Commission and the unions. This list must contain:

- name, residence, and age of the employee;
- number of members of the employee's family;

- qualification and level of employment; and
- method of application of the criteria.

In any event, the employee can challenge his/her dismissal within sixty days of receiving the written notice (see section 2.5 below).

Law No. 223/91 also provides that at the end of the procedure described above the redundant employees are entitled to receive from INPS an indemnity equal to:

- 100% of the 'Extraordinary Treatment of Salary Integration' (CIGS) (see section 1.1) for the first twelve months; and
- 80% of the CIGS for the following months.

As a rule, the employees are entitled to receive such indemnity from INPS for twelve months only. However, this period may be extended in consideration of the age of the dismissed employee, as follows:

- up to twenty-four months if the employee is between forty and fifty years old;
- up to thirty-six months if the employee is over fifty years old.

2.4   COST OF DISMISSAL

The employer must pay to INPS a fixed amount for each of the redundant employees – the so-called *contributo di ingresso* – as an advance on the total amount to be paid to the INPS at the end of the redundancy procedure. The aforementioned amount corresponds to the unemployment benefit and the sum is fixed year by year. For the year 2007, it was equal to EUR 84,406 for monthly salaries up to EUR 182,607, and EUR 95,523 for monthly salaries higher than EUR 182,607. The total amount of this charge is equal to nine months of unemployment benefits; that charge must be settled at the end of the dismissal procedure. It is important to highlight that this sum is reduced to one-third in case agreement is reached with the trade unions.

The notice period to be granted to employees depends upon the employee's level and seniority. The National Collective Agreement applied by the employer usually provides for specific terms.

During the notice period, the employee must continue to perform his/her duties. It is possible, however, to exempt the employees from working during all or part of the notice period. In such a case the employee is entitled to an indemnity in lieu of notice; the sum the employee will receive is equal to the aggregate salary that the employee would have been entitled to receive had he/she been working during the notice period. The payment of the indemnity is subject to social security contributions.

2.5   RISKS IN CASE OF UNFAIR DISMISSAL

Even the agreement with the unions cannot affect the rights of individual employees. In fact, should the employee deem the dismissal ungrounded or unlawful, he/she maintains the right to sue the employer. For this reason, only individual agreements can keep the company safe from the risk of reinstatement and suits for unfair individual dismissal. Nonetheless, if the company has reached an agreement with the unions, its position is much more defensible in case of a legal dispute.

If an agreement is not reached and the employee believes that he/she has been unlawfully dismissed, the employee can challenge his/her dismissal within sixty days by sending a registered letter to the employer. The employee must previously request a hearing with the Settlement Commission (established at the Provincial Labour Office); in the event that a settlement is not reached, he/she can sue the employer before the Labour Judge.

Should the judge declare the dismissal unfair, the provisions set forth in section 18 of Law No. 300/1970 will apply.

As a general rule, where a company employs more than sixty employees within Italian territory, or more than fifteen in one work unit, the employee who is found to be unfairly dismissed may demand reinstatement or, alternatively, accept an indemnity equal to fifteen months' salary. In any case, the employee is entitled to receive the payment of salary in arrears, as an indemnity, from the date of the unfair dismissal up to the date of the effective reinstatement, but it will be no lower than the equivalent of five months' gross salary.

3   ADVICE FOR LEGAL PRACTICE

3.1   NOTIFICATION AND INFORMATION

The notification should be prepared and carried out as carefully as possible. In fact, it is appropriate for the employer to provide the trade unions with all the information necessary to allow them a clear understanding of the company's position as well as the plan contemplated for each redundant employee. The absence of information could result in a declaration by a judge of illegitimacy in relation to the procedure, with all the consequences arising from an unfair dismissal.

For the sake of completeness, any redundancy proposals must be kept very confidential; a leak could theoretically invalidate the procedure.

3.2   CONSULTATION

It is advisable to reach an agreement with the unions for the following reasons:

- The criteria for selecting the employees involved in the redundancy procedure. Usually, reaching an agreement upon consultation with the unions allows the employer to use more favourable criteria of selection than those provided by law in the absence of agreement (i.e., organizational, technical, and productive criteria; employee's seniority and number of family dependants).

– The reduction to one-third of the *contributo di ingresso* due from the employer to the INPS. The saving of the *contributo di ingresso* usually comes into play in reaching an individual agreement with employees by way of an incentive payment.

3.3   DISMISSAL

Apart from the collective agreement with the trade unions, it is appropriate to reach an individual agreement, entered into between each employee involved in the collective dismissal procedure, so as to avoid any further claims against the employer.

LATVIA

Imants Jansons

1   OVERVIEW

In Latvia, redundancy schemes and employment contracts are regulated by the Constitution of the Republic of Latvia, international treaties, the Labour Law (and other regulatory enactments), collective agreements and working-procedure regulations.

Under the Labour Law, there is a distinction between individual and collective redundancy schemes. This chapter focuses upon collective redundancies.

1.1   Terminating an Employment Contract by Giving Notice

The Labour Law sets out an employer's rights to terminate an employment contract. It also sets out the permissible grounds for redundancy, notification requirements, procedural rules, terms, prohibitions, restrictions and the rules relating to severance payments.

In accordance with Article 101 of the Labour Law, an employer is entitled to terminate an employment contract unilaterally in the following circumstances:

- The employee has committed a serious breach of the employment contract (or specific working procedures) without justifiable cause.
- During the performance of his/her work, the employee acted illegally and has therefore lost the employer's trust.

©2008 Kluwer Law International B.V., The Netherlands.
Maarten van Kempen, Lisa Patmore, Michael Ryley, and
Robert von Steinau-Steinrück (eds), *Redundancy,* pp. 127-136.

- During the performance of his/her work, the employee has acted contrary to moral principles to the extent that the employment contract cannot continue.
- During the performance of his/her work, the employee is or was under the influence of alcohol, drugs, or other toxic substances.
- The employee has committed a serious breach of the employment protection regulations and jeopardized the health and safety of others.
- The employee lacks sufficient competence for the performance of his/her contractual duties.
- The employee is unable to perform his/her contractual work for health reasons (and this has been certified by a doctor).
- An employee who previously performed the relevant work has been reinstated.
- The employer (legal person or partnership) is in liquidation.
- The number of employees needs to be reduced.

Where the number of employees needs to be reduced, the grounds for dismissal may not relate to the conduct of an employee or his/her personal abilities. The decision must be based on urgent and genuine economic, organizational, technological, or other similar reasons.

1.2   TERMINATION BY COURT DECISION

In certain circumstances, a court may be requested to terminate an employment contract or acknowledge the validity of a notice of termination.
    Termination by the court can be divided into two categories:

(a) An employer's right to make a claim for termination.
      In accordance with Article 101 of the Labour Law, in exceptional circumstances, an employer has the right to bring a claim for termination of an employment contract. However, this must be done within one month and the employer must have good cause. Such good cause will exist where the employer claims, on grounds of fairness or morality, that the contract cannot continue. In each case, it will be for the court to decide whether or not good cause exists.
      In addition, where an employer wishes to terminate the employment contract of a trade union member, the employer must obtain consent in advance from the relevant trade union. If the trade union does not consent, the employer may bring a claim in court for termination (Article 110 of the Labour Law).
(b) An employee's right to make a claim for a declaration regarding the validity of the notice of termination.
      Where an employer's notice of termination has no legal basis or the relevant procedure for termination has not been followed, the notice may be declared invalid (Article 124 of the Labour Law).

Where an employee has been dismissed on the basis of an invalid notice (or the employer has otherwise breached the employee's rights), the employee must be reinstated pursuant to a judgment from the court.

1.3   COLLECTIVE REDUNDANCY

The regulations regarding collective redundancies are set out in Article 105 of the Labour Law. These provide that a collective redundancy occurs where an employer intends to make the following number of employees redundant within a thirty-day period:

- at least five employees, where the employer has a workforce of between twenty and forty-nine employees;
- at least ten employees, where the employer has a workforce of between fifty and ninety-nine employees;
- at least 10% of the workforce, where the employer has a workforce of between 100 and 299 employees;
- at least thirty employees, where the employer has a workforce of at least 300 employees.

The provisions regarding collective redundancies do not apply to crews of a sea-faring ship or employees of public administrative bodies.

2   LEGAL REGULATIONS

2.1   TIMING

2.1.1   Termination by Notice

Termination by notice can be divided into two categories:

(a) Termination by an employee
    In accordance with Article 100 of the Labour Law, an employee may terminate his/her employment contract by giving one month's notice in writing. A shorter notice period may be stipulated in the employee's employment contract or an applicable collective agreement.
    An employee is not required to give one month's written notice if he/she has good cause. As stated above, good cause is based on considerations of morality and fairness that prevent the employment contract from continuing.

(b) Termination by an employer
    In accordance with Article 103 of the Labour Law, the relevant period of notice depends on the grounds on which the employee's contract has been terminated. The Labour Law sets out three notice periods in the absence of an applicable collective agreement or contractual term

(which may specify a longer period). The relevant notice periods are as follows:

(i)   Termination without notice

This is where the employee, during the performance of his/her work:

     (a) has acted illegally and therefore lost the employer's trust; and/or

     (b) is under the influence of alcohol, drugs or other toxic substances.

(ii)   Notice period of ten days

This is where the employee:

     (a) has, without justifiable cause, committed a serious breach of his/her employment contract or specified working procedures;

     (b) has, during the performance of his/her work, acted contrary to moral principles to the extent that the employment contract cannot continue;

     (c) has committed a serious breach of the employment protection regulations and has jeopardized the health and safety of others; and/or

     (d) is unable to perform his/her contractual work for health reasons (and this has been certified by a doctor).

(iii) Notice period of one month

This is where:

     (a) the employee lacks adequate occupational competence for the performance of his/her contractual duties;

     (b) an employee who previously performed the relevant work has been reinstated;

     (c) the number of employees is being reduced; and/or

     (d) the employer (legal person or partnership) is in liquidation.

2.1.2   Termination by Court Decision

Termination by court decision can be divided into two categories:

     (a) Employer's claim for termination

An employer must bring a claim for termination within one month. In accordance with Articles 101 and 110 of the Labour Law, time starts to run from the date on which the 'good cause' arose or the date on which the trade union failed to agree to the notice of termination.

     (b) Employee's claim for a declaration of validity

In accordance with Articles 122 and 123 of the Labour Law, an employee may bring a claim for a declaration that the employer's notice of termination is invalid. Such a claim should be brought within one month from the date on which the employee received the notice of termination.

2.1.3   Collective Redundancies

An employer who intends to carry out collective redundancies must notify the State Employment Agency and local government office in writing. Notification must be sent at least sixty days before the proposed redundancies are due to take effect.

This notice must include the following information:

- the employer's name;
- the location and type of activity carried out at the undertaking;
- the reasons for the redundancies;
- the number of employees affected (together with job titles/descriptions and qualifications of each);
- the overall number of employees employed at the undertaking;
- the time period within which redundancies are intended to take place; and
- details of any consultation with the employee representatives.

The employer must send a copy of this notice to the employee representatives. The State Employment Agency and local government office may also request further information from the employer.

Where an employer submits an incomplete notice, administrative sanctions may be imposed. In accordance with the Administrative Offences Act, these sanctions may be in the form of a warning or a fine. The fine for a natural person is up to 250 Latvian lats (LVL), and for a legal person it is up to LVL 500.

An employer may not begin to dismiss employees until sixty days after submitting a notice to the State Employment Agency. This time period may be extended by agreement between the employer and employee representatives. However, the employer and employee(s) cannot agree to an earlier date.

In exceptional cases, the State Employment Agency may extend the time limit to seventy-five days. If it does so, the State Employment Agency is required to notify the employer and employee representatives of the extension and the reasons for it. This must be done in writing and two weeks before expiry of the time period. An employer can appeal against this decision on the basis that the circumstances are not exceptional. However, at present, there is no clear definition of what amounts to an 'exceptional case'.

2.2 INFORMATION AND CONSULTATION

2.2.1 Collective Redundancies

An employer who intends to carry out collective redundancies is required to commence consultation with employee representatives in good time. The aim of consultation is to agree on the number of employees to be made redundant, the procedure to be followed and the social guarantees for those affected.

During consultation, the employer and employee representatives must examine all possible ways of avoiding or reducing the number of redundancies. They must also consider ways of mitigating the effects of the redundancies by taking social measures to re-employ or retrain the affected employees.

The employer is required to inform employee representatives about the collective redundancies in a timely fashion. The employer must also notify the employee representatives in writing about the reasons for the redundancies, the number of employees affected, the names and job titles/descriptions and qualifications of each, the overall number of employees employed by the undertaking, the time period within which redundancies are to be made and the proposed method of calculating severance payments.

The duty to inform and consult must be complied with regardless of whether a decision about collective redundancies is taken by the employer or by an entity in control of the employer. Failure by the employer to comply with its duty to inform, consult and/or notify will not be justified where the reason for the failure is that the dominant undertaking has not provided the employer with the necessary information.

2.3   RISKS

2.3.1   Selection Criteria

In relation to collective redundancies, the Labour Law sets out selection criteria that are based on professional and social criteria.

Article 108 of the Labour Law provides that, where the number of employees must be reduced, it is preferable to retain employees with higher performance results and qualifications. If these do not differ substantially, it is preferable to retain those employees who (in no particular order of priority):

- have a long period of service;
- have suffered an accident or been taken ill with an occupational disease while working for the relevant employer;
- have children under fourteen years of age or a disabled child under sixteen;
- have two or more dependants;
- have family members without a regular income;
- are disabled or suffering from radiation sickness;
- participated in mitigating the effects of the accident at the Chernobyl Atomic Power Plant;
- have less than five years until they reach retirement age;
- without leaving work, are in the process of acquiring an occupation (profession or trade) in an educational institution; and/or
- have been granted the status of a politically repressed person.

2.3.2   Notice Restrictions

Certain notice restrictions apply to employees who are members of a trade union who are temporarily incapacitated or do not perform work for a justifiable reason.

As stated in section 1.2 above, an employer may not give notice of termination to an employee who is a member of a trade union without the prior consent of the trade union. However, the following situations are an exception to this rule:

- The notice is given during the probation period, during which both employer and employee have the right to give written notice of termination three days before the proposed termination.
- The employee is performing work under the influence of alcohol, drugs or other toxic substances.
- An employee who previously performed the relevant work has been reinstated.
- The number of employees is being reduced.

Where the number of employees is being reduced, the grounds for termination must not be related to the conduct of an employee or his/her abilities. Instead, termination must be for genuine and urgent economic, organizational, technological or other similar reasons.

In accordance with the Labour Law, an employer may not give notice of termination to an employee who is temporarily incapacitated, on leave, or not performing for other justifiable reasons.

2.3.3 Wrongful Dismissal

If an employer fails to give notice of termination, the affected employee may bring a claim in court for a declaration that the notice is invalid. As stated above, this must be done within one month. It is then for the court to decide whether the notice is valid. In doing so, the court will take into account the relevant notice requirements outlined above. Where a court finds that the relevant notice period has not been followed, it may declare the notice to be invalid, order reinstatement and require a the employer to make a payment based on the employee's average earnings during the period of absence.

2.3.4 Unfair Dismissal

Where an employer has failed to follow the correct redundancy procedures, employees are entitled to bring claims for a declaration that the dismissal is invalid. In doing so, an employee may ask the court to:

- declare the notice of termination invalid;
- reinstate him/her into his/her previous role; and
- make an order for the employee's average earnings during the period of absence to be paid by the employer.

The court will then decide whether the employer has complied with the necessary procedures and/or whether the employee's claim has been sufficiently established.

2.3.5 Collective Redundancy

If an employer fails to inform or consult employee representatives, or obtain required consents, it may face liability under the Administrative Offences Act. Under this Act, the employer may, as stated in section 2.1.3 above, face a warning or a fine.

2.3.6 Discrimination

Anti-discrimination is one of the general principles of employment law in Latvia. The Labour Law prohibits direct or indirect discrimination on grounds of race, colour, gender, age, disability, religious, political, or other beliefs, ethnic or social origin, property or marital status, or sexual orientation.

Where an employer terminates an employment contract on any of these grounds, the employee may bring a claim in court for a declaration that the termination is invalid.

2.4 COSTS

2.4.1 Compensation

In cases of redundancy, an employer must effect a severance payment to the affected employees where they have been dismissed on any of the following grounds:

– where the employees lack adequate occupational competence for performance of their contractual work;
– where the employees are unable to perform their contractual work for health reasons;
– where an employee who previously performed the relevant work has been reinstated;
– where the employer (legal person or partnership) is in liquidation;
– where the number of employees is being reduced; or
– where an employee terminates his/her employment contract without giving notice in circumstances where he/she has good cause.

Severance pay is as follows:

– one month's average earnings if the employee has been working for the relevant employer for less than five years;
– two months' average earnings if the employee has been working for the employer for between five and ten years;
– three months' average earnings if the employee has been working for the employer for between ten and twenty years; and

– four months' average earnings if the employee has been working for the employer for more than twenty years.

A collective agreement or terms contained in the employment contract may, of course, provide for a greater amount of severance pay.

In accordance with the Labour Law, average earnings must be calculated on the basis of the employee's salary during the previous six months. It may also include supplementary payments (as specified in certain regulatory enactments), payments provided for in an applicable collective agreement or employment contract and any bonuses.

2.4.2   Damages for Unfair Dismissal

In accordance with Article 126 of the Labour Law, employees who have been dismissed illegally and reinstated must be paid their average earnings for the whole period of absence imposed on them (following judgment by the court). Compensation for this period of absence must also be paid where a court terminates an employment contract at the employee's request. This may be done despite the existence of grounds for reinstatement.

2.4.3   Social Plan

In Latvia, all employees are members of the state's social security system. This system provides protection for employees against certain risks relating to age, maternity, sickness, work injuries, and unemployment.

There are no specific legal requirements for the parties to draw up a social plan as part of a redundancy scheme. However, the legislation does not prevent employers, trade unions and/or employee representatives from agreeing to draw up social plans when redundancies do arise.

3   PRACTICAL ADVICE

3.1   TIMING, INFORMATION, AND CONSULTATION

It is important to comply with all the legal provisions and procedures relating to redundancy schemes. In addition, it is important to plan each redundancy process carefully and comply with the various obligations to inform, consult and notify.

3.2   COST AND RISKS

An employer may incur costs where an employee brings a claim in court for a declaration as to the validity of a notice of termination and/or brings a claim for reinstatement. A Latvian court may well allow an employee's claim to succeed if the employer has breached provisions of the Labour Law. In such cases, the employer will be obliged to pay compensation to the employee for the period of absence imposed on him/her, in addition to the costs of litigation.

Accordingly, it is important to comply with all the provisions and procedures contained in the Labour Law in order to avoid the high cost of litigation.

LITHUANIA

Ieva Povilaitienė

1   OVERVIEW

Under the laws of the Republic of Lithuania, employment contracts may be terminated by mutual agreement between the parties, on the initiative of the employee or on the initiative of the employer.

Redundancy schemes in Lithuania are regulated by the Labour Code of the Republic of Lithuania (hereinafter 'Labour Code'). As a general rule, termination of the employment contract is legal if it is based on permitted grounds established by law; otherwise the termination will be invalid.

According to Article 129 of the Labour Code, an employer may lawfully only terminate an open-ended employment contract with an employee by giving him/her notice in accordance with the procedure established in Article 130 of the Labour Code. The dismissal of an employee without fault on his/her part is permitted if the employee cannot, with his/her consent, be transferred to other work. Transfer to other work, if there is a vacancy in the workplace and the employee agrees to be transferred, is compulsory.

An employment contract can only be terminated on the grounds established in Article 129 of the Labour Code, in two groups of circumstances:

- The first group of circumstances is related to the employee, i.e., circumstances which relate to the qualifications, professional skills or conduct of an employee.

©2008 Kluwer Law International B.V., The Netherlands.
Maarten van Kempen, Lisa Patmore, Michael Ryley, and
Robert von Steinau-Steinrück (eds), *Redundancy,* pp. 137-142.

- The second group of circumstances is not related to the employee, i.e., an employment contract may be terminated on economic or technological grounds or due to the restructuring of the workplace (hereinafter 'the restructuring of the workplace').

Under the terms of Articles 129 and 130 of the Labour Code, an employer is entitled to terminate a fixed-term employment contract before its expiry only in extraordinary cases where the employee cannot, with his/her consent, be transferred to other work, or alternatively, on payment of the average wage to the employee for the remaining period of the employment contract.

It is specially provided that an employment contract with employees who will be entitled to a full old-age pension within five years; persons under eighteen years of age; disabled persons; and employees raising two or more children under fourteen years of age may be terminated only in extraordinary cases, where retention of the employee would be of substantial detriment to the interests of the employer.

It is prohibited to terminate an employment contract and to dismiss an employee during a period of temporary illness, as well as during his/her vacation leave, or whilst called up to fulfil active national service.

2   MAJOR LEGAL REGULATIONS

2.1   TIMING

2.1.1   Pre-notice Information and Consultation

According to Article 130 part 4 of the Labour Code, before issuing a decision to terminate an employment contract pursuant to the restructuring of the workplace, the employer must, prior to giving notice of termination of an employment contract, hold consultations with employee representatives (i.e., the trade union or the works council) in order to seek ways of avoiding or minimizing the negative effects of the intended restructuring. It should be noted that whilst there is an obligation to consult with employee representatives there is no requirement to obtain their approval. If consultations with trade unions or the works council have not been held, the trade union (or works council) is entitled to apply to court for a declaration that the dismissals will be illegal.

Failure to consult will not render the dismissals unlawful if there are no representatives of the employees in the workplace.

2.1.2   Notice Period

According to Article 130 of the Labour Code, an employer must give two months' written notice of termination of employment (four months in the case of employees who will be entitled to the full old-age pension within five years; persons under eighteen years of age; disabled persons; and employees raising children under fourteen years of age), receipt of which must be confirmed by the employee in writing.

The notice of termination must specify:

- the reasons for the termination of the employment contract;
- the date of dismissal from work; and
- the procedure for settling accounts with the employee being dismissed.

The notice period must be prolonged by the period of any temporary illness or vacation of the employee, and by the period of the decision of the court in the event that the consent of the court to the dismissal of an employee representative/works-council member is sought.

If the employee is dismissed earlier than the expiry of the notice period, the date of dismissal may be deferred by the court to the last day of the notice period.

2.1.3 Collective Redundancies

EC Directives 75/129 and 98/59 on the approximation of the laws of the Member States relating to collective redundancies are implemented in the Labour Code of Lithuania.

Depending on the number of employees to be dismissed within a certain period of time (see below), advance notice of a mass lay-off may be required.

In the event of a reduction in the number of employees or cessation of the operations of an enterprise in accordance with the procedure prescribed by law, an employer must, two months in advance thereof, notify the territorial labour office, the municipal institution and representatives of the enterprise's employees in writing (Article 19 of the Labour Code) of the employer's intention to make redundant within a period of thirty calendar days:

- ten or more employees where an enterprise employs up to ninety-nine employees;
- more than 10% of the employees where an enterprise employs 100-200 employees;
- thirty or more employees where an enterprise employs 300 or more employees.

If a group of employees working under fixed-term employment contracts or seasonal employment contracts is dismissed on the expiry of the terms set out in those contracts, the same will not be treated as a collective dismissal.

2.2 INFORMATION AND CONSULTATION

2.2.1 Information and Consultation with the Representatives of the Employees in the Case of Collective Redundancies

As mentioned above, in the event of an intended dismissal of employees on the grounds of the restructuring of the workplace, the employer must, prior to giving notice of the termination of an employment contract, provide information to and hold consultations with representatives of the employees (i.e., with trade unions or the works council).

Following the Order of Social Security and Labour Minister No. 61 of 30 May 2005, in the case of reducing the number of employees, the employer is obliged to inform the trade unions or the works council in writing seven days prior to notifying the territorial labour office and the municipal institution (see section 2.1.3) concerning:

- the reason for the planned redundancy;
- the projected extent of the redundancies;
- the period over which the projected redundancies are to be effected; and
- the number of categories of workers to be made redundant.

The employer is obliged to hold consultations with the representatives of the employees, to outline its proposals, and to inform the representatives of the employees in writing about its decisions.

In the event that there are no representatives of the employees in the workplace, the employer is entitled to inform the employees personally or at a meeting of the employees.

2.3   RISKS

2.3.1   Notice Restrictions

It is prohibited to give notice of the termination of an employment contract and to dismiss from work an employee during a period of temporary disability (Article 133 of the Labour Code), during his vacation, or when an employee is called up to fulfil active national defence service or other duties of a citizen of the Republic of Lithuania, save for the cases specified in Article 136(1) of the Labour Code.

According to Article 132 of the Labour Code, an employment contract may not be terminated with a pregnant woman from the day on which her employer receives a medical certificate confirming pregnancy and for a month after maternity leave, except for the cases specified in Articles 136(1) and (2) of the Labour Code. An employment contract with employees raising a child under three years of age may not be terminated without fault on the part of the employee concerned (Article 129 of the Labour Code).

2.3.2   Selection Criteria

Following Article 135 of the Labour Code, in the event of a reduction in the number of employees on economic or technological grounds or due to the restructuring of the workplace, priority to retaining a job shall be enjoyed by those employees:

- who sustained an injury or contracted an occupational disease at that workplace;
- who are raising children (including adopted children) under sixteen years of age alone or caring for other family members recognized as disabled;

- whose continuous length of service at that workplace is at least ten years, with the exception of employees who have become entitled to the full old-age pension or are in receipt thereof;
- who will be entitled to the old-age pension in not more than three years;
- to whom such a right is granted in the collective agreement; or
- who are elected to the representative bodies of employees (Article 19 of the Labour Code).

2.4 Costs

2.4.1 Statutory Compensation

The cost of the termination of the employment contract at the initiative of the employer shall be these:

- compensation for unused annual leave;
- notice pay (two or four months);
- the rest of the remuneration for the period up to the date of dismissal;
- severance pay in the amount of his average monthly salary from one to six months (computed according to the three last monthly salaries of the employee), taking into account the continuous length of service of the employee, as follows (according to Article 140 of the Labour Code):

Months of Service	Months Worth of Salary
less than 12	1
12-36	2
36-60	3
60-120	4
120-240	5
more than 240	6

2.4.2 Costs as a Result of Unlawful or Unfair Dismissal

If the court establishes that the employee was dismissed unlawfully or without a valid reason and the employee cannot be reinstated in his previous job due to economic, technological, organizational, or similar reasons, or because he is faced with conditions not favourable for work, the court will recognize the termination of the employment contract as unlawful and award the employee:

- severance pay in the amount specified in Article 140(1) of the Labour Code; as well as
- the average wage for the period of involuntary idleness from the day of dismissal until the effective date of the court decision.

3   ADVICE FOR LEGAL PRACTICE

3.1   TIMING

The redundancy schedule should be prepared carefully, in order to ensure that representatives of the employees will have no cause for objection on legal grounds.

Notifications about dismissal should be issued to the employees on time and bearing in mind that the notice period may be prolonged in the case of certain employees (e.g., those absent due to illness or vacation).

3.2   COST AND RISKS

Breaches of the redundancy procedures can be very expensive, since the consequence in many cases is the invalidity of the termination.

Sometimes the possibility of terminating employment contracts by mutual agreement should be considered, in order to reduce the risk of the termination being held to be invalid, thus avoiding court hearings and the like. In the case of termination of the employment contract by mutual agreement, compensation in the sum agreed to by the parties should be paid. In this way, the need for giving notice and the restrictions relating to some groups of employees (e.g., pregnant women, employees raising children) are avoided. Such mutual agreement does not affect the employee's entitlement to unemployment benefits.

LUXEMBOURG

Guy Castegnaro
Ariane Claverie

1   OVERVIEW

Provisions regarding the termination of employment contracts, and, more specifically, redundancies, are contained in the Luxembourg Labour Code and in various
collective labour agreements. Redundancy refers to dismissals for reasons not
inherent to the particular employee(s). The redundancy may either be individual
or collective.

Luxembourg's legislation protects all categories of workers against unfair
and unlawful dismissal by providing precise procedures for both individual and
collective dismissals, as well as by requiring any dismissal to be founded on valid
grounds. Where termination is deemed to be unfair, the employee may claim
significant material and moral damages in addition to his/her possible rights to
a departure allowance.

It shall be noted that since the introduction of the Tripartite Law on 22 December 2006, to promote the maintenance of employment, it is no longer possible to
consider the issue of redundancies without considering the rules established for
the maintenance of employment. The Tripartite Law provides rules to be complied
with in the case of redundancies, such as a process of information centralization.
In addition, employers should try to avoid redundancies by establishing so-called
employment maintenance plans.

©2008 Kluwer Law International B.V., The Netherlands.
Maarten van Kempen, Lisa Patmore, Michael Ryley, and
Robert von Steinau-Steinrück (eds), *Redundancy,* pp. 143-150.

2   MAJOR LEGAL REGULATIONS

2.1   Timing

2.1.1   Duration of the Notice Period (Article L.124-3)

Except in the event of gross misconduct, the employee is entitled to be given notice prior to dismissal. The duration of the notice period is determined by reference to the employee's length of service in the undertaking or in the group of undertakings concerned.

Thus, in the case of employment for a period of less than five years, the notice period is two months. If the employee has been employed for more than five years but less than ten years, the notice period extends to four months. In the case of employment for at least ten years, the notice period is six months. It shall be noted that in the case of collective redundancies, the minimum notice period is seventy-five days.

2.1.2   Collective Redundancies (Articles L.166-1 to L.166-9)

2.1.2.1   Notification to the Labour Administration (Article L.166-4)

In the case of foreseen collective redundancies, namely, redundancies concerning at least seven employees within a period of thirty days or at least fifteen employees within a period of ninety days, the employer shall notify the labour administration of the collective redundancy proposal at the beginning of the negotiations at the latest. A copy of the notification shall also be sent to the Labour Inspectorate.

2.1.2.2   Collective Consultation (Articles L.166-1 to L.166-8)

Prior to any collective redundancy, a social plan must be established and negotiated with the staff delegation, the joint works council if any, and the trade unions if a collective bargaining agreement applies. The Labour Inspectorate must be informed of the outcome of the negotiations, at the very latest fifteen days from the beginning of the negotiations.

If the social partners do not agree on the content of the social plan within this fifteen-day period, they must sign a report stating their disagreement. They will then have to approach the National Conciliation Office, three days after the signature of the report at the latest. The National Conciliation Office will reach its decision within a twenty-day period, and will send its report to the Labour Administration and the Labour Inspectorate without delay.

Any individual notification of collective redundancy prior to the signature of a social plan or prior to the National Conciliation Office's report is void.

2.1.3 Individual Redundancies (Part V, Title I, Chapter I)

2.1.3.1 Notification to the Comité de Conjoncture (Committee of Economic Circumstances) (Article L.511-27)

An employer with more than fifteen employees who executes a dismissal for reasons not inherent to the employee's person, namely an individual redundancy, must notify such redundancy to the secretariat of the *Comité de Conjoncture* by, at the latest, the time the letter of dismissal is served.

2.1.3.2 Collective Consultation Aimed at Reaching an Employment Maintenance Plan (Articles L.513-1 to L.513-4)

The *Comité de Conjoncture* is entitled to invite the social partners to start discussions aimed at establishing an employment maintenance plan when it becomes apparent that dismissals are for reasons not inherent to the employee's person. The *Comité de Conjoncture* shall intervene when it notices, within the same undertaking, five redundancies within a reference period of three months or eight redundancies within a reference period of six months at the latest.

Where there is a lack of intervention on the part of the *Comité de Conjoncture*, the social partners may collectively take the initiative to begin discussions when they foresee economic or financial problems in the undertaking that may have a negative impact in terms of employment. The *Comité de Conjoncture* must be informed of the discussions.

The plan must contain provisions recording the result of the discussions between the social partners. In particular, these provisions should address the issues of short-term unemployment, training, early retirement possibilities and career transition. The full list of subjects to be discussed is set down in Article L.513-3 of the Labour Code. Once signed by the social partners, the employment maintenance plan is transmitted to the *Comité de Conjoncture*, which then submits it to the Labour Minister for approval.

If the discussions between social partners do not result in the establishment of an employment maintenance plan, a report containing the content and conclusions of the discussions, signed by all parties, is submitted to the board of the *Comité de Conjoncture*.

Companies that already have a maintenance plan need not undertake negotiations with social partners aimed at establishing a social plan in the case of collective redundancies. In such cases, negotiations are aimed at reaching a settlement agreement regarding financial compensation.

2.2   INFORMATION AND CONSULTATION

**2.2.1   Notification and Consultation Obligations in Cases
                of Individual Redundancies (Articles L.124-2 and L.124-5)**

Any employer with at least 150 employees must convene an interview with the
employee concerned prior to notification of the redundancy.

The preliminary meeting notification must contain the following information:

– the date, time, and venue of the interview;
– the fact that the employee may be assisted during the interview by a colleague or by a representative of a national trade union with which the
  company's staff representatives are affiliated; and
– the employer may indicate if he/she will be assisted by an employee or by
  a representative of an employers' association.

During the meeting, the employer must explain the reasons for the redundancy
programme, and must listen to the employee's comments and those of the person
who is assisting him/her. The employer then sends a letter of dismissal to the
employee, on the day following the preliminary meeting at the earliest, and no
later than eight days following that meeting.

The reasons for the redundancy need not be stated in the notification of dismissal, but the employee may request communication of the reasons for the redundancy by registered letter within one month of the date of being notified of the
dismissal. Within one month, the employer must provide detailed reasons as to the
grounds for the redundancy sent in a letter by registered post. The reasons must be
supported by demonstrable and explicit facts.

**2.2.2   Notification and Consultation Obligations in Cases
                of Collective Redundancies (Article L.166-2)**

In the case of collective redundancies, the employer must inform the employees'
representatives of the following information, in writing, preferably prior to the
negotiations and at the beginning of the negotiations at the very latest:

– the reasons for the anticipated collective redundancies;
– the number and categories of workers to be made redundant;
– the number and categories of workers employed;
– the period over which it is anticipated that the redundancies will be
  implemented;
– the criteria considered in choosing the workers to be dismissed, without
  prejudice to the competence of the joint works council and/or the employees' representatives; and
– the considered method, if any, of calculating any possible departure
  allowance exceeding that provided by the law or by collective bargaining

agreement, or the reasons, if any, justifying the employer's refusal to pay such allowance.

A copy of this written communication shall be sent to the Labour Administration, which will transmit it to the Labour Inspectorate.

In addition, as stated above, a social plan must be established by the social partners. The negotiations must cover possible ways in which to avoid or reduce the number of redundancies concerned, as well as ways to reduce their consequences through social measures, such as those facilitating the redeployment and immediate re-integration of the employees on the labour market. The law provides an exclusive list of subjects to be examined during the social partners' negotiations. These subjects are similar to those applicable to the establishment of an employment maintenance plan.

2.3   RISKS

2.3.1   Unfair Dismissal/Redundancy

Dismissal or redundancy is regarded as unfair and contrary to social and economic reason if the reasons for it are unlawful or if it is not founded on valid grounds, that is to say, grounds related to the employee's aptitude or conduct, or arising from the operating needs of the business, establishment or department.

Examples of dismissal for unlawful reasons include:

– dismissal notified during the period in which an employee on sick leave is protected;
– dismissal based on the transfer of an undertaking;
– dismissal based on the refusal of the employee to accept part-time/full-time employment;
– dismissal based on the refusal of the employee to accept overtime work under conditions other than those provided for in the employment contract; and
– dismissal based on the refusal of the employee to waive his/her right to early retirement indemnity.

In the case of collective redundancies, the redundancy of an employee prior to the signature of a social plan, or the production of a failure report from the National Conciliation Office, may be declared void.

2.3.2   Rights of the Employees' Representatives
(Articles L.415-11 and L.425-4)

If the employer foresees dismissing a staff representative (or a member of the joint works council) for economic reasons, the redundancy notice may only be given after the end of a six-month period following the end of the representative's mandate, at the earliest. The same protection applies to candidates for staff representative elections, for a three-month period following the elections.

The prior approval of the joint works council is required for the redundancy of a member of the joint works council.

2.3.3 Discrimination

In accordance with the law of 28 November 2006, the employer must not use discriminatory selection tools and criteria to determine the employees to be dismissed. This law prohibits any direct or indirect discrimination based on religion, convictions, handicap, age, sexual orientation, or real or supposed affiliation to a race or an ethnic origin.

2.3.4 Maternity Leave and Parental Leave (Article L.337-1)

The employee may not be dismissed for economic reasons during maternity and parental leave.

2.4 Costs

2.4.1 Departure Allowance (Article L.124-7)

Any employee dismissed for a reason not inherent to his/her person is entitled to a departure allowance following at least five years of service within the company.

As regards all employees, in the case of seniority of more than five but less than ten years, the departure allowance is equal to one month of gross salary; in that of ten but less than fifteen years, it represents two months of gross salary; and if the employee has been employed for more than fifteen but less than twenty years, it represents three months of gross salary.

As regards white-collar employees, in the case of employment of more than twenty but less than twenty-five years, the departure allowance represents six months of gross salary. For employment of over twenty-five but less than thirty years, it represents nine months of gross salary. Where someone is employed for more than thirty years, the allowance represents twelve months of gross salary.

2.4.2 Treatment during the Notice Period (Article L.124-9)

The employment contract remains in force until the end of the notice period. Thus, the employee is entitled to his/her usual salary during the notice period.

The employer may exempt the employee from working during the notice period. The employee is then entitled to begin to work for another employer. If the employee receives a lower salary than previously, his 'former' employer must pay the difference in salary until the end of the notice period.

In addition, during the notice period, the employee will be entitled to:

- the employer's contribution to hospital insurance and group insurance, if any;
- the use of a company car if such use was allowed for private reasons; and
- the payment of his fixed representation allowance, if any.

At the end of the employment contract, the employee will also be entitled to the payment of his/her remaining holidays and to a pro rata bonus provided that the latter can be considered as forming part of his/her remuneration.

2.4.3 Claims for Unfair or Unlawful Dismissal (Articles L.124-11 and L.124-12)

Luxembourg's legislation does not provide for pre-determined compensation for unfair or unlawful dismissal or redundancy. The labour courts have a wide discretion in determining the amount of compensation and will take into consideration the difficulties faced by an older employee in finding a new job.

As regards material damages, the court will attempt to put the employee into the financial situation he/she would have been in had the dismissal not happened. Additionally, the employer may be liable to reimburse the unemployment benefits which the employee received if the latter is a Luxembourg resident.

The employee may also request to be reinstated by the former employer. The court may only recommend the reinstatement to the employer. If the employer decides to proceed with the employee's reinstatement, it will not have to pay compensation to the employee. If the employer refuses to proceed with reinstatement, it is obliged to pay one month's salary in addition to the compensation outlined above.

As regards moral damages, they are fixed by the court in monetary terms after having considered the employee's personal situation and the circumstances of the dismissal. On average, amounts vary between EUR 500 and 12,500.

3 ADVICE FOR LEGAL PRACTICE

3.1 TIMING

In order to limit the employer's risk of unlawfully dismissing its employees, sufficient time should be allowed, in particular with respect to procedures such as that regarding the information and consultation between the employees' representatives and the employees who are the subjects of the anticipated redundancies.

3.2 INFORMATION AND CONSULTATION

The information to be given to the employees' representatives and/or to the joint works council shall be carefully prepared by the employer in order to provide them with sufficient information, as required by law, and thus avoid any additional delay due to a lack of communication.

3.3   RISKS AND COSTS

3.3.1   Alternative Employment

An employer may wish to transfer an employee to another position rather than to dismiss him/her.

Where the employment contract provides that the employee may be transferred to a different position for business purposes, such transfer may not always occur when it is not in the interests of the employee and where the employee's function is an essential element of the employment contract.

Any transfer effected without the employee's consent, in cases where the employee's function is an essential element of the employment contract, constitutes a breach of contract. Such breaches may be sanctioned by an indemnity paid to the employee if the employee expressed refusal to accept it by resigning. Alternatively, it may be sanctioned by the nullity of the contracts' modification if the employee is still employed by the company. Similarly, if the employer dismisses an employee on account of his/her refusal to accept a transfer of position, this may constitute an unfair dismissal.

To avoid such breaches, the employer must obtain the employee's consent prior to any transfer of position. Alternatively, the employer must respect the legal procedure by inviting the employee to an interview in advance and by sending him/her a notification as is the case for dismissals with notice.

Finally, it should be noted that employees' representatives may not be subject to a modification of their employment contract during their mandate.

3.3.2   Use of Settlement and Waiver Agreements in
          Cases of Claims

If there is a chance that a redundancy may be regarded by the court as unfair, it is advisable for the employer to reach an agreement with the employee in question. This agreement must state that the employer agrees to pay financial compensation to the employee. The indemnities provided for in the agreement are usually based on the amounts that could be awarded by the court.

A clause may be included in the agreement in order to prevent the employee from taking any actual or future judicial action in relation to the employment contract.

MALTA

Matthew Brincat

1   OVERVIEW

Maltese law specifies, in section 36 of the Employment and Industrial Relations Act (EIRA) of 2002 (Chapter 452 of the Laws of Malta), that a contract for an indefinite term may be terminated by the employer for reasons of redundancy.

By inference, it can be deduced that a fixed-term contract of employment may not be terminated for reasons of redundancy, and that redundancy may not be raised as a good and sufficient cause for terminating such a contract. In cases where an employer is seeking to reduce the workforce, and the employees in question are on fixed-term contracts, the employer is bound, under Article 36(11), to pay the employee an amount equal to half of the wages that the employee would have earned in the remaining contract period by way of legal penalty.

Under Maltese law, there is no definition of redundancy. The Industrial Tribunal in Malta has often referred to ILO Recommendation Number 119 on the Termination of Contracts of Employment, or, alternatively to English Law. The ILO Recommendation (supplemented by Termination of Employment Convention Number 158 of 1982) states that a contract of employment may be terminated for reasons based on the operational requirements of the undertaking, establishment or service.

It is therefore clear that termination by reason of redundancy is not in any way linked to the conduct or capacity of the employee, but rather with the organizational or financial affairs of the employer. As a result, the Industrial Tribunal has accepted as redundant an employee who is 'excessive', 'superfluous', or 'surplus to requirements'. The Tribunal has also held that the reason for a person being classed as excessive, superfluous or surplus to requirements must be a genuine one, linked to the operational requirements of the undertaking.

Typical reasons for redundancy, which have been accepted by the Maltese Tribunal, include:

- loss of clientele resulting in a loss of work;
- financial difficulties;
- complete abolition of the post; and
- genuine re-organization (a change of control does not amount to a genuine re-organization, although it may be a plausible reason for carrying out a genuine re-organization).

It is paramount that the redundancy is not perceived as an excuse to terminate the employment of the employee in question. The Industrial Tribunal remains competent at all times to examine the case in order to determine whether the redundancy was genuine or not.

2   MAJOR LEGAL REGULATIONS

2.1   Timing

2.1.1   Notice Periods (EIRA, Section 36(5))

Employment contracts are usually entered into for an indefinite period of time in Malta. For most employment relationships, an employment-at-will doctrine does not apply.

As regards termination, Maltese law distinguishes between termination for cause and termination due to redundancy.

The process leading to a declaration of redundancy is heavily regulated by EIRA. Prior to making an employee redundant, the employer is obliged to give due notice to the employee being made redundant. The notice periods are laid down in Table 1.

Table 1

Length of Service	Mandatory Notice Period
One to six months	One week
Six months to two years	Two weeks
Two years to four years	Four weeks
Four years to seven years	Eight weeks
More than seven years	An additional one week per year of service up to a maximum of twelve weeks

Once due notice has been given to the employee, in practice, the employer may *elect to either*:

- keep the employee in his employment during the term of the notice; or
- terminate the employee's employment immediately by paying the employee a sum equal to the full wages that the employee would earn during the notice period.

2.1.2   Selection of Employees to Be Made Redundant (EIRA, Section 36(4))

Article 36(4) of EIRA lays down the rule as to the sequence in which employees may be identified as redundant, and states that:

> [w]here an employer intends to terminate the employment of an employee on grounds of redundancy, he shall terminate the employment of that person who was engaged last in the class of employment affected by such redundancy.

The term 'class of employment' is in turn defined in Article 2 of EIRA as follows:

> '[C]lass' when used in the context of a group or a category of employees shall refer to the groups or categories listed in a collective agreement. Provided that where there is no collective agreement or where a collective agreement does not stipulate groups or categories of employees, it shall refer to the work performed or expected to be performed independently of the title or name given to the post.

If an employer deviates from this rule, the termination of employment for reasons of redundancy may be found to be invalid by the Industrial Tribunal, and compensation or re-instatement of the employee may be ordered.

2.1.3   The Possibility of Re-instatement (EIRA, Section 36(3))

Article 36(3) of EIRA provides that if the post formerly occupied by the employee made redundant is subsequently made available within one year of termination of the employee's employment, the employee is entitled to be re-employed in that post on conditions of employment that are not less favourable to him than those to which he was entitled previously. In cases of collective or group redundancies, the offer of employment should be given in the reverse order that the employees were made redundant, so that the employee with the most years of service with the employer is offered the job first.

With regard to this issue, the Industrial Tribunal has decided that it is important that, if and where possible, the employee be offered alternative employment prior to being made redundant. As regards those dismissed during injury or maternity leave, the Tribunal has made it clear that such persons may not be made redundant.

**2.1.4   Mass Lay-Offs Collective Redundancies
                   (Legal Notice 428 of 2002)**

The aim of the Collective Redundancies Regulations (Legal Notice 428 of 2002) is to make provision in order for employees or their representatives within an organization to be (a) informed in writing of possible future redundancies, and (b) given an opportunity to be consulted as specified below.

A 'collective redundancy' is defined in Article 2 of the Regulations as:

- ten workers, for employers employing 20-100 workers;
- 10% of the workforce, for employers employing 100-300; and
- thirty workers, for employers employing over 300 workers.

In order for there to be a 'collective redundancy', the employer must make the number of employees described above (calculated according to the size of the enterprise) redundant. All redundancies made over a period of thirty days are to be considered as one group with regards to calculating the above thresholds.

The Regulations specify that an employer planning to make redundancies may not terminate the employment of the employees affected by the redundancy before notifying the employees' representatives in writing of their intention to make collective redundancies and giving these representatives an opportunity to consult with the employer.

2.2   INFORMATION AND CONSULTATION

**2.2.1   Consultation with the Workers' Representatives
                   (Legal Notice 428 of 2002 & Section 37 of EIRA)**

Consultation must occur seven days after the notice of redundancy has been given to the employees' representatives. It must address the ways and means of avoiding the redundancies altogether; ways of reducing the number of employees affected and ways of mitigating the consequences of the redundancies. The employees' representatives are the union representatives in the case of a recognized union or the elected workers representatives in the case of a non-unionized workforce.

Prior to the expiry of the seven days mentioned above (i.e., prior to the commencement of the consultation process), the employee representatives must be given a written statement containing:

- the reasons for the redundancy;
- the number of employees which the employer intends to make redundant;
- the number of employees usually employed by the employer;
- the criteria proposed for the selection of the employees (the selection must be made whilst keeping in mind that the last in-first out rule is part of

Maltese law, which specifies that the last person to enter into a particular class of employment is to be made redundant first); and
– details regarding any redundancy payments due.

As far as information is concerned, the employer cannot withhold information on the basis that the decision to make the redundancies originated from an order of a parent company or another company having a connection with the employer. Moreover, the employer may not withhold the information required on the basis that the lack of information is due to the fact that the 'connected company' has not provided the necessary information to the employer.

An amendment to the Regulations, published in Legal Notice 442 of 2004, clarifies that the notice of termination to be given to the employees affected by the redundancy may be given to them from the date on which the consultations commence.

2.2.2　　　Mass Lay-Offs (Legal Notice 428 of 2002)

A copy of the notification and the written statement mentioned above must also be sent to the Director responsible for Employment and Industrial Relations. Such collective redundancies may not take effect prior to thirty days following the notification of the collective redundancy to the Director. Once the Director receives such a notice, he/she may opt to:

– grant the employer, in exceptional circumstances, a shorter period within which to make the redundancies; or
– lengthen the period of thirty days by adding a further period of thirty days, for a total of sixty days.

2.3　　　Cost and Risks

2.3.1　　　Protection against Unfair Dismissal

If the employer fails to give the appropriate notice periods for redundancy, the Labour Office may bring a criminal action against the employer for the non-payment of notice money. The employer may then be ordered to pay the notice money and may also be asked to pay a fine ranging from approximately EUR 235, to approximately EUR 2,350.

The employee may also contest the redundancy, claiming that his employment was terminated unfairly and that redundancy was not the real reason for termination, or that he was not the person that should have been selected for redundancy in accordance with Maltese law. Such a claim must be brought before the Industrial Tribunal within four months from the declaration of redundancy. The Tribunal may order compensation (there is no capping on the compensation that may be given) or it may order the re-instatement of the employee. Re-instatement is not possible if the employee held a position of trust.

The consent of the local authorities is not required prior to termination of an employment contract for redundancy.

Interestingly, there is no further protection under Maltese law for those employees who are pregnant, sick, disabled or for those employees that for any reason are not currently working at the employer's workplace. In these situations, the redundancy laws apply to this category of employees as they would to any other. For example, an employee who has entered the class of employment last would be made redundant, notwithstanding that she was pregnant.

2.3.2   Notice Periods

Regardless of whether employees are required to work during the notice period, costs are associated with notice periods, since some employees may have long notice periods during which they will be entitled to their salary. The notice periods must therefore be taken into account when planning redundancy schemes.

There are no additional statutory severance payments that must be made under Maltese law in cases of redundancy.

2.3.3   Consultation with the Workers Representatives

Non-observance of the Collective Redundancies Regulations (including the provisions on information and consultation with the workers representatives) results in a criminal offence. The Department of Employment and Industrial Relations may prosecute such offences, which are punishable with a fine set at a minimum of approximately EUR 1,175 per employee made redundant.

3   ADVICE FOR LEGAL PRACTICE

3.1   TIMING

Timing is of the essence in any redundancy process. Preparation for the declaration of redundancy provides the employer with the opportunity of discussing the various timings and selection parameters that must be met in order to avoid incurring unnecessary fines and/or compensation payments.

3.2   INFORMATION AND CONSULTATION

In order to avoid delay tactics by the workers representatives in the negotiations regarding redundancy plans, the notification to the representatives and to the Director should be prepared and processed as carefully as possible. Short notice tactics will only delay the process, since there is no timeframe for the negotiations to end, only one regarding when they should begin.

3.3   COST AND RISKS

As a general rule, the better the management of the preparation phase, the lower the costs and risks tend to be. In particular, breaches of formal requirements can only be avoided reliably if there has been sufficient preparation. Without the necessary preparation, costly crisis management will be required. This will not only increase the costs but will create unnecessary social tension which can only lead to further financial liability.

THE NETHERLANDS

Wouter Engelsman
Hannagnes Faber
Maarten van Kempen
Dave Sieler

1   OVERVIEW

Redundancy schemes in the Netherlands are subject to several labour law regulations, such as the Dutch Civil Code, the Extraordinary Decree on Labour Relations
1945, the Dismissal Decree, the Collective Redundancy (Notification) Act and the
Works Councils Act (WCA).

   In the Netherlands, redundancies are related to business reorganizations that
are either related to a business' financial situation or its organization. Reorganization is not a clear-cut concept. It can suggest downsizing, which will lead to job
cuts or closure of positions, or 'right-sizing', where fewer employees carry out the
same activities.

1.1   TERMINATION OF EMPLOYMENT AGREEMENT

In general, the Dutch Civil Code (DCC) provides two ways to terminate an
employment contract without an employee's consent.

1.1.1   Termination by Giving Notice

The first method requires an employer to give notice in accordance with the appropriate notice period. Before an employee gives notice, a pre-notice procedure should be followed because the Extraordinary Decree on Labour Relations 1945 (BBA 1945) prohibits an employer from giving an employee a notice of termination without first obtaining permission from the Dutch Centre for Work and Income (CWI). The CWI's permission is not required if:

- the employee gives a notice of termination;
- the termination relates to the dismissal of a managing director;
- the employment contract is terminated by mutual consent;
- the termination relates to the expiration of a fixed-term contract;
- the dismissal is made for an urgent cause which justifies dismissal with immediate effect as mentioned in DCC, Article 7:678;
- the dismissal results from the employer's bankruptcy; or
- the dismissal is carried out during the employee's probation period.

The BBA 1945 does not apply to:

- employees of public bodies;
- the teaching staff of educational institutes led by a natural person or body corporate;
- people holding ecclesiastical offices; and
- employees who only or predominately perform domestic work or personal services in private households for less than three days a week.

1.1.2   Termination by Court Decision

The second way in which an employment contract may be terminated without employee consent is if the court terminates the employment contract for important reasons at the request of either the employer or the employee (DCC Article 7:685). 'Important reasons' refer to circumstances that create an urgent cause for termination or those changes in circumstances that justify the termination of the employment relationship immediately or on very short notice. The court can grant compensation if it terminates the employment contract.

1.2   MUTUAL CONSENT

Until October 2006, unemployment benefits were granted to compensate employees who voiced opposition to their employer's decision to dismiss them. Therefore, termination by mutual consent was not an attractive option. As a result of the Unemployment Benefits Act, since October 2006 an employee is only prevented from obtaining unemployment benefits if he/she initiated the termination of his/her employment contract or in the case of an urgent cause, as mentioned in DCC

Article 7:678. Consequently, an increasing number of employers and employees try to reach settlements and terminate employment contracts by mutual consent.

1.3   INDIVIDUAL VERSUS COLLECTIVE REDUNDANCY

From a timing, information and consultation perspective, a distinction can be made between individual dismissals and collective dismissals. The European Collective Redundancies Directives 75/129 and 98/59 have been implemented into the Collective Redundancy Notification Act (*Wet Melding Collectief Ontslag*, or WMCO).

1.4   COMPENSATION

No Dutch legislation exists governing the calculation of compensation for employees in the event of redundancy. Guidelines for compensation and damages have instead been developed by case law.

2   MAJOR REGULATIONS

2.1   TIMING

2.1.1   Termination by Giving Notice

2.1.1.1   Pre-notice Procedure (BBA 1945)

This procedure should be followed by employers in order to obtain permission from the CWI to give notice of termination (see also section 2.2.1 below). The BBA 1945 does not provide for a specific timetable. In practice, it takes between six and eight weeks to obtain a decision from the CWI. If permission to give notice of termination has been given to the employer, the notice of termination should be given to the employee before the permission expires, which is two months after issuance.

2.1.1.2   Notice

As soon as the employer has received the CWI's permission, it can give notice of termination to the relevant employee, providing that it observes the appropriate notice period, which may be reduced by one month. After the one-month reduction, the notice period should still be at least one month. Termination can only become effective by the end of the month.

    The appropriate notice period can be statutory, or alternatively, the employer and the employee can agree upon a different notice period.

The statutory notice period is laid down in DCC, Article 7:672. The employer is required to provide the following notice periods:

- One month's notice, if the employee has been employed for five years or less.
- Two months' notice, if the employee has been employed between five and ten years.
- Three months' notice, if the employee has been employed between ten and fifteen years.
- Four months' notice, if the employee has been employed for fifteen years or more.

The statutory notice period given by an employee to the employer is always one month, regardless of the employee's length of service.

Provided that both the employer and the employee agree, the notice period may differ from the statutory notice period. However, the notice period given by the employer to an employee may not be less than the statutory notice period unless otherwise stated in an applicable Collective Labour Agreement. If the parties agree that an employee's notice period exceeds the statutory notice period of one month, the notice period required by the employer should be twice as long as that required of the employee. The maximum notice period that an employee can give to the employer is six months. If the notice period for the employee is longer than six months, it is considered to be null and void and will be converted into the statutory notice period.

2.1.2   Termination by Court Decision

Following a filing request for contract termination by either employer or employee, the court schedules a hearing. In practice, the hearing is scheduled within two to six weeks, depending on the availability of the parties and the judge. The employee can file a statement of defence for the court hearing. The judge usually reaches a decision within two weeks of the court hearing. The judge may terminate the contract at short notice and is not bound to observe the statutory or contractual notice period. It is not possible to appeal the judge's decision. (See also section 2.4.2)

2.1.3   Collective Redundancy

Under the WMCO, an employer who 'intends' to terminate the employment contracts of at least twenty employees in a certain area within a three-month period must give reasoned notice to CWI (WMCO sections 3 and 4). The notice should contain the following information:

- reasons for the collective redundancies;
- an estimate of the number of employees who will be made redundant;
- a timetable for the collective redundancies;
- selection criteria;

- methods for calculating possible compensation;
- information as to whether a works council is in place;
- information as to whether or not the decision is subject to the advice of the works council; and
- the stage at which the works council should become involved.

The information accompanying the notice should be complete, as the notice is only deemed to have been submitted once all information has been provided.

Once the CWI receives written notice of the proposed collective redundancies, it will observe a one-month statutory delay to assess the employer's request for the CWI's permission to give notice of employee termination. Unions and the works council should be informed and consulted during this period (see also sections 2.2.2 and 2.2.3). If such consultation has not taken place within this month and the unions have not been invited to a consultation meeting, the CWI will extend the statutory delay period until the invitation has been sent. The statutory delay will not apply and applications will be dealt with immediately by the CWI if the employer's notice of the proposed collective redundancies is accompanied by a statement by the relevant employee associations confirming that they have been consulted and waive the one-month statutory delay requirement. The courts are not bound by the WMCO, and assess requests filed to terminate employment contracts by court decision.

2.1.4   Works Council

Collective redundancies are subject to the advice of the works council under WCA, Article 25. The employer must seek this advice in writing at a time during which the works council can still influence the decision-making process (WCA Article 25 subsection (2)). The employer should take into account the works council's requirement of reasonable time to provide its advice. If the employer deviates from the works council's advice, implementation of the redundancy measures must be suspended for one month, unless the works council does not deem this necessary. During this one month, the works council may appeal to the Enterprise Section within the Amsterdam Court of Appeal under WCA Article 26. This procedure can take between one and three months.

2.2   INFORMATION AND CONSULTATION

2.2.1   Pre-notice Procedure

The CWI may grant permission to give notice of termination if the termination is for economic reasons. The CWI has issued guidelines as to what may comprise a business' economic reasons:

- the company is in financial trouble;
- the company has a structural need to reduce the number of its employees;
- termination of a business line within the company;

- relocation of business; or
- other organizational reasons.

An employer must substantiate these economic reasons by providing evidential documentation (for example, demonstrating the company's financial difficulties or the organizational need for the business relocation). In the event that the company intends to reorganize its business, it must submit documents explaining the 'new' business organization to the CWI.

The procedures to obtain permission from the CWI, as well as the criteria which must be satisfied in order to obtain permission, are laid down in the Dismissal Decree (DD) issued by the Dutch Ministry of Social Affairs. The CWI reaches its decision after communicating with the parties and obtaining the advice of a Redundancy Committee composed of representatives from both the workers' and employers' organizations. It is not possible to appeal the CWI's decision.

2.2.2   Collective Redundancy

WMCO Articles 3 and 4 provide that an employer must inform the relevant unions in writing of any proposed collective redundancies in time for the unions to influence the employer's decision-making process. The communication must explain the need for and the extent of the collective redundancies as well as set out the financial and social measures that the employer intends to take. The employer and the employee should discuss potential measures to be taken to avoid dismissal as well as the process by which the employment contracts will be terminated. In other words, the parties must negotiate a social plan. As a matter of practice, the CWI will not entertain any applications by employers for permission to give notice of termination during the one-month statutory delay.

2.2.3   Works Council

If a works council is in place, the employer must give the works council an opportunity to provide advice on any plans by the employer to substantially reduce, expand or change the company's business operations. At minimum, the employer's request for the works council's advice must explain the motive behind the plans, the anticipated effects on the employees and the measures proposed to deal with these consequences (for example, financial provisions such as a social plan) (WCA Article 25 subsection (3)).

The works council must discuss the issues in a consultation meeting at least once before it can give its advice. Advice with special stipulations is allowed; it can agree to a proposal provided that a number of conditions are satisfied (e.g., a social plan with the unions). This advice is given to the employer in writing and must be provided within a reasonable time. The law does not require that the request for the Work Council's advice be made in writing. An employer must decide to accept or reject the advice and then notify the works council of its decision in writing as soon as possible, with justification for any deviations from the works council's advice.

2.3   RISKS

2.3.1   Selection Criteria

If the CWI has granted permission to give notice of termination on economic grounds, either in relation to individual or collective dismissals, it must determine whether or not the correct employees have been selected. In March 2006, new selection criteria based on the reflection principle (*Afspiegelingsbeginsel*) were adopted and laid down in the Dismissal Decree (DD). The reflection principle has replaced the 'last-in-first-out' (LIFO) principle. The problem with the LIFO principle was that young employees tended to be selected for redundancy, which led to a disproportionately old workforce within certain companies. The reflection principle divides employees with similar positions into age groups. Within each age group, employees with the shortest term of employment are the first to qualify for dismissal. The relevant age groups are 15-25 years, 25-35 years, 35-45 years, 45-55 years, and over fifty-five years.

In cases of termination by court decision, judges are not formally bound by the selection criteria detailed in the DD because the DD follows the BBA 1945, which only applies to termination by giving notice. However, the courts tend to comply with the selection criteria in the DD in cases of requests for termination based on the economic reasons of a business unless there is a good reason for non-compliance – a matter which falls within the judge's discretion.

2.3.2   Notice Restrictions

Even if permission to give notice is granted by the CWI, an employer must observe the following restrictions and is not permitted to give notice to an employee:

- who is ill, unless the employee has been ill for at least two years without interruption (DCC Article 7:670 subsection (1));
- who is on maternity leave (in the case of a female employee) and for a period of six weeks after maternity leave (DCC Article 7:670 subsection (2));
- who is on military service or performing alternative service (DCC Article 7: 670 subsection (3));
- who is a member of a works council, European Works Council or one of its special committees, a member of the Negotiation Committee or a member of the SE or SCE works council;
- who is a member of a union (DCC Article 7:670 subsection (5));
- due to his/her political leanings (DCC Article 7:670 subsection (6));
- who is on a leave of absence (DCC Article 7:670 subsection (7));
- due to a transfer of enterprise (DCC Article 7:670 subsection (8));
- due to an employee refusing to work on Sundays (DCC Article 7:670 subsection (9));
- due to an employee filing a claim, whether or not brought to court, for sex discrimination or for unequal treatment based on the employee's working hours; or

– type of employment contract (fixed-term or permanent) (DCC Article 7:647 in conjunction with 646, 648, 649).

Further, pursuant to DCC Article 7:670a an employer cannot give a notice of termination without prior judicial approval to those employees who:

– are candidates to become members of the works council, European Works Council or other representative body or who have been members of such bodies in the two years prior to the notice;
– perform corporate health and safety duties; namely, supervisors, doctors and members of health and safety committees.

The restrictions on an employer giving notice as outlined in DCC Article 7:670, subsections 1-9, do not apply if the reason for the employment contract termination is that all or part of the company's activities have ceased (with the exception of women during maternity leave).

In addition, the restrictions on an employer giving notice as outlined in DCC Articles 7:670 and 7:670a do not apply during an employee's probation period and in the case of termination for an urgent cause. Although an employer is not allowed to give notice to an employee who is ill (DCC Article 7:670 subsection (1)), this restriction does not apply if the employee becomes ill after a request for permission to terminate the employee's employment contract was received by the CWI.

2.3.3   Wrongful Dismissal

A dismissal is considered wrongful if the correct notice period has not been given to an employee. The employee can either claim compensation, which is fixed by statute and equal to the amount of the salary that would have been paid had the correct notice period been given, or full damages. In cases of wrongful dismissal, an employer is also prohibited from enforcing any non-compete clauses that had previously been agreed upon (DCC Article 7:653 subsection (3)).

2.3.4   Manifestly Unreasonable Dismissal

Complying with the pre-notice procedure does not safeguard an employer against subsequent liability for damages. An employee has six months following the termination notice of his/her employment contract to commence proceedings for manifestly unreasonable dismissal. As a remedy, the employee can either seek damages or reinstatement. However, the claim for reinstatement is usually converted into a claim for damages by the court. DCC Article 7:681 provides a non-exhaustive list of circumstances which constitute unreasonable dismissal, such as a fabricated reason and the social consequences for the employee.

2.3.5   Discrimination

Several regulations under Dutch law govern the prohibition of discrimination on the grounds of religion, race, political views, gender, nationality, sexual orienta-tion, age, disability, contract term (temporary versus permanent), and working hours (part-time versus full-time). The relevant regulations are to be found in the General Act on Equal Treatment, the Equal Opportunities Act, DCC Articles 7:646-649, the Equal Treatment in Employment Act, the Equal Treatment for Temporary and Permanent Contracts Act and the Equal Treatment of the Disabled and Chronically Ill Act.

Discriminatory dismissals based on gender or working hours can be declared null and void in the two-month period following the giving of the notice of termination to the employee (DCC Article 7:647 subsection (2)).

Discrimination claims have been made on the basis of the alleged discriminatory selection of employees (for example, part-time versus full-time workers) and discriminatory social plans (for example, age, gender, part-time versus full-time), which have led to changes in the planned method of selection and adjustments to social plans.

2.4   COSTS

2.4.1   Damages in Case of Manifestly Unreasonable Dismissal

The court may grant damages to an employee if his/her dismissal by notice can be considered manifestly unreasonable. The court must consider all of the circumstances before determining a reasonable amount of damages. Many courts attempt to follow the court formula (see section 2.4.2 below) as it is an easy method for calculating damages. However, the Courts of Appeal are reluctant to apply the court formula because it was specifically developed for dismissals by court decision. Legal academics have concluded that compensation awarded to employees on the basis of a manifestly unreasonable dismissal is lower than similar cases in which an employee's employment contract was terminated by court decision.

2.4.2   Court Formula in Case of Termination
by Court Decision

The court formula is a set of recommendations developed by the national body of Dutch cantonal judges. The purpose of the court formula is to improve transparency when determining compensation for employees in cases where they have been dismissed by court decision.

The court formula is $A \times B \times C$, where:

A = amount of weighted years of service;
B = gross monthly salary (including holiday allowance, thirteenth month and other fixed salary components); and
C = correction factor.

For the calculation of the weighted years of service (A), each year of service completed whilst the employee was under the age of forty counts as one year of service; each year of service between the ages of forty and fifty years counts as 1.5 years of service; and each year completed over the age of fifty counts as two years of service. The age of the employee is determined on the date of termination of employment.

The court will apply a correction factor if it considers there are special circumstances in a particular case. The correction factor (C) will be 1 (one) if none of the parties is to blame for the termination.

In cases of dismissal due to economic reasons, the correction factor will generally be considered 1, unless the employer can prove that this factor would lead to financial difficulties (*habe wenig, habe nichts* defence). The court will then grant compensation based on a correction factor of less than 1.

2.4.3   Social Plan

Collective redundancies are mainly covered by a social plan. A social plan can either be agreed upon with the unions or the works council. Social plans usually contain formal procedures in relation to an employer's obligation to inform and consult during the process and details regarding social measures such as outplacement and financial compensation. The court formula explicitly states that in cases of termination by court decision, the courts shall not deviate from the provisions laid down in a social plan which have been agreed upon in writing with a union, unless the outcome in a specific individual case is considered disproportionately severe. The courts also tend to follow social plans in cases of manifestly unreasonable dismissal. The registration of the social plan as a Collective Labour Agreement with the Ministry of Social Affairs is a technique used to bind union members to the social plan.

Social-plan agreements with works councils are not binding on employees. However, case law shows that courts tend to follow these social plans as well.

3   ADVICE FOR LEGAL PRACTICE

3.1   TIMING

As the pre-notice procedure and requirements to inform and consult are different for collective redundancies, a step-by-step plan in relation to collective redundancies should detail the different stages in the employer's plans to inform and consult. The information and consultation process with the works council can be delayed if no social plan is agreed upon as the works council usually combines its advice with the outcome of negotiations regarding a social plan. If there is a procedure failure and permission from the CWI to give notice is not obtained, much time will be lost as the CWI cannot give permission unless all the procedures are completed. Careful preparation will keep the process on track.

3.2   INFORMATION AND CONSULTATION

The unions and the works council can use their powers to influence the timing of the reorganization process (namely, to delay the process). Unnecessary delay can be avoided if the unions are properly informed about the reasons for the redundancies, the consequences for employees and the measures taken to compensate employees.

3.3   RISKS

3.3.1   Termination by Notice or Court Decision

Both termination procedures have advantages and disadvantages.

Termination by notice is often used for collective redundancies in combination with a social plan agreed upon with the unions. The CWI is not authorized to award compensation to employees. In other words, the CWI cannot refuse to grant permission to give notice because the social plan does not contain a redundancy scheme. The disadvantages of termination by notice are:

- the bureaucratic procedure;
- CWI's lack of transparency when granting or refusing permission to give notice without the chance to appeal;
- notice periods; and
- notice restrictions after permission has been granted.

Termination by court decision occurs mostly in cases of individual dismissals. Some courts even refuse to accept requests to make collective dismissals by court decision. Since the courts are not formally bound by the rules regarding the selection criteria, notice restrictions, notice periods and the WMCO, yet can grant compensation, the courts and the parties have more flexibility in the termination of employment contracts. However, the amount of awarded compensation is at the sole discretion of the judge. As court proceedings are relatively short, a judge may not be able to thoroughly consider all the facts, which could affect the compensation awarded. The court's decision cannot be appealed and the employer only has the right to withdraw the termination request by court decision if the compensation granted deviates from the compensation offered.

3.3.2   Mutual Consent and Pro-forma Court Decision

Provided that an employer reaches a settlement with its employees to terminate their employment contracts by mutual consent, this can be effected by a pro-forma court decision. The advantage of this is that no court fee is due. Employees still tend to apply for a pro-forma court decision as the court decision can be enforced immediately if the employer decides not to comply with the agreed settlement.

3.4   COSTS

3.4.1   Outplacement

Costs can be minimized if an employer focuses on outplacement. Dutch courts do not tend to grant large amounts of compensation if an employee has been offered a suitable alternative position. In practice, most unions insist on outplacement provisions in social plans.

3.4.2   Court Formula

The court formula can be used as a tool to calculate a reasonable budget for a social plan. However, employers should be aware that in negotiations with employees, unions and works councils, an overall package should be negotiated. Other elements such as notice periods, restrictive covenants and alternative employment should be considered. If no agreement is reached, both the employer and the employees are at risk of an unfavourable outcome in court.

POLAND

Lukasz Kuczkowski

1   OVERVIEW

Redundancy schemes in Poland are subject to various labour law regulations, such as the Labour Code Act dated 26 June 1974 (the Labour Code), and the Special Terms of Terminating Employees' Employment for Reasons Not Related to the Employees Act dated 13 March 2003 (the Act).

In Poland, termination of an employment agreement is a complex issue, particularly in the case of individual dismissals. Polish courts have been playing an increasingly important role in this field. As legal awareness of Polish employee rights has grown, Polish courts increasingly exercise judicial control over employment termination matters. Thus, whenever employment is terminated (whether with respect to individual employees or a group of employees dismissed as part of a collective redundancy), one should consider not only the direct costs of the employment contract's termination (remuneration for the notice period, monetary equivalent for outstanding annual leave, additional benefits or mandatory severance pay), but also potential future (mainly financial) burdens resulting from control exercised by courts over employment termination. Such burdens may be very high, depending on the extent of the redundancies. Therefore, it is necessary to duly prepare, from a legal point of view, the procedure of employment termination to minimize the likelihood of such additional burdens.

2   MAJOR LEGAL REGULATIONS

2.1   Timing

2.1.1   Termination

The Polish Labour Code provides for the following methods of terminating an employment contract:

- upon mutual agreement of the parties;
- with notice; and
- disciplinary dismissal (without notice).

These methods apply to employment contracts made for a non-fixed term, a trial period and a fixed term. In the last case, an employment contract made for a term exceeding six months may be terminated with notice provided that it stipulates such an option.

2.1.1.1   Mutual Agreement

The mutual agreement of the parties must be a mutual declaration of the employer's and the employee's will. It must be made in writing, but it need not include a justification. Hence, any potential subsequent judicial control of the employment termination is very limited. This is because generally, the employee may only challenge the effectiveness of his/her declaration of will (consent to terminate the employment contract by mutual agreement of the parties) by demonstrating that he/she made the declaration without full consent, such as by having been threatened or misled. The court does not examine the actual reason for the termination of the employment contract. Hence, termination of an employment contract by mutual agreement of the parties is the most desirable form of terminating employment (from the employer's perspective).

2.1.1.2   Unilateral Termination

Termination of employment with notice or without notice (disciplinary dismissal) is effected by the employer's unilateral declaration of will aimed at terminating an employee's employment. The employer's declaration should meet the following formal requirements:

- It should be executed in writing.
- It should clearly and precisely specify to the employee the reason, which should be actual and justified, for the employment termination (this does not apply to contracts made for a fixed term).
- It should include an instruction about the possibility of challenging the termination at a labour court and name the competent court.

The declaration should be handed to the employee. The employee is neither required to acknowledge its receipt by signing it, nor even to read it. It is sufficient for the employer to provide the employee with the opportunity of acquainting himself with the written declaration (such as by placing it in front of the employee).

It must be emphasized that, whether or not it meets the above formal requirements, the notice is effective; that is, it leads to the termination of the employment contract. Hence, even if the written notice does not include the reason for termination, for example, the employment is terminated.

2.1.2   Notice Periods

In the event of standard termination, an employment contract is terminated only after the notice period ends. The statutory notice period is laid down in Articles 33 and 34 of the Labour Code and depends on the length of the employee's service with a given employer (except an employment contract for a fixed term):

- In the case of contracts made for a trial period, the notice period is (i) three business days, if the trial period is up to two weeks; (ii) one week, if the trial period is longer than two weeks but shorter than three months; and (iii) two weeks, if the trial period is three months.
- In the case of contracts made for a fixed term, the notice period is two weeks. However, this applies only to contracts made for a term exceeding six months and provided that the contract may be terminated with notice. Contracts for a fixed term of less than six months and those for a term exceeding six months, which do not provide for termination by notice, may not be so terminated.
- In the case of contracts that are not for a non-fixed term, the notice period is: (i) two weeks, if the employee has been working for the employer for less than six months; (ii) one month, if the employee has been working for the employer for more than six months but less than three years; and (iii) three months, if the employee has been working for the employer for more than three years.

2.1.3   Collective Redundancies

2.1.3.1   Scope of Collective Redundancies

In Poland, collective redundancies are governed by the Special Terms of Terminating Employees' Employment for Reasons Not Related to the Employees Act, dated 13 March 2003, which implements Directive 98/59. The Act applies to employers of twenty or more employees. It is irrelevant whether the employees are engaged by the employer on a full- or a part-time basis. The type of the employment contract between an employee and the employer (for example, a contract for a fixed or non-fixed term, trial period or replacement) is not relevant.

The Act applies to both private employers and public employers funded by the State Treasury. The Act applies only if the employment contract is terminated for a reason unrelated to an employee. Typical instances include restructuring or reduction of the number of jobs at the employer's company, combined with their liquidation.

The provisions of the Act must be observed in the case of termination of employment by an employer of at least twenty employees for reasons not related to employees, if within a maximum of thirty days, the redundancy applies to at least:

- ten employees, if the employer employs less than 100 employees,
- 10% of employees, if the employer employs a minimum of 100, but less than 300 employees,
- thirty employees, if the employer employs a minimum of 300 employees.

In establishing whether a given case involves a collective redundancy, the manner of terminating employment is irrelevant as long as employment is terminated for reasons not related to employees. This means that employment may be terminated with notice or by the mutual agreement of the parties. In the latter case, if the agreement is executed on the employer's initiative, the number of dismissed employees only includes cases where at least five employees are laid off by mutual agreement of the parties.

2.1.3.2   Notifications

The employer should notify the trade unions as well as the county labour office of the planned collective redundancies. If trade unions represent employees at the employer's company, the employer must consult them about planned collective redundancies. The main purpose of such consultations is to avoid or reduce the scope of the collective redundancies and safeguard the interests of the dismissed employees.

The employer must inform the trade unions and the county labour office of: the reasons for the planned collective redundancies, the number of employees affected, the classification of such employees, the criteria for selecting such employees, the duration of the planned collective redundancies process, and methods of resolving employment issues related to the collective redundancies.

As a result of consultations with trade unions, the parties should enter into an agreement. Such agreement should set out the rules for carrying out the collective redundancies, including redundancy criteria and the employer's actions aimed at minimizing the adverse consequences of the redundancies, the level of severance, and so forth. The agreement should be entered into within twenty days of the information referred to above being provided to the trade unions.

If two or more trade unions operate at a given employer's company, the employer should hold consultations and enter into an agreement with all the trade unions. If this proves impossible, the agreement should be executed with representative trade unions within the meaning of the Polish Labour Code.

Following this, the employer should notify the county labour office of the agreement executed with the trade unions and governing the collective redundancies or collective redundancy by-laws implemented by the employer (independently or upon agreement with the employee representative). This second notice should specify the scope of the redundancies, among other things.

2.1.3.3   *Carrying out the Redundancies*

Only after the employer has notified the county labour office of the extent of the collective redundancies and arrangements made following consultations may the employer start dismissing individual employees by giving them notice or executing agreements concerning termination of employment. Notice of employment termination may be given and employment may end thirty days after the county labour office has been given the second notice at the earliest.

Dismissals as part of collective redundancies follow the rules applicable to standard dismissals. Thus, the same notice periods apply, the notice should meet specific legal requirements, and the employer should issue an employment certificate to the dismissed employee.

The fact of a collective redundancies is no basis for the employer to shorten notice periods unilaterally, even when providing compensation. General rules apply in such cases. According to these rules, the employer may unilaterally shorten the notice period to one month if the reason for the redundancy is the liquidation or bankruptcy of the employer.

Generally, the employer may commence dismissals as part of collective redundancies thirty days after the second notification to the county labour office at the earliest.

2.2   INFORMATION AND CONSULTATION

2.2.1   **Individual Redundancy**

2.2.1.1   *Trade Unions*

According to Article 38 of the Labour Code, if trade unions operate at the employer's company, the employer must consult them about the intended termination of employment with or without notice in the following two cases:

- if the dismissed employee is a member of a trade union; or
- if a trade union agreed to defend a given employee (who is not a union member).

In these cases, the employer must notify the trade union of the intention to terminate the employment contract and must specify the reason for its termination. The trade union may express its opinion on this matter within five days. The opinion is not binding on the employer and even if it is negative, the employer may nonetheless terminate employment. If the above time limit expires and the employer does not receive any opinion, it may proceed to terminate employment.

It must be emphasized that the consultation requirement only applies to non-fixed term contracts.

2.2.1.2   *Works Council*

In the event of dismissing individual employees, the employer is not required to consult the employee council about the intended termination of employment.

2.2.2   Collective Redundancies

The main obligation of an employer intending to carry out collective redundancies is to consult employees' representatives about its intention. The scope and binding force of such consultations depend on the type of organization representing employees at the employer's company; this may be a trade union, a works council or a representative elected by employees.

2.2.2.1   *Trade Unions*

Consultations with trade unions include the following stages:

(a) All trade unions represented at the employer's company are informed of the intended collective redundancies. Such information should be provided to trade unions in writing in advance (namely, before the planned commencement of collective redundancies), so that it is possible to enter into an agreement governing the collective redundancies with the trade unions. As part of performing that obligation, the employer informs the trade unions about the reasons for the planned collective redundancies, the number of employees affected by them and the professional groups such employees belong to, the criteria for selecting such employees, the dura-tion of the planned collective redundancies, the way of resolving employ-ment issues related to the collective redundancies (such as the level of severance or professional training) and so forth.

(b) The trade unions make proposals concerning the planned collective redun-dancy in connection with the above information provided by the employer.

(c) The employer and the trade unions hold consultations and, consequently, enter into an agreement governing the planned collective redundancies. The parties should hold consultations in good faith, namely, with the intention of reaching an agreement.

2.2.2.2   *Employee Representative*

If there are no trade unions operating at the employer's company, trade union rights related to the collective redundancy procedure are available to an employee representative elected by employees in the manner adopted at the employer's company. Such employee representative may not be imposed upon employees by the employer; he/she must be elected by employees themselves.

The employer must inform the employee representative about the planned collective redundancies in the same way as applies to trade unions. The employee representative may make proposals related to information provided by the employer. The purpose of the consultations is to agree on collective redundancy by-laws with the employee representative.

2.2.2.3   *Works Council*

Whether or not trade unions operate at the employer's company, the employer must also consult a works council about the planned collective redundancies, provided that such a council exists at the employer's company. It may be created by employees or trade unions according to the Employee Information and Consultation Act dated 7 April 2006 (this Act implements Directive 2002/14 in the Polish legal system). At present, only an employer with a workforce of at least a 100 employees must inform employees that they may create a works council.

The consultation obligation results from the fact that a works council should be consulted about, among other things, the employer's planned changes to the employment level. Collective redundancies undoubtedly represent such a change.

Consultations with the works council should precede the planned commencement of the collective redundancies. They are aimed, by analogy with consultations with trade unions, at minimizing the adverse consequences of collective redundancies; however, their effects are not binding on the employer.

2.2.2.4   *By-laws*

If the employer carries out consultations with trade unions but the two parties do not agree on the wording of the agreement, the employer must unilaterally determine by-laws in relation to the collective redundancies, reflecting, as far as possible, representations made by the trade unions during consultations.

The employer should also implement collective redundancy by-laws if there are no trade unions at the employer's company, and in situations where consultations are held with the employee representative. In such cases, the employer should agree on the substance of the by-laws with the employee representative.

2.3   RISKS

2.3.1   **Individual Redundancy**

2.3.1.1   *Unfair Dismissal*

In connection with termination of his/her employment with or without notice (disciplinary dismissal), an employee is entitled to judicial control of such termination. As part of this entitlement, an employee may sue his/her employer and claim reinstatement or compensation. Judicial control is instituted upon request, by way of a statement of claim, by the employee. As part of such control, the court examines both whether formal requirements were met concerning the employer's declaration of will to terminate the employment contract, and whether the reason for the employment contract termination, as it appears in the declaration, is actual, specific, clear, and justified.

The main risk an employer faces in relation to an individual redundancy is that an employee will bring an action to a labour court claiming reinstatement or compensation. An employee may lodge such a claim primarily if he/she concludes that the reason for employment termination is untrue, as well as where the employer violated general rules concerning individual redundancy (for example, the termination notice did not include all mandatory elements). Depending on its findings, the court may reinstate the employee or award compensation (in principle, equal to a maximum of three months' salary; the compensation level is defined by the Labour Code and the court may only award such compensation up to this maximum level).

2.3.1.2 Consequences of the Employer's Failure to Follow the Procedure

Polish laws do not guarantee the continuity of employment in the event that the employer breaches the Polish Labour Code provisions concerning employee dismissals. Thus, even if the employer fails to follow the applicable procedure but communicates its intention to dismiss an employee to such employee in any way, employment is effectively terminated under law. The effects, namely, termination of employment, may only be mitigated if the employee brings an action to a labour court and is reinstated. However, in principle, if the employee does not take such action, employment will not be automatically restored.

2.3.1.3 Notice Restrictions

Some employees are protected against individual redundancies, and thus their employment contracts may not be terminated with notice. In principle, however, such protection does not apply in the event of disciplinary dismissals.

Protected employees include, for instance: trade union activists; pregnant women; employees taking annual, maternity, child-raising, and sick leave; members of a work council; and employees with less than four years remaining until retirement age. Nonetheless, it must be emphasized that if the employer violates these protection rules, for example by terminating an employment contract with a pregnant woman by giving notice, the termination is effective. However, if the dismissed employee in question brings an action to court, the likelihood that he/she will be reinstated is very high.

2.3.2 Collective Redundancies

2.3.2.1 *Selection Criteria*

Generally, the employer determines the selection criteria concerning employees to be dismissed during collective redundancies itself. Such criteria should be objective, so that the employer does not violate the laws prohibiting discrimination in employment. During consultations with trade unions, the works council and employee representatives, the employer may change these criteria or set new ones.

2.3.2.2 *Unfair Dismissal*

A collective redundancy does not preclude an unfair dismissal, since it cannot be guaranteed that the reason for the collective redundancy, as given by the employer, is based on fact. In such cases, the employee's entitlements are identical to those available in the event of collective redundancies (compare to section 2.3.1.1 above).

2.3.2.3 *Notice Restrictions*

In general, various provisions affording employees special protection against termination of employment with notice or otherwise do not apply to collective redundancies. In principle, the employer is not obligated to consult trade unions regarding the intention to dismiss any individual employee (if an agreement with trade unions was entered into). Additionally, the employer enjoys greater freedom to dismiss an employee who is absent due to annual leave or for other valid reasons.

Some employee groups, though protected in the event of individual redundancies, are not protected against collective redundancies. These include employees who are absent due to annual leave or for other justified reasons, as well as those who are four years away from retirement age.

On the other hand, the employer may not give notice of employment termination as part of collective redundancies to other employees who enjoy special protection, such as trade unionists, members of an employee council or pregnant women. In such cases, in the event of collective redundancies, the employer may only terminate terms of work and pay, subject to the proviso that if such employees' salaries are reduced, they are entitled to receive a compensatory benefit by the end of the protection period.

2.3.2.4 *Re-employment*

An employee dismissed as part of collective redundancies may notify the employer about his/her willingness to be re-employed if the employer hires new employees. Such notice should be given in writing within a year of the end of employment.

If such notice is given, the employer must re-employ the dismissed employee if it hires employees in the professional group to which the dismissed employee belongs. This obligation applies to the employer for a period of fifteen months following the end of the employee's employment. Once such a period has elapsed, the employer is no longer obligated to re-employ the dismissed employee.

The purpose of such regulation is to minimize the number of cases where the employer carries out collective redundancies and shortly thereafter hires new employees for the same positions but usually at lower salaries.

If the employer does not re-employ the dismissed employee despite meeting the statutory requirements (notice and time limit), the dismissed employee may claim re-employment by the employer in court.

2.3.2.5   *Consequences of the Employer's Failure to Follow the Procedure*

The employer's failure to follow the collective redundancy procedure does not entitle an employee to lodge a claim for reinstatement or a compensation payment. However, if the employer fails to follow the collective redundancy procedure, the employer (management board members or other people in charge) may be fined by a labour inspector.

2.3.2.6   *Discrimination*

Anti-discrimination legislation affects the collective redundancy procedure only as regards to setting the criteria for selection of the employees to be dismissed. Such criteria may not violate the laws prohibiting discrimination in employment. Therefore, such criteria should be objective.

If non-objective criteria violating the laws prohibiting discrimination are set down, the employee dismissed on the basis of such criteria may be awarded compensation of not less than the national minimum wage (in 2007, this was about EUR 250). The Labour Code does not specify any compensation cap.

2.4   Costs

2.4.1   **Individual Redundancy**

Individual redundancy costs generally include: (i) the costs of remuneration paid to the employee during the notice period (employees often submit medical exemptions from work and do not work during such period), and (ii) the costs of a monetary equivalent of any leave not taken, if the employee is still entitled to such leave at the end of the notice period.

Some provisions of the Act also apply if, though collective redundancies do not take place (due to a small number of dismissed employees), the reasons for terminating a given employee's employment with notice or by mutual agreement of the parties are related to the employer only. In such cases, the employer must pay statutory severance pay to the dismissed employee. For the severance pay level, see section 2.4.2.1 below.

2.4.2 Collective Redundancies

2.4.2.1 Mandatory Compensation

The employer's main obligation related to collective redundancies resulting from Article 8 of the Act is to pay statutory severance pay to the dismissed employees. The severance level depends on the dismissed employee's length of service, but may not exceed fifteen times the national minimum wage applicable in a given calendar year (the national minimum wage changes every calendar year). Thus, in 2007, statutory severance pay could not exceed approximately EUR 3,500.

The level of severance pay available is as follows:

(a) one month's salary, if the employee has been employed with the employer for less than two years;
(b) two months' salary, if the employee has been employed with the employer for more than two years and less than eight years;
(c) three months' salary, if the employee has been employed with the employer for more than eight years.

The employer may not reduce such statutory severance pay. Severance pay is paid when employment ends.

2.4.2.2 Social Plan

The employer is free to grant additional benefits to dismissed employees. These benefits may be monetary (such as premiums, bonuses, or additional severance pay) and non-monetary (such as professional training courses and sessions). Such additional benefits may be granted by the employer on a discretionary basis, unless they are granted under an agreement or by-laws determined following consultations.

3 ADVICE FOR LEGAL PRACTICE

3.1 INDIVIDUAL REDUNDANCIES

3.1.1 Timing

The main issues as regards individual redundancies are whether the formal requirements were met concerning the substance of the employer's declaration of will to terminate an employment contract, and whether there is a specific, actual, clear, and justified reason for termination of an employee's employment. If these fundamental rules are violated, the employer usually loses in a court action in which the employment contract termination is controlled by the court.

3.1.2   Risks

The main risk to the employer in the event of individual redundancies is that an employee will be reinstated or awarded compensation. This risk cannot be fully eliminated, but it can be reduced considerably, provided that the termination of the employment contract is duly prepared in legal terms. However, Polish employees are increasingly aware of their rights in this respect, and thus they request labour courts to examine employment termination more and more frequently.

3.2   COLLECTIVE REDUNDANCIES

3.2.1   Timing

The most important issues related to collective redundancies are timing and the execution of an agreement with trade unions, or the determination of by-laws with an employee representative. If the employer reaches this stage of the collective redundancy procedure swiftly, the procedure may be shortened and the redundancies themselves may take place earlier. However, since third parties (trade unions or an employee representative) are involved, sometimes the time needed to complete the collective redundancy procedure cannot be shortened, regardless of how well prepared the employer was. Where this is the case, there are often additional costs to the employer whilst being obliged to maintain the existing level of employment.

3.2.2   Costs

When planning collective redundancies, one should primarily take into account costs of additional severance pay, which render such redundancies much more expensive. Additionally, one should consider the costs of potential court claims by employees challenging their dismissal. If the reasons for collective redundancies are well justified in legal and economic terms, the likelihood that such a claim will be resolved to the benefit of the employee is small, but it cannot be fully disregarded due to the complex redundancy procedure and the risk of the employer having made an error.

The employer's liability is essentially limited to financial liability in connection with employee claims. If redundancies are duly prepared, this liability may be minimized.

PORTUGAL

Luís Miguel Monteiro
Joana Almeida

1   OVERVIEW

The main legal regulations governing redundancy schemes in Portugal are (i) the Labour Code (LC), approved by Law 99/2003; and (ii) the Labour Code Regulation (LCR), approved by Law 35/2004. The LC has implemented Council Directive 98/59 CE of 20 July 1998 in relation to collective redundancies.

Redundancy schemes, based on objective criteria, follow one of two procedures, depending on the number of employees to be made redundant and on the number of employees employed by the employer. These two procedures are: Collective dismissal (*despedimento colectivo*) or individual redundancies (*extinção do posto de trabalho*), which literally translated means the extinction of the post.

The two procedures referred to above must be based on the grounds set out by the LC, which differ depending upon which procedure is being followed. Broadly speaking, the following stages are common to both procedures:

(1) intention to dismiss;
(2) information and consultation duties; and
(3) the communication of dismissal.

In both individual and collective redundancies, the planned termination of the contract must be communicated by the employer to the redundant employees

©2008 Kluwer Law International B.V., The Netherlands.
Maarten van Kempen, Lisa Patmore, Michael Ryley, and
Robert von Steinau-Steinrück (eds), *Redundancy,* pp. 183-191.

sixty days prior to dismissal. The employees must also be informed that they are entitled to compensation.

Both collective redundancy dismissals and individual redundancies may be challenged in court, either because of lack of grounds or failure to comply with the relevant legal procedure. If the court finds the dismissal unlawful, the employee may be reinstated.

2   MAIN LEGAL REGULATIONS

2.1   TIMING

2.1.1   Threshold

Employers with more than fifty employees must conduct a collective dismissal procedure whenever they wish to dismiss five or more employees within a three-month period. The same applies to employers with fifty employees or fewer that wish to dismiss two or more employees within the same given period (LC, Article 397/1).

Where a particular position within a company is eliminated, the procedure that applies is individual redundancy; for example, an employer with more than fifty employees who intends to dismiss two employees (LC, Article 397/1).

2.1.2   Grounds

All redundancies may be based on either market, structural or technological grounds (LC, Articles 397/2 and 402).

2.1.2.1   *Market Grounds*

Market grounds are grounds relating to a reduction in the employer's activity caused by a decrease in demand for its goods or services or the impossibility, whether legal or practical, of getting those goods or services to market.

2.1.2.2   *Structural Grounds*

An economic-financial imbalance, a change of activity, the restructuring of the business organization and/or the replacement of the employer's main product lines may constitute structural grounds.

2.1.2.3   *Technological Grounds*

Technological grounds relate to changes in production techniques, the automation of production tools, the computerization of services or the automation of the means of communication.

2.1.3 Additional Requirements

The elimination of an employment position or individual redundancies is subject to additional legal requirements (LC, Article 403):

- Grounds for dismissal may not result from either the employer's or the employee's fault.
- The employer may not hire employees under fixed-term contracts who will execute functions similar to the job positions to be made redundant.
- The maintenance of the employment contract, i.e., retaining the redundant employee, must be impossible, in the sense that the employer does not have an alternative job position in which to place the relevant employee.

Under this procedure, the law sets out criteria for selecting employees to be made redundant. The general rule is that the employees with the least number of years of service will be the first to be made redundant.

2.1.4 Notice Periods

Upon completion of the relevant procedure, the employee must be notified of the decision to dismiss sixty days prior to termination (LC, Articles 398/1 and 404). Portuguese law allows for indemnification payments in lieu of notice, thus allowing for an immediate dismissal (LC, Articles 398/2 and 404).

2.1.5 Intention to Dismiss

2.1.5.1 Collective Redundancy Dismissals

Employers who intend to conduct a collective redundancy dismissal procedure must initially notify the employees' representative bodies of their intention to do so. The employees' representative body may be the works council (*comissão de trabalhadores*), should it exist, or the trade-union representatives (*comissão intersindical* or *comissão sindical*). Where these representative bodies do not exist, the initial communication is addressed to each employee affected by the dismissal and the employees may form a representative committee (*comissão representativa*).

The notification of the intention to dismiss must be accompanied by certain information – a description of the grounds for dismissal, the criteria for selecting the employees to be made redundant and the criteria for determining the compensation to be paid.

Copies of these documents must be sent to the relevant department of the Ministry of Employment (LC, Article 419).

2.1.5.2 Individual Redundancy Dismissals

Where the employer wishes to terminate an individual employee, the intention to dismiss is sent to both the relevant employee and the existing employees' representative body. This notification must include, among other elements, the grounds for dismissal (LC, Article 423).

2.1.6   Information and Consultation

2.1.6.1   Collective Redundancies

Within ten days from the date that the notification of the intention to dismiss is delivered/received, the employer and the employees' representative body should engage in negotiations with the aim, where possible, of agreeing upon the scope of the collective dismissals and the potential alternatives (e.g., suspension or reduction of work, early retirement). There is no time limit for these negotiations, which may involve (and normally do) the participation of representatives from the Ministry of Employment. As a rule, the LC imposes an obligation for minutes of the meetings to be recorded (LC, Articles 420 and 421).

2.1.6.2   Individual Redundancy Dismissals

In the case of the elimination of a post, both the employee and the existing representative bodies may present their written opinion on the dismissal. There is a ten-day window for this, which runs from the delivery/receipt of the intention to dismiss and the presentation of any other required information. At the request of either the employee or his representatives, the relevant department of the Ministry of Employment may issue a prior (non-binding) opinion on the dismissal (LC, Article 24).

2.1.7   Decision to Dismiss

2.1.7.1   Collective Redundancy Dismissals

Where collective redundancy dismissals are to occur, the employer must not formally announce the decision to dismiss until at least twenty days have elapsed since the intention to dismiss notice was delivered.

The dismissal notice must be sent to each relevant employee and must include, amongst other details, the dismissal grounds, the termination date and the compensation amount due (LC, Article 422).

2.1.7.2   Individual Redundancy Dismissals

The same procedure noted above in section 2.1.7.1 applies in individual redundancy dismissals but with two key differences. First, the decision to dismiss may be communicated after only five days have elapsed from the end of the period for the employees or their representative bodies, to issue their opinion as described above in section 2.1.6.2. Secondly, the communication must expressly confirm that the additional legal requirements referred to above are met (LC, Article 425).

Depending on the procedure, there are additional information requirements that must be communicated to the Ministry of Employment (LC, Articles 422 and 425).

2.2   INFORMATION AND CONSULTATION

2.2.1   Prior Information and Consultation Duties

If the employer has a works council, the employer must request the works council's prior non-binding written opinion before starting the redundancy procedure (LCR, Article 357).

If there are trade union representatives (*delegados sindicais*), the LC sets out information duties that must also be observed prior to carrying out the redundancy procedure (LC, Article 503).

Employers that belong to a European group of companies must check whether there is a need to consult with the European Works Council (*conselho de empresa europeu*), should the restructuring affect employees in several countries.

A collective bargaining agreement may also set out additional obligations on the matter.

2.3   RISKS

2.3.1   Selection Criteria

2.3.1.1   Collective Redundancy Dismissals

At the same time that the intention to dismiss is communicated to the employees or their respective representative bodies, the employer must also disclose the criteria for selecting those to be made redundant (LC, Article 419/2/c).

The LC does not specify selection criteria, which means that the employer does retain some freedom in this regard provided that the criteria adopted are objective and non-discriminatory. In any case, the employer's criteria must be consistent with the grounds for dismissal, which in some cases may constitute the criteria itself. For example, if a company's department is closed, presumably all employees in that department will be selected for redundancy even if other departments have job positions similar to the ones in the department that has been previously selected for redundancy and it is these positions that the employer would prefer to eliminate.

2.3.1.2   Individual Redundancy Dismissals

In contrast to collective redundancy dismissals, the LC in Article 403/2 sets out the criteria for selecting the positions to be made redundant under individual redundancy schemes, and the order of these criteria:

(1) Employees with fewer years of service in the job position.
(2) Employees with fewer years of service in a professional category.
(3) Employees with an inferior professional category.
(4) Employees with fewer years of service with the employer.

These are mandatory criteria and failure to observe them causes the dismissal to be unlawful (LC, Article 432/c).

2.3.2   Notice Restrictions

Employees under maternity or paternity protection (e.g., pregnant employees; employees during the 120-day period following childbirth; employees who breast-feed a child; male parents during the five-day period of paternity leave) cannot be dismissed on redundancy grounds without the employer first seeking the opinion of the Commission for Equality in Work and Employment (*Comissão para a Igualdade no Trabalho e no Emprego*). If the Commission opposes the proposed dismissals, the employer must apply to the court in order to obtain the court's authorization to dismiss (LC, Article 51 and LCR, Article 98).

2.3.3   Judicial Proceedings

Within five days from the day on which the employees received the communication of dismissal, employees may file for an injunction in court (*procedimento cautelar*) to suspend the dismissal. If the courts find that the dismissal is likely to be found unlawful, employees will be reinstated and will continue to receive their salary until the conclusion of the judicial proceedings which will determine the matter (LC, Article 434).

Employees have six months from the termination of the employment contract to file proceedings to determine the lawfulness of the collective dismissal. In the case of the elimination of a post, the period in which to bring proceedings is one year (LC, Article 435).

2.3.4   Unfair Dismissal

A dismissal will be considered unlawful or unfair where there are no grounds for dismissal; where an employer is unable to demonstrate such grounds in court; where an employer fails to comply with the respective redundancy procedure; or where an employer does not pay the compensation until the date of termination (LC, Articles 429, 431, and 432).

2.3.5   Discrimination

The Portuguese Constitution, the LC and the LCR prohibit discriminatory treatment. In terms of redundancies, the LC specifically states that the dismissal will be unlawful if it is based on political, ideological, ethnic or religious motives (Article 429/b).

If the court finds that the dismissal is unlawful on the grounds that it is discriminatory and assuming that the employee did not choose to be reinstated, monies awarded to the employee are on an indemnity basis and approximate the maximum set out by the law – forty-five days of base remuneration and seniority premiums for each year of service or fractions thereof, starting at a minimum of three months' wages (LC, Article 439/1 to 3). In addition, in this case, employers may not oppose reinstatement (LC, Article 438/4).

2.4   Costs

2.4.1   Statutory Redundancy Payment

Employees whose job positions are made redundant are entitled to a statutory redundancy payment equal to one month's base remuneration, plus premiums based on the employee's level of seniority (*diuturnidades*) for each year of service, starting at a minimum of three months' wages. Fractions of years of service are compensated proportionally (LC, Articles 401 and 404).

There is a legal presumption that employees who accept the statutory redundancy payment also accept the dismissal and are therefore prevented from challenging it in court afterwards. However, employees may turn to the courts to disprove the presumption (LC, Articles 401/4 and 404).

In addition, employees are entitled to any credits/benefits normally due at the time the employment contract ends, e.g., those which relate to salary, holiday pay and holiday and Christmas allowances.

Failure to pay the statutory redundancy payment or credits/benefits will render the dismissal unlawful (LC, Articles 431/1 and 432).

2.4.2   Damages in the Case of Unfair Dismissal

In the case of a finding of unfair dismissal, employees are entitled to loss of salary from the date of dismissal until the date of the court's decision (including the courts of appeal) and they are also entitled to choose between reinstatement and receiving damages awarded on an indemnity basis (LC, Articles 436-439).

Damages are determined by the court and vary from fifteen to forty-five days of base remuneration and seniority premiums for each year of service or fractions thereof (starting at a minimum of three months' wages). The LC criteria for determining what is due in each case include the amount of the remuneration and the degree to which the dismissal is unlawful (LC, Article 439/1). For example, dismissals implemented without an employer conducting the required procedures are more likely to generate damages higher than a situation where the relevant redundancy procedure was observed but a minor formality was not met.

There is no element of double recovery. Damages are either paid as a lawful statutory redundancy payment or as damages based on an unlawful dismissal.

Employees under maternity and paternity protection (as explained above in section 2.3.2) and employees who are members of employees' representative bodies are entitled to greater damages, varying from thirty to sixty days of base remuneration (LC, Articles 51/7 and 456/5). The criteria for determining the amount of damages due are the same (amount of remuneration and the degree to which the dismissal is unlawful).

Although, as a rule, it is up to the employee to choose between reinstatement and damages, there are situations in which the employer may oppose reinstatement – for example, employers with fewer than ten employees or, regardless of the number of employees, when the employee who was unlawfully dismissed carries out a management function (LC, Article 438). The decision in all cases remains with the court. This option does not apply in situations where the employee is under maternity or paternity protection (LC, Article 51/8) or to situations where the dismissal was based on political, ideological, ethnic or religious motives (LC, Article 438/4).

If the court decides not to order reinstatement, damages due will also vary from thirty to sixty days of base remuneration, starting at a minimum of six months' wages (LC, Article 439/4 and 5).

Within the limits set by the LC, collective-bargaining agreements may determine the damages due in the event of unlawful dismissal (LC, Article 383/2 and 3).

2.4.3   Social Plan

Portuguese law is unfamiliar with the 'social plan' concept. However, the information and negotiation phase of collective dismissals is the appropriate stage to agree upon the scope of the collective dismissals; on potential alternatives (e.g., suspension or reduction of work, early retirement); and on the compensation to be paid (LC, Article 420).

3   ADVICE FOR LEGAL PRACTICE

3.1   Timing

The most important advice in regard to redundancy schemes is the need to prepare for them in sufficient time in order to ensure that all legal requirements are met. Complying with the relevant legal procedure is crucial if an employer wishes to ensure a favourable ruling in any potential court proceedings.

3.2   Cost and Risks

Apart from the advice provided above, the best way of preventing the cost and risks associated with redundancy proceedings is to enter into a written termination agreement with the relevant employees. There are two additional benefits. Firstly, termination agreements are not subject to specific grounds and do not require the need to comply with a specific procedure. Secondly, termination agreements may be immediately effective, thus avoiding the need to provide a period of notice during which the employee continues to work or receives a payment in lieu of notice. In addition, litigation risks are much lower in situations where the employee has agreed to contract termination. Finally, the payment of a global compensation sum (*compensação pecuniária de natureza global*), together with the employee's statement that all credits have been duly paid, constitutes a legal presumption that the compensation includes all credits due to the employee at the termination date (LC, Article 394/4).

The only disadvantage to termination agreements is that compensation tends to be greater than that which may be awarded through following the appropriate redundancy procedure set forth in the LC. As a general rule, compensation under termination agreements usually represents forty-five days of remuneration for each year of service. It is generally no more than this amount because this limit is tax-exempt. Nevertheless, only a certain number of employees (from each employer) may enter into termination agreements and remain entitled to the unemployment allowance. Such number depends on the total number of employees employed by the relevant employer and on the number of termination agreements that were entered into in a three-year period (Decree-Law 220/2003, of 3 November).

ROMANIA

Cristina Bazilescu

1   OVERVIEW

The procedure an employer must follow when making redundancies is established by Romanian legislation. Romanian employment legislation is generally drafted with a view to protecting employees from any potential discriminatory and abusive measures which may be taken by the employer. The legal framework relating to the termination of employment contracts is contained in the Romanian Labour Code ('the Labour Code') and the National Collective Bargaining Agreement.

The National Collective Bargaining Agreement represents the written agreement between the employer or the employer's organization, and the employees, represented by their trade unions or in any other manner stipulated by law. The agreement regulates working conditions and wages as well as other rights and obligations deriving from labour relationships. Such an agreement may be concluded at national level, industry level or employer level. In accordance with Article 3(a) of the National Collective Bargaining Agreement, its provisions apply to all employees.

1.1   REDUNDANCY

An individual employment contract may be terminated as follows:

- rightfully;
- by mutual consent; or

- unilaterally, in the cases and under the limitation terms stipulated by the law.

According to the National Collective Bargaining Agreement, employees dismissed for reasons not related to them personally (for example, misconduct or capability) shall benefit from a notice period of twenty working days.

Nevertheless, the parties can agree to a shorter period.

Romanian employment legislation distinguishes between individual and collective dismissals. These differ mainly in terms of timing and consultation requirements.

Article 68 of the Labour Code defines collective dismissals as dismissals of employees for reasons not related to them personally, where the dismissals occur within thirty calendar days of each other and:

- at least ten employees are dismissed, where the employer has more than twenty but fewer than 100 employees;
- 10% or more of the employees are dismissed, where the employer has more than 100 but fewer than 300 employees; and
- at least thirty employees are dismissed, where the employer has more than 300 employees.

When calculating the number of employees dismissed, one must also take into account the employees whose employment contracts have been terminated by the employer for one or more reasons not related to the employee personally, provided there have been at least five dismissals.

The Labour Code has been amended in order to transpose the provisions of Council Directive 98/59/EC of 20 July 1998 on the approximation of the laws of the Member States relating to collective redundancies.

2   LEGAL REQUIREMENTS

2.1   Timing

2.1.1   Notice Periods

Article 73 of the Labour Code sets out a mandatory notice period in the case of dismissal, except where the dismissal is due to a serious disciplinary offence or where the employee is in custody as a result of criminal proceedings for a period exceeding thirty days.

The notice period to be given by an employer is no less than fifteen working days. However, a longer notice period may be agreed upon in individual employment contracts or applicable collective bargaining agreements. In practice, employment contracts carry a fifteen-day notice period.

The National Collective Bargaining Agreement stipulates that a twenty-working-day notice period needs to be observed. Since a longer notice period is in the employee's favour, the provisions of the National Collective Bargaining Agreement shall apply in this case.

2.1.2   Collective Redundancies

In the case of collective dismissals, the employee is required to give several prior notifications to the labour authorities and trade unions. The time limits for such notifications depend on the size of the business and the number of employees to be dismissed.

Thus the trade union or the employees' representatives must be notified as follows:

- Fifteen days prior to the notification of the labour authorities related to the dismissal decision, where the employer has fewer than 100 employees.
- Twenty days prior to the notification of the labour authorities related to the dismissal decision, where the employer has between 101 and 250 employees.
- Thirty days prior to the notification of the labour authorities related to the dismissal decision, where the employer has more than 250 employees.

The dismissal decisions shall only be issued once thirty calendar days have elapsed since the notification of the labour authorities. Following a well-reasoned request of the trade union or employer, this period may be reduced without infringing upon the individual rights regarding the prior notice period.

Nevertheless, where the issues regarding the collective dismissal cannot be solved in the above-mentioned period of time, the labour authorities may postpone issuing the dismissal decisions by a maximum of ten calendar days. (See further in section 2.2.2 below.)

2.2   INFORMATION AND CONSULTATION

2.2.1   Individual Redundancies

In the case of individual dismissals due to serious disciplinary offences, a preliminary disciplinary inquiry must be carried out. To this end, the person authorized by the employer to make the inquiry shall write to the employee inviting him/her to a meeting, stating the reason, date, time, and place of the meeting. Where the employee fails to attend the meeting, and does not give an objective reason for his/her failure to attend, the employer is entitled to impose sanctions without the need to carry out a preliminary inquiry.

During the preliminary disciplinary inquiry, an employee shall have the right to submit all evidence in his/her defence and to be assisted, at his/her request, by a representative of the trade union of which he/she is a member.

Should an employer fail to carry out the requisite procedure, the dismissal shall be considered null and void. Consequently, a legal action filed against the dismissal decision may lead to the reinstatement of the relevant employee to the same position. It may also lead to the back payment of any salary due to the employee for the previous relevant period.

2.2.2   Collective Redundancies

According to the Labour Code, when an employer intends to proceed with collective dismissals, it is obliged to initiate, in good time, consultations with the trade union, with the aim of reaching an agreement as well as notifying the labour authorities.

Such consultation shall at least refer to any ways to avoid the collective dismissals or minimize the number of employees subject to dismissal. Such consultation should refer to the mitigation of the consequences through social measures such as support for professional re-qualification or redeployment of the dismissed employees.

Depending on the size of the business and the number of employees to be dismissed, the employer is obliged to notify the trade union within a certain period of time prior to notification of the labour authorities.

The notice must be in writing and should include all the following relevant information:

- The total number and categories of employees.
- The reasons for the prospective dismissal.
- The number of employees affected by the dismissal.
- The selection criteria considered, according to the law and/or any collective bargaining agreements.
- The measures considered for limiting the dismissals.
- The measures for mitigating the consequences of dismissal and the compensation which will be granted to dismissed employees, according to the law and/or any applicable collective bargaining agreement.
- The date from which, or the period in which, the dismissal will take place.
- The period in which the union can submit proposals for the avoidance or limitation of the number of dismissed employees.

A copy of the above-mentioned notice should be sent to the labour authorities on the same date on which the notice is sent to the trade union.

The trade union may suggest measures in order to avoid the dismissals or to limit the number of dismissed employees within ten calendar days of receiving the notification. The employer is obliged to draft a written and well-reasoned reply to the suggestions made by the trade union within five calendar days of receiving the suggested measures.

Furthermore, if the employer decides to proceed with the collective dismissal, it is obliged to notify the territorial labour inspectorate and the territorial employment agency in writing, at least thirty calendar days prior to issuing the dismissal decisions. This notification must contain all of the relevant information regarding the intention to carry out a collective dismissal mentioned above, as well as the conclusions of the consultations with the trade union, in particular:

- the reasons for the dismissal;
- the total number of employees;
- the number of employees affected by the dismissal; and
- the date from which or the period in which the dismissals shall occur.

A copy of the notification which was submitted to the labour authorities should be provided to the trade union on the same date. The union or the employees' representatives may submit their points of view to the territorial labour inspectorate.

2.3   RISKS

2.3.1   Selection Criteria

During the consultation phase, the employer must inform the trade union of the technical/economic justification for its proposed measures as regards the opportunities for relocation of the personnel, modification of the labour schedule, and the organization of qualification, re-qualification or professional re-orientation classes.

If the dismissals cannot be avoided, the management of the company shall inform, in writing, all employees whose positions will be terminated regardless of whether or not they will be offered alternative positions within the company or whether they will be enrolled in a form of professional retraining in order to be eligible for new positions in the same company.

Several criteria must be followed regarding the particular order in which the dismissals take place – for example, age, number of persons under care, retirement, and so forth.

Thus, the employer must dismiss the employees in the following order:

(a) Employees currently holding two or more jobs, as well as those who already have a pension as well as a salary.
(b) Employees who fulfil the retirement conditions but have not requested retirement according to the law.
(c) Employees who fulfil the retirement conditions upon their request.

In addition, the National Collective Bargaining Agreement sets out some minimum criteria to be taken into consideration during the dismissal procedure:

- Where the dismissal measures may affect a husband and wife employed within the same company, the employee with the lower salary shall be dismissed; this provision cannot be applied if it would mean the dismissal of an employee whose position is not subject to the collective dismissal.
- The dismissal measure first affects all employees who do not have children in their maintenance and care.

– The dismissal measure only affects, at the last stage, women with children in their care; widowers or divorcees with children in their care; or sole family breadwinner; as well as employees, male or female, who have a maximum of three years remaining until retirement, upon their request at the last stage.

2.3.2   Notice in Writing

In a situation where the employees cannot be offered other positions or if they refuse the positions offered or enrollment in retraining, the company's management shall inform them in writing as to the notice provisions. An important aspect that must be taken into consideration is the dismissal decision. This must be communicated to the employees in writing and must contain the grounds for the dismissal, the duration of the notice period, the selection criteria, the list of available positions and the period in which the employees may decide to fill a vacant position.

A dismissal decision which does not contain all the information mentioned above is null and void.

2.3.3   Notice Restrictions

Pursuant to the Labour Code, dismissals cannot be ordered:

– for the duration of an employee's temporary labour disability, as established in a medical certificate according to the law;
– for the duration of quarantine leave;
– for the duration of an employed woman's pregnancy, as long as the employer was aware of this fact before issuing the dismissal decision;
– for the duration of an employee's maternity leave;
– for the duration of an employee's leave for raising a child up to the age of two, or, in the case of a disabled child, up to the age of three;
– for the duration of an employee's leave to care for a sick child aged up to seven years, or, in the case of a disabled child, for illness, until he/she turns eighteen years of age;
– for the duration of an employee's military service;
– for the duration of an employee's exercise of an elected position in a trade-union body, except when the dismissal is ordered for a serious disciplinary offence; or
– for the duration an employee's rest leave.

Where a dismissal is ordered in the above-mentioned circumstances, it is not valid and labour courts may rule in favour of the employee, ordering his/her reinstatement and the back payment of salary.

2.3.4   Other Employee Protection

It is also important to take into consideration the fact that, in cases of individual dismissal for physical/mental incapacity and professional unfitness, the employer is under an obligation to offer that employee other vacant positions in the company, consistent with his/her professional training or, as applicable, his/her work capability as assessed by an occupational physician.

If there is no such vacant position, the employer will be under an obligation to ask the territorial employment agency for support in reassigning the employee in question according to his/her professional training or, as applicable, his/her work capability as assessed by an occupational physician.

The employee must reply to the employer's offer regarding a new position, in writing, within three working days of receipt of the employer's offer. If the employee fails to reply/agree to the offer within the three-day period and after the employment agency has been notified, the employer may dismiss the employee.

2.3.5   Rehiring

The National Collective Bargaining Agreement forbids an employer who has made collective dismissals from hiring new employees and placing them in the positions vacated through the collective dismissal, for nine months after the dismissal date. If, within this period, the activities which ceased and led to the collective dismissal are resumed, the employer is obliged to inform the trade union in writing and to send the dismissed employees written notice in order to rehire them in their former positions without any pre-conditions or trial period. The employees have a maximum term of ten working days from the date they received the employer's notice in which to respond to the re-employment offer.

Only once employees with the right to be rehired have either notified their interest in writing within this term or have refused the position offered, can the employer can hire new employees to fill the vacant positions.

2.3.6   Wrongful Dismissal

Dismissals not ordered in compliance with the procedure stipulated by law are void. As a consequence, the whole procedure must be re-started.

2.3.7   Unfair Dismissal

In the case of unfair dismissal, the employee may claim reinstatement to the same job and payment of the increased salaries and other payment rights they would have been entitled to. In addition, the employee may ask for the payment of damages for injury to feelings, provided that he/she can prove the prejudice which he/she suffered on account of the unfair dismissal.

2.3.8   Discrimination

The Labour Code stipulates that the principle of equal treatment for all employees and employers shall apply within work relationships. All direct or indirect discrimination towards an employee, based on factors such as gender, sexual orientation, genetic characteristics, age, national origin, race, skin colour, ethnic origin, religion, political opinions, social origin, disability, family conditions or responsibilities, or trade-union membership or activity shall be prohibited.

In addition, Romania has adopted several laws against discrimination, such as Government Ordinance No. 137/2000 on the prevention and sanction of all types of discrimination, and Law No. 202/2002 on the equality of opportunity and treatment between women and men. The provisions of these laws apply to the employment sector as well, thereby forbidding any kind of discrimination based on criteria such as race, nationality, ethnic origin, language, religion, social status, convictions, gender, sexual orientation, age, and disability.

2.4   Costs

2.4.1   Mandatory Compensation

Under the National Collective Bargaining Agreement, upon termination of an individual employment contract for reasons other than personal reasons (both for individual and collective dismissals), the employee is entitled to compensation of at least one month's salary, besides his/her salary to date.

In addition, the employees should be granted compensation paid from the social security fund, which varies based on the length of service of the respective employee as follows:

- six months' salary (average net wage) for employees with up to five years of service;
- nine months' salary (average net wage) for employees with between five and fifteen years of service;
- twelve months' salary (average net wage) for employees with more than fifteen years of service.

However, this is the minimum compensation that an employee may receive. The individual employment contract or the collective bargaining agreement concluded at company level may provide for higher compensation.

Moreover, during the consultation phase of a collective dismissal procedure, the trade union and the employer may agree to pay additional compensation to that which is provided for by the law.

2.4.2   Damages

An employee cannot claim additional damages besides those mentioned above.

2.4.3   Social Plans

The notification mentioned in section 2.2.2 above has the characteristics of a social plan, although it is not expressly defined as such by law.

3   PRACTICAL ADVICE

3.1   TIMING

All the time limits stipulated by the law with respect to redundancy are mandatory and must therefore be strictly observed. An employer implementing a redundancy procedure will need to adhere carefully to all the steps provided by the law in order to ensure that such procedure is valid, although it is a long process.

In addition, in order to avoid any delays on the part of the trade union or the labour authorities, the notification related to this procedure must be carefully drafted and well reasoned.

3.2   INFORMATION AND CONSULTATION

The purpose of informing a trade union and the labour authorities with respect to redundancy procedures is to ensure that the employees' rights are not infringed. This is a sensitive matter which labour courts always treat carefully. Every breach of the above-mentioned procedure could trigger a court ruling in favour of employees.

3.3   COSTS AND RISKS

Redundancies carried out without observing the procedure provided for by law will be null and void, and the court may declare the redundancies unlawful and order the employer to compensate the employees for the amount of salary and other payment to which the employee would have been entitled, had the employee still been employed. In addition, the court may reinstate the employee to his/her previous position upon request.

RUSSIA

Nadezhda Bulatova
Nadezhda Serova
Sergey Stefanishin

1   OVERVIEW

The amended Labour Code of the Russian Federation, Federal Law No. 197-FZ dated 30 December 2001, (the Labour Code), distinguishes between dismissals made because of a 'reduction in the number of employees' and dismissals made because of a 'staff reduction'. Dismissals because of a 'reduction in the number of employees' means dismissals made because of a reduction in the number of employees within a specific group, e.g., a reduction in the number of secretaries from nine to five, whereas dismissals because of 'staff reduction' means dismissals made because of the abolition of a specific role, e.g. deputy chief engineer or office manager. Despite this, both of these terms are used in Russian legislation to mean redundancy.

The starting point in Russian law is that an employer has the right to determine staffing levels within his own business, but must follow the obligatory procedures established by the Russian employment legislation if it wishes to avoid claims when dismissing employees.

The regulations governing redundancy dismissals are contained primarily in the Labour Code. In addition, other statutes have set out provisions relating to specific protection and compensation, such as the amended Russian Federation

Law No. 1032-1 dated 19 April 1991, 'On Employment of the Population in the Russian Federation'.

The Labour Code provides that an employment contract may be terminated by an employer where there is a 'reduction in the number of employees' or a 'staff reduction' in its business, i.e., a redundancy situation. 'Employer' is defined broadly to cover legal entities and individuals, including registered entrepreneurs and individuals hiring employees to assist with household duties.

2   MAIN REQUIREMENTS AND CONSIDERATIONS

2.1   TIMING

2.1.1   Notice Periods

An employer is obliged to give an employee at least two month notice before terminating his employment (Labour Code, Article 180). The notice must be given in writing, and proof that the employee has received it must be retained. However, if the employer obtains the employee's written consent, the employer can terminate the employment contract before the expiration of the notice period by paying the employee compensation equal to the employee's average earnings for the remaining notice period. In terms of the Labour Code, the average earnings are calculated as follows:

- An employee's average salary is figured using the paid base salary and the actual work hours for the preceding twelve calendar months. A calendar month is considered to be the period from the first day up to and including the last day of a particular month.
- Average daily earnings for the purposes of leave payment and unused leave compensation are calculated for the last twelve calendar months by dividing the salary paid by twelve and then by 29.4 (the average number of calendar days per month).
- Average daily earnings for the purpose of leave payment and compensation for unused leave as envisaged by the code are granted in working days and determined by dividing the salary paid by the number of working days based on a six-day work week.

A collective agreement may stipulate other bases for the calculation of average salary, provided that this does not worsen the position of the employees.

The Labour Code provides that, in the case of agreement between the parties on early termination, the employer must still pay the employee the salary due plus compensation equal to the amount that the employee would have received had early termination not taken place.

Labour Code, Article 81 places further restrictions on an employer's ability to dismiss by reason of redundancy, stating that dismissal on the grounds of redundancy is only permissible if the employee cannot be transferred (with his written consent) to another job with the employer. The idea behind this provision is that in the case of redundancy, the employer is obliged to offer redundant employees other available vacant positions and must transfer them to other positions if they consent. If the employee does not consent, his employment will be terminated pursuant to Article 81.2 (redundancy) in accordance with the specified procedure. The employer must, therefore, offer the employee any vacant position that arises at his place of work and which matches the employee's qualifications as well as a lower qualified position or a lower paid job. The employer will only have to offer vacancies in other locations if there is a provision to this effect in any collective agreement with the works council or in the employee's employment contract. The obligation to transfer the employee to alternative employment continues throughout the notice period.

2.1.2 Collective Redundancies

In terms of the Labour Code, when an employer proposes to make collective redundancies, specific provisions apply. Collective redundancies include the liquidation of a company with fifteen or more employees, a reduction in the number of employees or staff positions (fifty or more individuals within thirty calendar days, 200 or more individuals within sixty calendar days, 500 or more individuals within ninety calendar days) or the termination within thirty calendar days of 1% of the employed persons in a region where the total number of employed persons is less than 5,000. In cases of collective redundancies where there is a works council, the employer must notify the representatives of the relevant works council in writing of its proposal at least two months before making any dismissals. Where the proposal is to make 'large-scale' redundancies, the employer must give no less than three months prior notice to the relevant works council, and in the same form and terms the employer must notify the local state employment authority. What constitutes a 'large-scale' redundancy will be determined by industry sector and/or territorial agreement.

Such agreements (accords) are legally binding agreements regulating social and labour relations and establishing the general principles of the regulation of associated economic relations concluded between authorized representatives of employees and employers, at federal, interregional, regional, sectoral (intersectoral) and territorial levels of social partnership within the limits of their competence.

Agreement between the parties participating in collective bargaining may be bilateral and trilateral.

Accords that envisage full or partial financing from particular budgets shall be concluded with the mandatory participation of the corresponding executive bodies or local government bodies that are party to the accord.

Depending on the scope of the social and labour relations that are regulated, accords of the following types may be concluded:

– The general accord establishes the general principles of the regulation of social and labour relations and associated economic relations at federal level.

- The interregional accord establishes the general principles of the regulation of social and labour relations and associated economic relations at the level of two or more constituent entities of the Russian Federation.
- The regional accord establishes the general principles of the regulation of social and labour relations and associated economic relations at the level of a constituent entity of the Russian Federation.
- The sectoral (intersectoral) accord establishes general conditions of payment for labour and guarantees and compensations and benefits for employees in a sector. A sectoral (intersectoral) accord may be concluded at federal, interregional, regional and territorial levels of social partnership.
- The territorial accord establishes general conditions of payment for labour, and guarantees and compensations and benefits for employees in the territory of a particular municipality.

Other accords may be concluded by parties at any level of social partnership in particular areas of the regulation of social and labour relations and other directly associated relations.

The 'Regulations for Organizing Work and Promoting Employment on Mass Redundancy of the Work Force', endorsed by the Russian Federation Government Resolution No. 99 dated 5 February 1993, states that, despite what is stated in any industry sector and/or territorial agreement, there will be a 'large-scale redundancy' when:

- fifty or more employees are to be dismissed during a period of thirty calendar days;
- 200 or more employees are to be dismissed during a period of sixty calendar days;
- 500 or more employees are to be dismissed during a period of ninety calendar days; or
- in a region (administrative district) where the total number of employed persons is less than 5,000, 1% of the total number of employees are to be dismissed during a period of thirty days.

The employer must send a draft of the redundancy proposals and the reasons for them to the works council. The works council must, not later than five business days from the day it receives the draft, send the employer a reasoned opinion on the draft in writing. In the event that the works council's reasoned opinion does not agree with the draft or contains proposals for improving it, the employer may agree with it or else is required, within three days of receiving the reasoned opinion, to hold additional consultations with the works council for the purposes of reaching an acceptable decision. If no agreement has been reached, a protocol must be drawn up indicating the disagreements. The employer will then be entitled to adopt a decision that is subject to appeal by the work council at the relevant state labour inspectorate or in court. Moreover, the works council is entitled to commence collective bargaining negotiations according to the procedure established by the Labour Code. Upon receiving a complaint (petition) from a works council, the state labour inspectorate is required to conduct an audit within one month of receiving the complaint (petition) and in the event that violations are discovered, issue a binding injunction ordering the employer to repeal the above mentioned decision.

The employer must notify the local state employment authority of his redundancy proposals. Russian Federation Law, Article 25.2, 'On the Employment of the Population in the Russian Federation' No. 1032 dated 19 April 1991, stipulates that upon the adoption of a decision on liquidation of the company or redundancy (reduction in the number of employees or staff positions) and possible termination of employment contracts, the employer is obliged to notify the employment authority in writing no later than two months before carrying out the relevant measures, and to specify the title, name, speciality and qualification requirements for the employees being dismissed and payment terms for each particular employee. Should such decision result in employment lay-offs, the notification must be filed three months in advance.

2.2   INFORMATION AND CONSULTATION

2.2.1   Collective Consultation

If there is a collective bargaining agreement with a works council, it may establish an alternative procedure for informing and consulting on redundancies.

2.3   FORMALIZING THE DISMISSAL

An internal notice of termination of employment should be given to employees on the date of their dismissal and a receipt should be obtained. If this is not possible or if an employee refuses to sign the notice as acknowledgment of his dismissal, a note to this effect must be made on the notice or, alternatively, a separate document confirming the above must be signed by a representative of the employer and two witnesses.

The employer should, on the date of termination, make a record of the employee's dismissal in the labour book and then give it to the employee. The employee should sign the book to acknowledge that he has seen the records made by the employer in the labour book. He should also acknowledge receipt of the labour book by signing the internal order of dismissal whilst at the same time signing a copy of the special registration journal of labour books kept by the employer.

If the employer fails to make a record in the labour book and gives it to the employee on his last working day, or if the employer makes an incorrect record of the employee's dismissal, the employer is obliged to pay the employee his average salary until the date when the employer gives the labour book to the employee or rectifies the error made in the labour book. In this case, the date of dismissal will be the day of making the correct record in the labour book, and the employer shall issue a new order of dismissal specifying a new dismissal day. When this happens, the date of the employee's dismissal will be the date when the correct record is made in the labour book, and the employer will need to issue a new order specifying the new dismissal date. In addition, the employer is required to correct the previous record. If the employee is absent from work or has refused to accept or acknowledge receipt of the labour book and it is therefore impossible for the employer to make a record in it and to give it to the employee on his last working day, the employer is required to send a notice to the employee by registered mail, advising the employee to either collect the labour book or agree to accept delivery by post. In these circumstances, the employer is not obliged to obtain the employee's signature.

The employer is obliged to pay the employee all amounts due including salary, holiday pay and any severance payment, on the day of dismissal.

2.4   RISKS AND COSTS

2.4.1   Protected Employee Categories

In Russia, there are certain employee categories that are afforded greater protection from redundancy. In particular, where there is a proposal to make certain employees redundant, employers have to comply with rules concerning the 'preferential right to remain at work' (Labour Code, Article 179). A preferential right to remain at work is afforded to employees with 'higher productivity and skills'. In a case in which employees being considered for redundancy are equally skilled and productive, the preference will be to retain:

- employees with two or more dependants;
- employees with an incapacitated family member who is dependent on the employee;
- employees who provide the only family income;
- employees who have sustained a severe injury or become ill whilst working for the employer;
- invalids of the Great Patriotic War between Germany and Russia (1941-1945); and
- disabled persons as a result of combat in defence of Russia.

A collective bargaining agreement with a works council may also stipulate other employee categories that give the employees a preferential right to remain in work.

Besides the 'preferential right to remain at work', the following categories of employee are entitled to additional protection and compensation when they are made redundant:

- employees injured as a result of the Chernobyl accident or through radiation at the Semipalatinsk range;
- individuals working permanently as state secret agents;

- heroes of the Soviet Union;
- heroes of the Russian Federation;
- full knights of the Order of Glory;
- inventors;
- spouses of military men in government bodies or military units; and
- orphans and children without parental custody.

Additionally, if provided for in a collective bargaining agreement with a works council, employees may be entitled to 'remain on the waiting list' for free housing with their former employer. Further, the employees' children may continue to attend the infant school on equal terms with the children of those still employed by the company.

2.4.2 Legal Redundancy Requirements for Certain Employee Categories

2.4.2.1 Employees Located in the Far North and Equated Localities

Under the Labour Code, employees made redundant from an organization located in the far north or equated localities (there is a special list of areas which are classified as Far North/Equated Localities including certain regions of Murmanskaya Oblast, Arkhangelskaya Oblast, Karelia, Tyumenskaya Oblast, etc.) are listed and approved by the Russian Government and are entitled to receive a severance payment equivalent to their average monthly salary while looking for a new job. This average monthly salary will be for a period not exceeding three months after dismissal (against which the severance pay will be set off). In exceptional cases, the average monthly payment will be paid to the employees for a maximum of six months after the date of dismissal whilst they are looking for a job. Employees will only be entitled to a payment in excess of three month's average salary if they applied to a state employment authority and no job was found for them within one month of their dismissal.

2.4.2.2 Employees on Fixed-Term Contracts of Two Months or Less

The Labour Code provides that an employer must give employees with fixed-term contracts of less than two months written notice of at least three calendar days before dismissing for redundancy. On being made redundant, such employees are not entitled to a severance payment unless otherwise established by federal law, a collective bargaining agreement or the employment contract.

2.4.2.3 Employees under the Age of Eighteen

Special protection is given to employees under the age of eighteen. An employer must follow special procedures before making such employees redundant, and may only do so with the prior permission of the state labour inspectorate and the commission for children and the protection of their rights.

2.4.2.4   *Seasonal Workers*

Seasonal workers, as defined in inter-industry agreements that have been concluded as part of government partnerships, also have special protection. Employers must give seasonal workers at least seven days prior written notice of their dismissal by reason of redundancy. Seasonal workers are also entitled to severance pay equivalent to two weeks' average salary.

2.4.2.5   *Directors and Chief Accountants*

A director can be dismissed for the following reasons:

- company insolvency;
- pursuant to a decision of an authorized body of a legal entity or the owner of the assets of the organization or by a person (body) authorized by the owner; or
- in circumstances provided for in their employment contract.

A director is entitled to such compensation as is set out in his employment contract. However, a director is entitled to a minimum of three months' average salary, provided he has not acted in contravention of the law or of his employment contract.

The Labour Code also provides that in the case of dismissal of a director, deputy director and/or a chief accountant following a takeover, the new management must pay a minimum of three months' average salary as compensation.

The Labour Code provides that a takeover does not constitute a reason to make employees redundant unless the change in ownership has been registered with the government authority.

In the event of a change of ownership of the assets of an organization, the new owner shall have the right to terminate the employment agreement with the director and deputy directors of the organization and the chief accountant no later than three months from the day on which it acquires ownership rights.

2.4.2.6   *Works Council Members*

Before a works council member can be made redundant, the employer must give notice to the works council representative of the proposed redundancy together with copies of any supporting documents. Within seven business days of receiving the notice and documents, the works council's representatives must review the documents and send the employer their written opinion on the employer's proposal. Opinions not submitted within the seven-day period do not have to be considered by the employer.

If the representatives do not agree with the employer's proposed decision to dismiss, the representatives must engage in further consultations with the employer, the results of which must then be set out in a report. If agreement cannot be reached, the employer is entitled to dismiss at the end of ten business days from the date on which the notice of the proposed redundancy and supporting documents were provided.

The dismissal can be appealed by the employee to the state labour inspectorate. The state labour inspectorate must consider the appeal within ten days of receipt. If it finds the dismissal to be unlawful, if the stipulated procedures and formalities had been violated, it will order the employer to give the employee his job back and pay him for the period he did not work. The court may rule that the employee must be reinstated to his position and the employer must follow the ruling. The employer may appeal this ruling to a court.

The dismissal of the employee must be effected within one month of the employer receiving an opinion from the works council's representatives. Such a period does not include sick leave, holiday, or other periods of absence.

2.4.3   Unlawful Dismissal

If an employee brings a claim for unlawful dismissal, the court will, above all, wish to determine whether the dismissal was in fact by reason of redundancy. The employer should seek to prove that the dismissal was by reason of redundancy by producing a copy of the order of dismissal. However, the court will also examine the employer's list of employees before and after the dismissal to see if the job carried out by the employee was replaced with a similar role following his dismissal. If the name of the position has changed but the volume of work and the nature of work remains the same, the redundancy could be an unlawful dismissal. The employer should get a list of employees accepted before dismissing. In the absence of an employee list, employers may have to rely on payroll statements to prove the legitimacy of the redundancy. A list of employees means the 'staff schedule' – an internal document which lists staff levels, positions and employee duties. Absence in the list of employers of redundant positions is the evidence of a real process of redundancy. A new version of the list of employees should be approved by the employer before starting to implement the redundancy.

The Labour Code provides that it is unlawful to make certain categories of employees redundant. These categories include:

- pregnant women;
- women with children under the age of three years;
- single mothers with children under the age of fourteen years or disabled children under the age of eighteen years; and
- individuals responsible for bringing up children under the age of fourteen years or disabled children under the age of eighteen years where there is no mother.

It is also unlawful to dismiss an employee on sick leave or vacation.

2.4.4   Reinstatement of the Employee

If an employee considers his dismissal unlawful, he may apply to a court for an order of reinstatement. If the employee's claim is upheld, the court will, in terms of the Labour Code, oblige the employer to reimburse the employee for his unpaid salary and benefits for the period he was out of employment. It can also declare the dismissal void and order the reinstatement of the employee.

The court may also award the employee damages for injury to feelings. The Labour Code provides that damages to be paid to the employee for injured feelings caused by the employer's illegal actions or inactions shall be such sums as may be agreed between the parties. If the parties do not agree on the amount of compensation, then it will be determined by the court.

2.4.5   Severance Pay

Where an employee is dismissed by reason of redundancy, the employer is obliged to pay the dismissed employee a minimum severance payment equal to one month's average salary plus an additional month's average salary whilst the employee seeks new employment. In exceptional cases, the state employment authorities may decide to pay the employee a third month's average salary, provided that the employee registered with such authorities within two weeks of dismissal and did not find new employment during the third month after termination of his employment.

The employment contract or collective bargaining agreement with the works council may provide for higher amounts of severance pay to be paid to employees who are made redundant.

3   REDUNDANCY IN PRACTICE

The following list summarizes redundancy in practice:

- An employer must notify the employee of his forthcoming redundancy and simultaneously offer another suitable job, if there is one available.
- An employer should comply with the rules relating to the 'preferential right to remain at work' when selecting employees for redundancy.
- Where there is a works council, an employer should notify it or obtain its consent to the dismissal due to redundancy.
- An internal order on dismissal should be issued.
- The severance payment and any other amounts due to the employee should be paid on the day of dismissal.
- A relevant record should be made in the employee's labour book, and the labour book should be handed to the employee on the day of dismissal.

The employer should document his actions throughout the redundancy process. For example, the employer should keep a written record of any job offer made to the employee or the fact that the employer had no alternative vacancy for the employee. This is particularly important given that, where a job offer is not made, the court will investigate what vacancies existed at the time the employee was given notice and when his employment terminated. If, within the two months between the date of notification and the date of dismissal appropriate vacancies became available and were not proposed to the employee, the court will be likely to reinstate the employee.

SLOVAK REPUBLIC

Tomáš Čermák
Zuzana Majerčáková
Karin Šturdíková

1   OVERVIEW

For the purposes of this chapter, the term 'organizational reasons' shall mean:

- the employer (or part of the employer) has ceased to exist or has been relocated;
- there have been changes to the tasks performed by an employee or changes to technical equipment, leading to a reduction in the number of employees needed, with the aim of increasing work efficiency; or
- other organizational changes.

The legislation that governs dismissals for organizational reasons and collective redundancies includes:

- Act No. 311/2001 Coll., the Labour Code, as amended ('Labour Code);
- Act No. 125/2006 Coll., on Inspection of Work, as amended (Act on Inspection of Work);
- Act No. 5/2004 Coll., on Employment Services, as amended (Act on Employment Services); and
- Act No. 365/2004 Coll., on Equal Treatment in Selected Areas and on Protection against Discrimination (Antidiscrimination Act).

©2008 Kluwer Law International B.V., The Netherlands.
Maarten van Kempen, Lisa Patmore, Michael Ryley, and
Robert von Steinau-Steinrück (eds), *Redundancy,* pp. 213-221.

The provisions of the Labour Code are mandatory and, therefore, the parties to a contract of employment cannot determine their own terms.

The ways in which a contract of employment can be terminated are set out in the Labour Code. These are:

- by agreement;
- with notice;
- termination with immediate effect; and/or
- termination within the probation period.

These methods of termination are described in more detail in section 2 below, which focuses on termination by agreement and termination with notice. These two methods of termination are common when a contract of employment is terminated for organizational reasons.

In addition, an employment contract will automatically terminate in the event that the employee dies. However, the death of an employer, where the employer is a natural person, does not automatically cause the contract of employment to terminate. In such cases, the Labour Code provides that the rights and obligations contained in the employment contract will transfer to the employer's heirs.

Conversely, where an employer that is a legal entity ceases to exist, the rights and obligations contained in the employment contract will either be transferred to its legal successor (where applicable) or terminated by the employer before it ceases to exist.

2   MAIN REQUIREMENTS AND CONSIDERATIONS

2.1   TIMING

2.1.1   **Individual Redundancies**

Where an employment contract is terminated by agreement [section 60 of the Labour Code], the date of termination is determined by the parties. Any such agreement must be in writing and, if requested by the employee, must state the reasons for the termination. These reasons must also be included if the parties have entered into an agreement for the termination of the contract of employment for organizational reasons.

When an employment contract is terminated by agreement between the parties, there is no requirement for the employee representatives to participate in the termination process. For example, there is no obligation to consult employee representatives or obtain their consent. This is not the case with other methods of termination.

When an employment contract is terminated by giving notice, the notice must be in writing and must be delivered to the employee. In such circumstances, the contract will terminate when the notice period expires. In each case, the notice period must be the same for both the employer and the employee.

Usually, the notice period must be at least two months. However, where an employee's length of service is five years or more, the notice period must be at least three months. In each case, the notice period will start on the first day of the month following delivery of the notice. The notice period will expire on the last day of the relevant month, unless otherwise determined.

There is one exception to these rules. This is contained in section 49(6) of the Labour Code and provides that the notice period for part-time employees who work less than fifteen hours per week is thirty days. In such cases, the notice period begins when notice of termination has been delivered to the employee.

An employer may only serve a notice of termination for specific reasons (see below), and, in order to be valid, any notice issued by an employer must clearly specify the reason for dismissal.

The specific reasons for which an employer can serve notice of termination on an employee are contained in section 63 of the Labour Code and include termination for organizational reasons.

Where organizational reasons exist, an employer may only serve notice of termination in one of the following circumstances:

- The employer cannot continue to employ the employee at the agreed location (even for a shorter working time).
- The employee is not willing to perform other suitable work that has been proposed by the employer at the agreed location or to undergo a prior training for such other work.

If the employer has served notice of termination on the employee on grounds of redundancy, the redundant position must not be refilled. In addition, the employer must not recruit another person to fill this position for three months following the dismissal (section 61(3) of the Labour Code).

If the employee breaches his/her obligation to stay with the employer during the notice period, the employer is entitled to compensation in the amount of the employee's average monthly earnings for one month, provided the employer and the employee so agreed in the employment contract. Unless such agreement is in writing, it shall be invalid.

2.1.2 Collective Redundancy

Under the Labour Code, a collective redundancy exists where an employer (or part of the employer) terminates the employment contracts of at least twenty employees for organizational reasons or another reason not vesting in the employee, either by giving notice or by mutual agreement, during a period of ninety days (section 73 of the Labour Code).

Where there are collective redundancies, the procedure to be followed is more onerous. For example, the employer must comply with a large number of information and consultation obligations, as described below.

2.2   INFORMATION AND CONSULTATION

2.2.1   Individual Redundancies

In accordance with section 74 of the Labour Code, an employer is obliged to
discuss with the employee representatives any notice of termination or termination
with immediate effect, in advance of issuing any notice or making such dismissals.
Failure to meet this obligation will lead to the invalidity of the notice or termination. If the employee representatives participate in these discussions, they must do
so within ten days of receiving an invitation from the employer. Otherwise, it shall
be deemed that the discussions have taken place.

In addition, strict rules apply when contracts of employment of employee
representatives are terminated. In such cases, the prior approval of the employee
representatives is required (section 240(8) of the Labour Code).

Under section 66 of the Labour Code, an employer may only terminate the
employment contract of a disabled employee if it has obtained prior consent from
the competent authority of labour, social affairs and family (labour authority). In
the absence of such consent, the notice will be deemed to be invalid.

2.2.2   Collective Redundancy

At least one month before a proposed collective redundancy, the employer must
discuss with the employee representatives – or, if no employee representatives
operate at the employer, directly with the involved employees – potential measures
to prevent or reduce the number of redundancies. These representatives include
members of a trade union, employee council or employee fiduciaries. The aim of
the consultation is to reach agreement on relocating the employees and providing
them with suitable alternative work (even if training is required). The discussions
must also be with a view to agreeing on measures to reduce the adverse impact of
the redundancies on the employees.

To aid consultation, an employer is obliged to provide the employee representatives with specific information ('Notice 1'). This information primarily relates to:

- the reasons for the redundancies;
- the number and categories of employees affected;
- the aggregate number and categories of all employees;
- the period during which the redundancies will take place; and
- the criteria for selecting the redundant employees.

A copy of Notice 1 must be provided to the labour authority. The employer is also
obliged to discuss any measures to prevent or reduce the number of collective
redundancies with the labour authority.

After discussing the collective redundancies with the employee representatives, the employer is obliged to provide both the employee representatives and the
labour authority with a written statement outlining the result of these consultations
('Notice 2').

The employer is entitled to start making the employees redundant one month after delivering Notice 2 to both the employee representatives and the labour authority. The employer can affect a redundancy by delivering either notices of termination for organizational reasons or notices containing proposals for mutual agreements in relation to dismissals for organizational reasons.

Where the court has declared an employer bankrupt, the one-month period for delivering notices is not applicable, and the employer is not obliged to discuss measures to prevent or reduce the number of collective redundancies with the labour authority.

2.3   Risks

As outlined above, the termination of a contract of employment (either on an individual or collective basis) is subject to a number of specific legal requirements.

In the event that these requirements are not fully met, the following statutory risks may arise:

- invalid termination of the contract of employment;
- increased costs (connected with invalid terminations or as a result of non-compliance with the statutory requirements);
- claims (e.g., compensation for damages or discrimination claims); and
- fines levied by the state authorities.

A number of specific circumstances could have a significant impact on the degree of risk that may arise, and which, therefore, need to be considered carefully. These are listed below.

2.3.1   Protected Groups of Employees

In accordance with section 64(1) of the Labour Code, certain specific groups of employees are protected against dismissal. An employer may not serve notice of termination (whether by reason of an individual or collective redundancy) to employees who, for example:

- have been declared temporarily incapable of work due to illness or injury;
- have been released to perform a position of civic or public duty;
- are pregnant, are on maternity or parental leave, or are a solitary employee[1] caring for a child younger than three years of age; or
- are temporarily unable to work night shifts (should the employee work night shifts).

---

1. A solitary employee, pursuant to the LC, shall be understood as an employee who lives alone and is a single, widowed, or divorced man or a single, widowed, or divorced woman.

There are, however, certain exceptions to these rules. In particular, section 64(3) of the Labour Code provides that the ban on dismissal does not apply when the notice of termination arises out of the following circumstances:

- There are organizational reasons (being either cessation or relocation of the employer or part of the employer).
- The conduct of the employee entitles the employer to terminate the contract of employment with immediate effect, for example, when the employee has been found guilty of committing an intentional criminal offence or the employee has committed an act of gross misconduct. However, this exception does not apply if the employee is on maternity or parental leave. If notice is served prior to the commencement of maternity or parental leave (so that the notice period would expire during maternity or parental leave), the notice period will expire when the maternity or parental leave ends.
- The employee was guilty of a less serious disciplinary offence. Again, this exception does not apply if the employee is on maternity or parental leave.
- As result of his/her own fault, the employee loses the prerequisites for the performance of agreed work according to special regulations. This covers situations when, due to the employee's fault, his/her preconditions for the performance of the agreed work pursuant to special regulations cease to exist, e.g., when an employee whose scope of employment is driving (for which, pursuant to special regulations, possession of a valid driving licence is required) is disqualified from driving because of his/her own fault.

As stated above, in accordance with section 66 of the Labour Code, an employer may terminate an employment contract of a disabled employee by notice, if it has obtained prior consent from the labour authority. Failure to obtain consent will result in the notice being deemed invalid.

2.3.2   Invalid Termination by the Employer

Any failure to meet all of the statutory requirements will result in the termination being invalid.

The question of the validity of a termination by notice, termination with immediate effect, termination during the trial period [probation period], or termination by agreement may be challenged by an employer and/or employee in court, provided the application to the court is made within a period of two months from the date the employment contract was (thought to be) terminated.

If the employer has served an invalid notice on the employee, invalidly terminated the employment contract with immediate effect, or invalidly terminated the employment contract within the trial period, the employee may inform the employer that he/she wants to continue to work for the employer. Where this happens, the employment contract will continue, unless a competent court decides that it is 'unjust' to require the employer to continue to employ the employee.

An employee's employment contract will terminate if he/she does not inform the employer that he/she insists on the continuation of the employment within the following time periods:

- where notice has been given, by the expiry of the notice period; or
- where the employment was terminated with immediate effect or termination during the trial period, by the date of delivery of the termination with immediate effect or termination during the probation period. However, an employee is entitled to receive compensation equal to two months' salary (the notice period).

2.3.3   Discrimination

The principle of equal treatment, introduced by the Antidiscrimination Act, applies inter alia to employment relationships and consists of three main provisions:

(a) prohibition of discrimination on any grounds;
(b) a duty to adopt measures aimed at protecting against discrimination; and
(c) a duty to perform rights and obligations in line with good morals.

The principle of equal treatment does not begin with the commencement of the employment relationship. It applies to the recruitment of employees and continues throughout the duration of the employment relationship, including selection criteria and recruitment conditions, e.g., advertisements and interviews, and working conditions including remuneration, promotions and dismissals.

Any detrimental treatment on the grounds of gender, religion or belief, race, national or ethnic origin, disability, age, or sexual orientation may be considered to be discriminatory.

Anyone who believes he/she has suffered a detriment as a result of his/her employer's failure to apply the principle of equal treatment may seek judicial relief. If the employee submits evidence to the court that suggests that the principle of equal treatment was breached, the employer will have the burden of proving that the breach did not, in fact, occur.

2.4   Costs

2.4.1   Severance Payments

Where the employment contract has been terminated for organizational reasons, an employer must make a severance payment to an employee. In accordance with a strict interpretation of the Labour Code, employers and employees cannot agree on severance payments under any other circumstances of termination.

The amount of the severance payment is not prescribed or limited by law and is, therefore, at the employer's discretion.

An employer is obliged to make a severance payment to an employee, regardless of whether the employer and employee agree on immediate termination of the employment contract or its termination within a notice period. If the employee has been employed for less than five years, the severance payment should be equal to two months' salary. Otherwise, the severance payment should be equal to at least three months' salary.

Where organizational changes lead to a transfer of rights and obligations contained in an employment contract but not to dismissal, the employee will not have any claim to a severance payment.

2.4.2   Compensation for Invalid Termination

If an employer invalidly terminates an employment contract, and the employee informs the employer that he/she would like his/her employment to continue, the employment continues unless a court decides that this would be unjust.

In such circumstances, the employee can claim compensation from the date the employee's notice was delivered to the employer until either the date on which the employer begins to re-assign work to the employee or the date on which the employee's employment is validly terminated.

If the period of time between these dates exceeds twelve months, the court, at the request of the employer, has discretion to decrease, or not award, the compensation.

2.4.3   Payments for Breach of Collective Redundancy Provisions

If an employer fails to comply with its obligations with regard to:

(a) discussing the intended collective redundancies with employee representatives;
(b) providing them with Notice 1;
(c) providing a copy of Notice 1 to the labour authority;
(d) providing employee representatives and labour authority with Notice 2; or
(e) keeping the period of one month from the delivery of Notice 2 to employee representatives and labour authorities before starting collective redundancies,

an employee whose contract is terminated as part of a collective redundancy will be entitled to receive compensation equivalent to two months' salary.

2.4.4   Penalties under Labour Law Regulations

If an employer fails to comply with the provisions of the Labour Code or related labour law rules, the Labour Authority may impose a penalty.

Moreover, if senior employees or statutory bodies of the employer breach their obligations under the Labour Code, related labour-law rules or collective bargaining agreements; give instructions to commit such a breach; or conceal facts relevant to the performance of an inspection, they may face a penalty of up to four months' salary.

3   PRACTICAL ADVICE

3.1   Timing

The timing of dismissals for organizational reasons, both individual and collective, is key to the efficiency of the termination process. This is particularly the case with respect to the involvement of employee representatives. Therefore, in order to ensure efficient and successful implementation of a redundancy process, the statutory periods during which employee representatives are obliged to comment on or give consent must be planned at an early stage.

3.2   Information and Consultation

As specified above, the need to communicate with employee representatives or the labour authority by way of consultation, provision of information, or obtaining consent must be borne in mind. Any failure to meet this obligation may have significant consequences for the employer, including the invalidation of termination of contracts (see section 2.3.2 above) or an obligation to pay compensation to the affected employees.

In addition, any failure to comply with the LC or relevant labour-law regulations may result in administrative sanctions being imposed on the employer.

3.3   Risks and Costs

The potential risks and consequences of invalid terminations – increased costs, claims, or fines levied by the state authorities – may be avoided by complying with the statutory obligations imposed on employers.

In this context, and aside from the formal requirements imposed on both employers and employees in relation to the form, content, and/or delivery of documents, a well-prepared redundancy process that takes into account the relevant time requirements and notification obligations is essential for successful implementation of proposed redundancies.

SLOVENIA

Ralf Pescheck
Melanie Taufner

1   OVERVIEW

Labour law in Slovenia provides for strict rules regarding termination. In general, employees are protected against termination by the provisions of the Employment Relationships Act *(Zakon o delovnih razmerjih)* (ERA).

Employment relationships may be ended unilaterally by ordinary or extra-ordinary termination or by mutual agreement. In addition, a court judgment may terminate an employment relationship or it can be unilaterally terminated *ex lege* due to an employee's disability.

Whilst an employee may ordinarily end the employment relationship without having to cite a reason for doing so, ordinary termination by an employer requires a reason which may, inter alia, be a business decision. A business reason exists when the need for the employee's work ceases due to economic, organizational, technological, structural or similar reasons. Such reasons may be, for example, the result of changes in the economic and/or financial conditions of the business, a reorganization of the company or technological improvements with a view to increasing efficiency. However, a business reason will not be accepted if the employee is employed in a department of the company where employees have to work overtime on a regular basis or if 'cheaper' employees are to be employed after terminating others. Employers must bear in mind that they may be required to

©2008 Kluwer Law International B.V., The Netherlands.
Maarten van Kempen, Lisa Patmore, Michael Ryley, and
Robert von Steinau-Steinrück (eds), *Redundancy,* pp. 223-230.

substantiate a business reason before a court. Accordingly, employers should ensure that the reasons for any termination are thoroughly documented.

A Slovenian employer, like in many countries, has to follow a set of preliminary steps before it may actually give notice to an employee. The extent of these notification and warning obligations depends on the employer's reason for terminating the employee.

It is important to bear in mind the rule that a mutual dissolution of the employment relationship requires a written agreement between the parties to the employment agreement, which must include information regarding the consequences of termination, in particular those with respect to claims vis-à-vis unemployment insurance, as an employee will not be entitled to any unemployment benefits in the case of a mutual termination.

2   MAJOR LEGAL REGULATIONS

2.1   TIMING

2.1.1   Examination of the Possibility of Continued Employment (ERA Article 88, paragraph 3)

If an employer intends to base the termination of an employee with at least six months' service on business reasons, the employer must examine whether such employee can be employed under changed circumstances, be re-assigned to another workplace or be retrained and continue with the same employer after the retraining.

If so, the employer must offer a 'new' employment agreement to the employee. Although this only represents a change in the employee's obligations within the framework of the existing employment relationship, the formal approach of Slovenian law requires the signing of a new contract.

The employee has to respond to the offer of a new employment contract within thirty days. Should the employee refuse to accept an adequate new employment contract, the employee loses entitlement to severance pay. If the new contract is unfavourable compared to his/her previous employment, the employee is entitled to a proportionate amount of severance pay. However, should the employee accept the offer, he/she does not lose the right to challenge the reason for termination and thus the offer of the new employment agreement (ERA Article 90).

Small employers, i.e., those with ten employees or fewer, are not subject to this obligation.

2.1.2   Ex ante Information (ERA Article 83, paragraph 3)

If an employer intends to effect an ordinary termination of an employment relationship for a business reason, it must inform the employee of the envisaged termination in writing. The law does not stipulate a particular time limit for fulfilling this obligation. It is recommended that this *ex ante* information also confirm that the employer has examined the possibility of continued employment of the employee.

Accordingly, an employer must prepare two letters for terminating an employment relationship: The first letter to provide the employee with the *ex ante* information and the second letter as the actual notice of termination.

2.1.3   Notification to the Trade Union (ERA Article 84)

An employee may request that the employer inform the applicable trade union of its intention to terminate his/her employment. If so, the trade union is authorized to offer its opinion regarding the intended termination within eight days.

If the trade union opposes the termination, this does not bar the employer from initiating the termination procedure. While an employee may request that any effect of the termination notice be suspended, if the reason for the termination is anything other than business, he/she is not entitled to such a suspension.

2.1.4   Periods of Notice (ERA Articles 91 et seq.)

In general, an employment agreement must be for an indefinite term. A fixed-term agreement is justifiable only for certain reasons (e.g., employment of executive employees or seasonal work), but this is further restricted by the rules on the admissible length of a limited term. A fixed-term employment agreement generally ends upon the expiration of the envisioned limited term. However, a termination before expiration of the fixed term is permissible.

In the event of an ordinary termination, the employer must comply with the minimum notice periods stipulated in the ERA. The employment agreement may, however, extend the notice periods to be adhered to by the employer, as may also be the case with the applicable collective bargaining agreement. The duration of the individual notice period depends on the employee's length of service, on the one hand, and on the reason cited for termination on the other. If the employment relationship is to be terminated for a business reason, the notice period ranges from thirty to 120 days, depending on the length of service of the individual employee. Notice periods start to run on the day following service of the notice letter.

The law provides for specific notice periods for certain situations: Upon termination of the employment relationship associated with insolvency or judicial liquidation, the liquidator may terminate the employment relationship by adhering to a notice period of only fifteen days. Likewise, a notice period of only thirty days generally applies in other cases involving termination of the business.

Further, the employer has to meet a six-month deadline as the opportunity to terminate an employment agreement for a given reason lapses after that time period.

Any termination must be announced in writing. The employer must include information regarding the reason for the termination. In addition, it must inform the employee of the legal remedies available and rights vis-à-vis unemployment insurance. As a rule, the employer must hand over the notice letter to the employee personally at his/her work place.

2.1.5   Mass Lay-Offs (ERA Articles 96 et seq.)

Mass lay-offs lead to an increase in the administrative and financial efforts required by an employer during the termination procedure. These additional rules apply if the employment of a large number of employees is to be terminated for business reasons within any thirty-day period (ERA Article 96). The threshold for a mass lay-off lies at ten employees in companies that employ more than twenty but fewer than 100 employees; at 10% of the employees in companies that employ more than 100 but fewer than 300 employees and at thirty employees in companies that employ more than 300 employees. In addition, the threshold is exceeded if at least twenty employees are terminated for business reasons within any three-month period.

If the threshold is exceeded and, thus, a mass lay-off is to take place, the employer must prepare a termination programme for all employees affected. This termination programme must comprise a certain minimum content (ERA Article 99). It must set out:

– the reasons for the terminations and the actions implemented in order to avoid or reduce the terminations;
– a list of redundant employees;
– the measures implemented in order to mitigate the harmful consequences of the terminations (e.g., financial support in the form of higher severance payments, assistance in starting a self-employed activity); and
– the criteria for selecting such measures.

In the event of mass lay-offs, an employer is under an obligation to apply certain criteria in determining which employees will become redundant. In this respect, maintaining the jobs of employees who are in a disadvantaged social position will take priority.

The employer may make a final decision on the termination programme only when it has consulted with the trade union and dealt with suggestions for the programme made by the employment service.

2.2   INFORMATION AND CONSULTATION

2.2.1   Notification to the Trade Union

As mentioned above (see section 2.1.3), an employee may generally request that the employer inform the applicable trade union of the intended termination.

2.2.2 Consultation Rights of the Works Council (The Law on Worker Participation in Management, Articles 91 et seq.)

Slovenian employment law is characterized by the coexistence of trade unions and works councils, although it is more common for employees to be represented by trade unions rather than by works councils. The participation rights of the works council is regulated by the Law on Worker Participation in Management *(Zakon o sodelovanju delavcev pri upravljanju)* (LWPM).

Besides other participation rights, the works council has a right to information and consultation with regard to personnel issues. These include the termination of a significant number of employees (i.e., 10%). A specific time frame applies for the termination process. The employer must forward the information to the works council at least thirty days before it makes its decision. The joint consultation serving to harmonize the positions of the employer and the works council must be organized at least fifteen days before the employer makes its decision. Since the works council has the right to stay decisions ('veto') if it was not duly informed of the measure at hand and invited to consult with the employer, it is crucial to comply with this obligation. Furthermore, administrative fines of at least approximately EUR 1,000 may be imposed on the employer for non-compliance. Further participation rights, in particular rights of the works council to information, apply with respect to measures often connected to terminations for business reasons, e.g., changes in the company's activity, changes in the organization relating to production or technological changes.

2.2.3 Mass Lay-Offs

In the event of mass lay-offs, an employer is obligated to provide certain information to the trade union (ERA Article 97). This information, which must be provided as soon as possible, must comprise:

- the reasons for the termination;
- the number and categories of all employees;
- the prospective categories of the affected employees;
- the planned date on which the employment will be terminated; and
- the criteria for determining those employees to whom notice will be given.

The employer must forward a copy of this information to the employment service.

In addition, the employer is obligated to enter into consultation with the trade union regarding the criteria for determining which employees are redundant and the measures for avoiding or reducing terminations as well as mitigating the harmful consequences of such terminations.

Subsequently, the employer must fulfil information obligations vis-à-vis the employment service which relate to the procedure for determining the terminations; the results of the consultation with the trade unions; the number and categories of all affected employees; proposed categories of redundant employees; and the date on which the termination of employees is planned. The trade union is entitled to receive a copy of this information (ERA Article 98).

The notification of the employment service initiates a blocking period of thirty days during which the employer may not give notice. The employment service is authorized to extend this period to sixty days. The higher the number of employees being terminated and the harder it will presumably be for them to find a new job, the greater the risk of such extension by the employment service. In contrast, the employment service seems to abstain from extending the blocking period if the employer presents a termination programme involving generous aid for employees.

The employer is required to address the suggestions of the employment service regarding measures to be taken for avoiding or reducing terminations and mitigating the harmful consequences of such terminations, as set out in the termination programme.

2.3   COST AND RISKS

2.3.1   Severance Payment

In the event of a termination for business reasons, an employee is entitled to severance payment if his/her service time amounted to at least one year. The highest possible amount of severance payment is ten times the employee's average salary during the last three months of employment.

If the employee receives a job offer from a new employer during this notice period and the new employer credits the service time spent with the former employer, the employee has no claim for severance payment against the former employer.

2.3.2   Protection against Unlawful Termination

If an employee considers his/her termination unlawful, he/she may file a lawsuit within thirty days of delivery of the notice letter. Insofar as the employee wishes to assert purely financial claims and does not seek reinstatement, the lawsuit must be filed within five years.

As discussed above, the employer bears the burden of proof that the reason cited in the notice of termination is substantiated (ERA Article 82). If the employer is unable to prove the existence of the termination reason, the court will conclude that the employee's termination was unlawful. If so, the employee is authorized to continue his/her employment relationship with the employer. As a consequence, the employee is entitled to receive salary and social security contributions for the period between the unlawful termination and the conclusion of the proceedings. On the other hand, the employee may decide that he/she does not wish to continue the employment relationship. If so, he/she may request that the court rule that the employment relationship existed until the judgment of first instance was issued. The court will then calculate the employee's claims up to this date. Further, the court may award compensation to the employee up to an amount of eighteen monthly salaries. The court may also take this route if it comes to the conclusion that the continuation of the employment relationship is not reasonable for either party.

Bearing in mind that the court usually issues the judgment of first instance after approximately two years, the employer should calculate the risk and compare it carefully with the costs of a mutual dissolution, including a voluntary severance payment. The employer is not entitled to any compensation for the costs of litigation, even if the court confirms that the termination is valid.

The law provides for special protection against termination for employee representatives, pregnant employees, employees on parental leave, disabled employees and older employees.

2.3.3   Right to Re-employment (ERA Article 102)

If the employer cited a business reason as the basis for terminating the employment relationship, the employee has a preferential right to re-employment if the employer hires new employees within one year of such employee's termination. This should be taken into account to avoid any claims for damages by an affected employee when an employer hires new employees during this period.

2.3.4   Consultation with the Works Council

As mentioned above, failure by an employer to duly inform the works council authorizes the latter to stay the decision (see section 2.2.2). In parallel, the works council must initiate procedures to settle the dispute, which additionally delays the implementation of the measures adopted by the employer. The employer is not allowed to execute its decision until the final decision of the competent court has been issued.

2.3.5   Mass Lay-Offs (ERA Article 96)

Regarding the potential additional costs associated with mass lay-offs, please refer to the comments in section 2.1.5 above. Further, the employer should pay particular attention to following all the steps required in the case of mass lay-offs. Otherwise, the employer faces the risk that the terminations may be deemed invalid.

3   ADVICE FOR LEGAL PRACTICE

3.1   Timing

It is particularly important to give notice of termination before the time limit for asserting the reason for termination has lapsed, when the reason may no longer be a basis for termination.

With respect to mass lay-offs, the employer should dedicate sufficient time in advance to drafting the termination programme, since a well-prepared termination programme may considerably speed up the required information and consultation process with the trade union and the employment service.

3.2   INFORMATION AND CONSULTATION

Informing the employment service as early as possible usually reduces the risk of the employment service extending the blocking period from thirty to sixty days. As the employer may not give notice during the blocking period, the running of the notice periods is significantly delayed by such an extension.

3.3   COST AND RISKS

Since an employer bears the burden of proof for the existence of the reason cited as the ground for termination, it is essential that the employer thoroughly record all circumstances relevant to such reason.

Furthermore, it is extremely important to follow carefully the prescribed steps of the termination process. Any mistake in this respect may lead to the invalidation of the termination and thus cause additional costs. Moreover, the time limit for acting upon the reason for termination may lapse in the meantime (see section 2.1.4).

SPAIN

Jesús Domingo Aragón
Eva Sainz Cortadi

1   OVERVIEW

Redundancy schemes in Spain are subject to several labour law regulations.

1.1   TERMINATION OF EMPLOYMENT AGREEMENTS

In general, Spanish law provides for the following ways to terminate an employment contract:

- mutual agreement between the concerned parties;
- valid causes set down in the contract, if reasonable and justified;
- in the case of temporary contracts of limited duration, the expiration of the period contracted for or the completion of a special task or service for which the contract was drawn up;
- death, retirement or the winding up of the contracting party;
- resignation of the employee;
- death, permanent total or severe disability of the employee;
- employee retirement;
- *force majeure*;
- termination for just cause on the initiative of the employee;

- objective causes which are legally permitted;
- dismissal for disciplinary reasons; and
- redundancy proceedings based on economic or technical reasons and those based on reasons related to the company's organization or production plans.

1.2   REDUNDANCY

Redundancy is regulated by Workers Statute *(Estatuto de los Trabajadores)* Article 51, which defines it as the termination of employment contracts based on economic, technological, organizational or production-related grounds.

These grounds are understood to arise when collective dismissal helps to improve the company's economic position, assures the future viability of employment at the company through a suitable reorganization of resources or when the company has no prospects of viability.

1.3   COLLECTIVE REDUNDANCIES

Collective redundancies require a special procedure in order to obtain authorization from the Labour Authorities to terminate employment contracts.

2   MAJOR LEGAL REGULATIONS

The relevant legal regulations are found in Workers Statute Article 51 and the Royal Decree 43/1996 of 19 January.

2.1   TIMING

2.1.1   Notice Periods

An employer should observe a one-month notice period to dismiss, which must be communicated in writing.

2.1.2   Collective Redundancies

According to the labour law, the collective redundancy procedure *(Expediente de Regulación de Empleo)* must be followed when, over a period of ninety days, a certain minimum number of employment contracts (according to company size) will be terminated as follows:

- ten workers in companies employing fewer than 100 workers;
- 10% of workers in companies employing 100-300 workers; and
- thirty workers in companies employing more than 300 workers.

These special proceedings take place before the appropriate Labour Authority. The collective dismissal procedure is as follows:

(1) An authorization application for the redundancy proceedings is made to the appropriate Labour Authority.
(2) Negotiations are opened by means of a written notice to the legal representatives of the workers, a copy of which is attached to the application and submitted to the Labour Authority.
(3) Negotiations between the company and the workers' legal representatives should last thirty calendar days (if the company has more than fifty workers) but this period is understood to be over, irrespective of its duration, if the parties have reached an agreement.
(4) The Labour Authority shall be notified of the outcome of the negotiations at the end of the period.
(5) The Labour Authority then makes a ruling on the filed application.

In practice, if the period of negotiation ends without agreement between the parties, the Labour Authority will probably refuse the application and the collective dismissals will not be approved unless there are serious and justified causes that make the redundancy dismissals clearly necessary.

The application to the Labour Authority mentioned above under (1) should be accompanied by the following documents:

- a report explaining the grounds for the proceedings;
- financial documents covering the last three years (balance sheets, profit-and-loss statements, corporate income tax returns), if the alleged reason for dismissal is economic;
- technical plans, projects, or reports which may be used in order to justify the redundancies, the measures to be taken and the projected impact of the redundancies on the future viability of the company, if the alleged ground is technical, organizational or related to production;
- number and categories of the workers employed in the last year, criteria used to determine the employees whose contracts are to be terminated and the period of time over which it is expected that the termination of the employment contracts will be carried out, if applicable;
- a report by the chartered auditor, if the proceedings involve companies with more than fifty workers and the terminations are on economic grounds;
- written notice to the employees' legal representatives relating to the report that, according to Spanish law, the employee representatives are entitled to issue before the company carries out a collective redundancy; and
- a copy of the written notice of negotiations with the workers' legal representatives. This implies that prior to the application to the Labour Authority, a negotiation period must have been opened with the workers.

The Labour Authority should be notified of the outcome of the talks and negotiations held at the end of the negotiation period under the following circumstances:

– If the period of talks ends in an agreement between the parties, the Labour Authority will then authorize the termination of the employment contracts within fifteen calendar days (except if they consider that some fraud has been perpetrated in reaching the agreement).
– If the period of talks ends *without* an agreement between the parties, the Labour Authority must decide within fifteen calendar days from the notification of the cessation of the round of talks whether it accepts or rejects, in full or in part, the contract terminations.

If the Labour Authority's decision authorizes the collective dismissal, the decision must state the date on which the compensation for the workers is to be paid and declare that the affected workers are now in circumstances of statutory unemployment, which entitles them to receive unemployment benefits. The decision of the Labour Authority may be appealed before the courts.

2.2	INFORMATION AND CONSULTATION

2.2.1   Collective Redundancies

Negotiations between a company and the workers' legal representatives must last thirty calendar days; if the company has fewer than fifty workers it must last only fifteen days. The employer and the legal representatives must negotiate in good faith with a view to reaching an agreement. In the event that the workers do not have employee representatives, the workers themselves can take part in the proceedings. If there are more than ten employees, they must appoint representatives (up to a maximum of five) to negotiate for them before the Labour Authority.

Any agreement requires the approval of a majority of the members of the workers' committee.

2.3	RISKS

2.3.1   Collective Redundancy

If a company dismisses more than thirty workers without following collective dismissal procedures, the courts will declare the dismissal null and void and demand reinstatement of the dismissed employees. The dismissed workers are entitled to be paid any lost salary. Furthermore, the company is fined according to a penalty established by the Labour Authority, which can be up to EUR 180,000.

If the employer does not comply with a reinstatement order issued by the court, it can be fined and its managers prosecuted.

2.3.2 Selection Criteria

Since redundancy is based on either economic, organizational, technical or pro-duction-related reasons, the affected employees must be those whose positions are threatened by such causes. As long as several employees' positions are similarly affected, the employer may choose whom to dismiss as long as anti-discrimination rules and regulations are respected. For instance, an employee's age, pregnancy, race, and gender are all considered unlawful discriminatory causes for dismissal.

2.3.3 Special Protection

Special protection is due to workers' representatives because they have a priority claim to remain in a company when redundancies are being executed. In the event they are dismissed and the court finds that their dismissals were unfair, they are entitled to choose between being reinstated or receiving legal compensation for the unfair dismissal. If it can be proved that they were dismissed because of their role as workers' representatives, the court may declare such dismissals null and void.

2.3.4 Wrongful Dismissal

An employee may file a claim for unfair dismissal when there are not enough objective and serious reasons to justify termination. If the court decides that the dismissal is unfair, the employer has the option of reinstating the employee or paying him/her legal compensation for unfair dismissal – forty-five days of salary per year of service.

2.3.5 Null and Void Dismissals

If the dismissal is due to discrimination based on age, gender, race, pregnancy, a violation of an employee's constitutional rights, or an employer not following fair redundancy procedures, the employee may petition the court to void the dismissal. If the court declares the dismissal null and void, the employee must be immediately reinstated to his/her former position and compensated for lost wages.

2.3.6 Unfair Dismissal

An employee may file an unfair dismissal claim on the grounds that there are no objective and serious reasons sufficient to justify the dismissal. If the employee's suit is successful, the employer will have the option of reinstating the employee or paying compensation.

2.3.7 Discrimination

As noted above in section 2.3.5, the court may declare the dismissal null and void when the dismissal is based on gender, race, pregnancy, other forms of discrimination, or when it violates the employee's constitutional rights. If the court declares the dismissal void in those circumstances, the employees must be immediately reinstated to their former positions and compensated for their loss of wages.

In case of discrimination, the courts may also impose compensation for additional damage suffered by the employees.

Furthermore, beyond all the compensation referred to above, the Labour Authority may penalize the companies with fines of up to EUR 187,000 for discriminatory acts.

2.4   Costs

2.4.1   Statutory Compensation

The statutory redundancy pay in Spain is equal to twenty days' salary per year of service, up to a maximum of twelve months' salary.

2.4.2   Unfair Dismissal

The compensation for unfair dismissal is equal to forty-five days' salary per year of service (any period of less than one year's service being pro-rated by months employed) and subject to a maximum of forty-two months' pay. In addition, an employee must be paid the accrued salary from the effective date of dismissal up to the date when the court decision is issued – usually a period of four months. In some circumstances, the employee must also be paid for the period up to the date of the hearing before the Labour Authority (one month's salary).

2.4.3   Social Plan

In practice, it is common for the parties to negotiate higher compensation than the formulas established in the labour law provide.

Regarding the amount of compensation for a collective dismissal, there are two possibilities:

- If an agreement is reached with legal representatives of the employees, the amount of the compensation will be the sum agreed upon.
- If no agreement is reached and the labour authorities authorize the collective dismissal, the amount of the compensation per employee will be the legal minimum, that is, twenty days of salary per year of employment up to a maximum of twelve months' salary.

In practice, the labour authorities normally do not authorize collective dismissals without an agreement between the parties and for that reason, it is very advantageous to reach an agreement between the parties early on in the redundancy process.

3   ADVICE FOR LEGAL PRACTICE

3.1   Reaching an Agreement with the Unions

As noted above, in practice, the labour authorities will not authorize collective dismissals if an agreement between the parties is not reached because even political reasons can be taken into account in reaching a decision. It is therefore advisable for the company to reach an agreement with the unions and the employees.

3.2   Timing

From a timing perspective, redundancy schemes should always follow the statutory procedure laid out above in section 2.1.2 and be well-prepared in every instance. It is important to allow enough time in the preparation phase. If the redundancy scheme is well prepared, the works council will have little opportunity to prevent the measures being taken by the employer, although in all cases they have the chance to delay implementation.

In a similar vein, if the collective dismissal is well prepared and the grounds are justified, it is less likely that strikes will crop up in the company.

To reach agreement, it is important to offer the employees higher compensation than that required by law. Compensation of fifty-five days of salary per year of service, and even higher, is not unusual.

3.3   Information and Consultation

It is convenient to initiate an informal period of negotiation with the workers' representatives before the official talks start, for the purpose of reaching an agreement and thereby obtaining the required authorization from the Labour Authority without difficulty.

3.4   Cost and Risks

3.4.1   Minimum Statutory Compensation versus Unfair Dismissal Compensation

In practice, unfair dismissal compensation is normally paid instead of 'statutory redundancy pay' because it is easier to dismiss an employee by paying him/her forty-five days of his/her salary per year of service than to dismiss him/her by reasons of redundancy and paying him/her only twenty days per year of service up to twelve months. The company must take into account that, unless very clear and dire economic reasons for redundancy can be proven, reaching an agreement acceptable to the workers will be necessary.

During the negotiations with the unions and in order to ameliorate the social impact of the collective dismissal on the employees, additional payments are normally also agreed to by employers.

That is not surprising as the employees and the unions threatened by the restructuring/transfer/dismissal process may retaliate by organizing strikes or public demonstrations and may even block entry into the company's plant and offices. Most employers will therefore negotiate additional severance payments with unions or individual employees. The payments are usually made in return for the unions'/employees' consent to the dismissals, to avoid the risk of legal claims, further strikes or other inconveniences.

As a general rule, costs and risks always tend to be lower in relation to the care and time devoted to the preparation phase. Breaches of the formal requirements of the redundancy process are very costly, since the consequence in many cases is the invalidity of the termination, which results in the entire process having to be re-initiated.

SWEDEN

Jessica Stålhammar

1   OVERVIEW

Employment relationships in Sweden are subject to numerous legal requirements that are contained in employment contracts, collective agreements and statutes. On the whole, the laws are designed to protect employees, particularly in connection with job transfers within the company; and protecting employment positions during the transfer of a business, the dismissal period and the resolution of disputes between the employer and employee.

The Act on Security of Employment (*lagen om anställningsskydd*) ('the Act') applies where an employee is to be dismissed. Under the Act, an employer can only dismiss an employee where there are objective grounds for doing so. This may be on the basis of 'reasons peculiar to that individual' or because of a shortage of work. In circumstances where it is reasonable for an employer to provide the employee with an alternative role in the company, the employer will not have objective grounds for dismissing that employee for redundancy. The concept of what constitutes objective grounds for dismissal has been developed through case law.

Collective redundancies are regulated in the same way as individual redundancies.

Legislation does not specify how many employees must be dismissed for there to be a collective redundancy. However, a dismissal of employees for reasons relating to the employees themselves (for example, misconduct or incompetence) cannot be a collective redundancy. Rather, to be a collective redundancy, the dismissals must be based on reasons affecting the employer's business.

2   MAIN REQUIREMENTS AND CONSIDERATIONS

2.1   TIMING

2.1.1   Notice Periods

Before making an employee redundant, the employer must give the employee a written notice of dismissal. The notice must include the date; the name of the employer and the employee; the reason for dismissal; an explanation of the procedure the employee must follow to make a claim and seek a declaration that the dismissal is null and void; and information about 'preferential rights'. The notice of dismissal has to be personally delivered to the employee.

The period of notice given to employees depends upon when the contract of employment was entered. New rules, introduced by the Act, specify revised minimum notice periods for contracts of employment entered into after 1 January 1997 while the old rules on notice periods continue to apply to contracts entered into before 1 January 1997.

The notice period stipulated in the Act may only be departed from if there is a collective bargaining agreement which sets out an alternative notice period.

Under the old rules, notice periods are determined by reference to age; under the new rules, notice periods are determined by reference to length of service. The period of notice required to be given is:

New Rules	Old Rules	
LENGTH OF SERVICE	*AGE*	*PERIOD OF NOTICE*
<2 years	Any	1 month
2-4 years	25	2 months
4-6 years	30	3 months
6-8 years	35	4 months
8-10 years	40	5 months
>10 years	45	6 months

An employee is entitled to salary and benefits during the notice period. However, the employer is entitled to deduct from such salary and benefits any income which the employee receives from employment elsewhere during the notice period.

2.1.2   Collective Redundancies

Where five or more employees are to be made redundant, the County Employment Board (*Länsarbetsnämnden*) (LAN) must be notified. The minimum period of notification is set out in the Recruitment Promotion Act. These are:

Number of Redundancies	*Advance Warning to LAN*
5-25	2 months
26-100	4 months
101 +	6 months

2.2   INFORMATION AND CONSULTATION

2.2.1   Collective Consultation

Prior to giving an employee a notice of termination of employment (whether to one employee or to a number of employees as part of a collective redundancy), the employer must inform the relevant trade union of its proposal to make redundancies and enter into negotiations as required by the Codetermination at Work Act (*lagen om medbestämmande i arbetslivet*) ('the Codetermination Act'). The Codetermination Act also contains detailed provisions regarding information that an employer is required to supply to the relevant trade union.

Furthermore, notice cannot take effect before the negotiations with the trade union have come to an end.

The employer and the trade union are obliged to negotiate on the reasons for the proposed redundancies, their possible consequences and the list of proposed candidates for dismissal. The employer is required to comply with the agreement reached with the trade union when dismissing the employees. A failure to follow the above procedure or to negotiate with the trade union could result in the employer facing a claim for damages. Given that there are no works councils in Sweden, there is no obligation to inform and consult with them. However, there are rules in relation to consultation with the European Works Council where an employer's workers are located in different countries. Swedish law, however, does not require the employer to draft a 'social plan'.

2.2.2   Individual Consultation

The rules that apply to collective redundancies described above in section 2.2.1, also apply to individual employees faced with dismissal.

2.3   RISKS

2.3.1   Legal Requirements

Prior to dismissing an employee by reason of redundancy, the employer must first try to find the employee an alternative job within the company. The employee should be offered a vacancy within the company that is both suitable for him/her and which he/she is qualified to carry out. If the employer has such a vacancy, it is required to offer the job to the employee in writing. If the employee declines the offer, the employer is deemed to have fulfilled its obligations and is not required to take any further steps to find alternative employment for the redundant employee. If the employer does not have any suitable alternative employment, the employer must still be prepared to prove that it attempted to find suitable alternative employment for the employee.

2.3.2   Selection Criteria

When there is a redundancy situation, the employer must use the 'last-in-first-out' (LIFO) principle when selecting candidates for redundancy. If there are several employees being made redundant but there is no suitable alternative employment for all of them within the company, the employer should draw up selection criteria which must include length of service. The employer must apply the criteria to all of the employees slated for redundancy. Those who have the longest service with the company should not be selected for redundancy except where the LIFO principle has been modified by a relevant collective bargaining agreement. As a result, if a particular position or occupational group is identified for redundancy, it does not necessarily mean that all the employees assigned to that position or occupational group will be made redundant. Also, certain groups of employees are particularly protected, such as employees on parental leave or union representatives.

To determine who should be made redundant, the employer must refer to the order of priorities. This must include looking at which employees within the operational unit are affected by the work shortage. For example, an 'operational unit' can be a factory or a restaurant. For every operational unit within each area governed by a particular collective agreement, the employer should draw up a short list which consists of both unionized and non-unionized employees (or blue-collar workers and white-collar workers).

Who should be made redundant can be decided purely on a mathematical basis or based on the tasks performed by the employee. For example, at a workplace:

- where there are fifty employees who all carry out the same or similar tasks; and
- where there has been a 10% reduction in productivity,

the employees with the shortest length of service will be dismissed. But, if there is reduced productivity related to one employee's specific work tasks, the employer must consider who ought to be dismissed on that basis. In a redundancy situation, an employee who has a longer period of service (seniority) than other employees being considered for redundancy must be offered the role over one of the employees with a shorter period of service, provided he/she has sufficient qualifications. The term 'sufficient qualifications' means that the longer-serving employee would be able to carry out his/her new role immediately or after a short training period.

The short list can be negotiated to a certain extent, if the employer and trade union agree on what constitutes 'sufficient qualifications'.

If the employer employs ten employees or fewer, then the employer, under the Act, may, at its discretion, choose two employees to exempt from the LIFO principle, provided that the employees in question are of special value to the business.

2.3.3 Redundancies and the Sale of a Business

Swedish law prevents employers from dismissing employees because of, or for a reason connected with, a business transfer. Where there is a sale of a business, the workers employed by the business are transferred to the buyer on their existing contracts of employment, i.e., on the same terms and conditions.

Following the transfer, the new employer is free to change the contracts of employment of its employees, including newly transferred employees, as long as it complies with the Act. The employer may, however, only change the terms and conditions of employment if the changes are accepted by the employees or if the new employer offers a new position which has different terms and conditions of employment to the employee and the employee accepts. If the employee does not accept the offer, he/she will continue to be employed by the transferee but, in accordance with the Act, can be made redundant. Where terms and conditions relating to an employee are included in a collective agreement, they can be terminated. However, in accordance with the Codetermination Act, the new employer is obliged to apply the terms and conditions of the seller's collective bargaining agreement for a period of one year from the date of the transfer.

2.3.4 Unlawful Dismissal

A dismissal by reason of redundancy is unlawful if it does not fall within one of the reasonable grounds. If, following a claim brought by an employee, the court finds that the employee has been unlawfully dismissed, it may declare the dismissal invalid. The employee may then be permitted to continue his employment or, if he has already left, be reinstated. Compensation and punitive damages may be awarded in connection with the dismissal itself and in respect of any procedural breaches. In certain circumstances, the union, as well as the individual employee, may be entitled to damages for procedural breaches.

Where the employer refuses to implement the court decision to retain or reinstate an employee, the employer will be obliged to pay an increase in damages. However, where an employee does not ask the court to order that he/she be allowed to continue employment or be reinstated, the employee's only remedy is compensation.

Claims by employees are usually brought with the support of the employees' union, through the Labour Court (*Arbetsdomstolen*) in Stockholm. However, if the employee is representing him or herself; is not a union member or is not bound by a collective bargaining agreement, the appropriate court will be the employee's district court (*tingsrätt*). Some collective bargaining agreements provide that any dispute should be referred to arbitration instead of litigation.

An employee looking to have his/her dismissal declared invalid must give notice of same to his/her employer within two weeks of receiving the employment termination notice and must file court proceedings within two weeks of the end of the notice period or upon the conclusion of any negotiations between the trade union and the employer. In circumstances where an employee has not been sent a termination notice or notice of the right to challenge the dismissal, the time allowed for serving notice on an employer and filing court proceedings is extended from two weeks to one month.

Where the employee does not want a declaration that his/her dismissal is invalid, his/her only remedy is compensation. In this circumstance, the employee must give notice within four months of receiving his/her notice of termination of employment that he/she is going to apply to the court for compensation and then he/she must file court proceedings within four months of the end of the notice or the conclusion of any negotiations between the trade union and the employer. The time period is increased from four to eight months where the employee has not been informed, in the notice of termination, of his/her right to challenge his/her dismissal. Court proceedings must then be commenced within four months of the end of the notice period or at the conclusion of negotiations between the employer and the trade union.

Compensation awarded in cases of unlawful dismissal are linked to length of service and age. They can provide damages for loss of earnings and emotional injury. The maximum damages that can be awarded by law are as follows:

Service	Months of Salary
Less than 5 years	16
Between 5 and 10 years	24
10 years or more	32

2.3.5   Discrimination

Dismissals based on the employee's gender, physical or mental disability, sexual orientation, or ethnic background are considered discriminatory under Swedish laws.

2.3.6   Rehiring Employees after Redundancy

Should an employer find itself in a position where it needs to hire staff after making redundancies, those employees who were dismissed by reason of redundancy have the right to be rehired over other candidates not previously employed by the employer. This preferential treatment continues for the period of nine months after notice of termination has been given to the employee. Again, priority is given to those who had longer service with the employer. Employees eligible for re-hiring must be informed in writing of any vacancies that arise in that nine-month period.

2.4   Costs

2.4.1   Severance Payments

During the employee's notice period, the employer must continue to pay the employee's salary and benefits, regardless of whether he/she is required to work or not. This can be costly, given that some employees may have long notice periods.

In Sweden, employees do not have any statutory right to receive a severance payment. However, an employee whose employment has been terminated because of redundancy may be entitled to receive a severance payment under the terms of his/her employment agreement or under a relevant collective bargaining agreement.

2.4.2   Damages/Compensation

An employee may claim damages that arise from being given insufficient notice; where he/she successfully shows that the notice given was invalid; or the court-ordered reinstatement is not complied with. The compensation may be awarded as discussed in detail in section 2.3.4 above.

3   PRACTICAL ADVICE

Swedish employment law is complicated and it is advisable for employers to seek the advice of a seasoned labour lawyer before implementing any redundancies. There are numerous issues to consider and a considerable scope for error.

For example, it is difficult to determine how long a redundancy consultation with the unions should last, as it will often depend on how many employees are affected and if the parties can agree on the selection of the list of candidates for dismissal.

Redundancies are often settled by negotiation. For various reasons, the employer often ends up giving its employees greater benefits than those required by statute or in accordance with the employment contract. The employer will usually give additional salary and paid leave in exchange for the employee waiving his/her preferential right of re-employment. The employer may also choose to 'buy out' employees who have a preferential right to remain at work, usually for substantial amounts of money.

SWITZERLAND

**Andrea Bantle
Andrea Kaiser
Sara Licci**

1   OVERVIEW

Compared to the laws of most other European countries, Swiss employment law is fairly liberal, particularly in relation to the termination of contracts of employment. There is, therefore, limited protection for employees against dismissal. An employer who wishes to terminate a contract of employment may do so without needing any specific reason, except when such termination would constitute a 'misuse of rights.'

The focus, therefore, in Swiss employment law, is not when (and in what circumstances) an employee can be dismissed but when a dismissal should be with, or without, notice.

To terminate without notice, the employer must have a 'valid reason'. A valid reason would exist in any circumstances where the terminating party cannot be expected, in good faith, to continue the employment relationship. This would not, however, include dismissals by reason of redundancy (meaning termination for economic reasons). As there is limited protection for employees against dismissal, there is, accordingly, no statutory definition, in Swiss employment law, of 'redundancy' or 'economic reason'. The only requirement, except where the dismissal requirement would constitute misuse of rights, is that the employer must give written reasons for dismissal if the employee requests them. An exception to this, however, is where an 'abusive notice' is given. This is where notice of termination of employment is given by an employer because of a personality trait of the employee. Even if there is an 'abusive notice', the employment relationship is effectively terminated and the only remedy available to the employee is compensation.

In addition to the general laws governing dismissals, specific legal provisions apply when it is proposed to make collective redundancies and, whilst the employer is free to dismiss employees for economic reasons, it must follow a special procedure before doing so. This special procedure includes informing and consulting with the employees and/or the employees' representatives, where appropriate, in order to reach an agreement. However, the employer is not obliged to negotiate a social plan or any payment to be made to employees on redundancy (except the salary for the notice period).

2   MAIN REQUIREMENTS AND CONSIDERATIONS

2.1   TIMING

2.1.1   Notice Periods

2.1.1.1   General Position

Swiss law distinguishes between employment contracts entered into for a fixed period of time and employment contracts entered into for an indefinite period of time, but terminable on notice. A fixed-term employment contract ends, without the requirement to give notice, at the end of the fixed term. As a general rule, therefore, no notice can be given to terminate the contract before the fixed term expires. The exception to this is where there is a 'valid reason.' Employees who are on employment contracts for an indefinite period of time, but terminable on notice, can be given notice to terminate their employment at any time.

In case of an employment contract entered into for a fixed period of time, in principle there is no requirement to give notice at the end of the fixed term. As a general rule, therefore, termination with notice period/ordinary termination is not possible before the fixed term expires. An employment contract entered into for a fixed period of time therefore may only terminate without a notice period, i.e., when a valid reason is given. As an exception to this rule, such contracts may be terminated by dismissal with a notice period of six months as of the eleventh year of employment, i.e., that they become contracts of an unlimited duration with the possibility to give notice.

An employer may only terminate without notice where it has a 'valid reason' to do so. The Swiss courts, though, are reluctant to find that there is a valid reason justifying termination of employment without notice. Depending upon how serious the grounds of dismissal are, a previous formal warning is usually required before termination without notice can be justified. Furthermore, an employer seeking to rely upon the fact that there is a 'valid reason' to terminate without notice will have to demonstrate that it terminated the employment relationship, without notice, as soon as possible after it became aware of the event which it will rely upon to justify immediate termination. As a general rule, no more than two working days may elapse between the event relied upon and the dismissal itself.

The statute sets out the minimum notice period to be given to terminate an employee's contract of employment. This is one month's notice during the first year of employment; two months' notice for employees who have worked between two and nine years; and three months' notice for employees who have worked nine years or more. However, these notice periods do not apply to employees who are still in their probationary period. It should be noted that a different notice period can be agreed upon by the parties in the contract of employment, provided it is no less than the statutory one month's notice. The notice period must be the same for both the employer and the employee and if a contract of employment contains a different notice period for each party, the longer period of notice will apply to them both. However, shorter notice periods can be agreed upon in circumstances where the employer intends to terminate the employee's employment because of economic reasons. The shorter notice period must be set out in the contract of employment, a collective agreement or an agreement entered into between the employer and employee at the time of the actual, or proposed, dismissal.

The notice will only start to run at the end of the month it was given.

During the employee's probationary period, which can be no more than the first three months of employment, the employment contract can be terminated on seven days' notice.

2.1.1.2 *Notice of Termination at Improper Time*

Whilst the employer can terminate the employee's employment for any reason during the probationary period, once this has expired the employer is subject to certain limitations and may not terminate the employment of the employee (the 'Prohibited Periods'), in the following circumstances, as follows:

– Whilst the employee, under federal legislation, is on either compulsory military, civil or civil protection service, or serves in the Red Cross services. Furthermore, if the employee is on such service for more than twelve days, his/her employment must not be terminated during the four weeks preceding and the four weeks following such service.
– For a specified period of time, which is linked to the length of service of the employee, when the employee is off work due to sickness or accident, through no fault of the employee. This period is either, continuous or in aggregate, thirty days in the first year of employment, ninety days in each year for the second to the fifth year of employment and 180 days of each year for the sixth year of employment and thereafter.
– During pregnancy and the sixteen weeks after the birth of the child.

Any notice given by an employer during any of these Prohibited Periods is void. If notice is given before the start of a Prohibited Period with the result that the employee's employment would terminate during the Prohibited Period, the notice period is suspended during the Prohibited Period and will only start to run again when the Prohibited Period has come to an end.

2.1.1.3   *Abusive Notice of Termination*

An employer does not need to provide written reasons for dismissal unless the dismissed employee requests the same, in writing. The fact that an employer may not comply with the request, or gives a false reason for the dismissal, will not affect the fact that a dismissal has taken place. However, in the event that an employee brings a claim, a court may take into account the employer's failure to respond, or the provision of a false reason, when determining if there is an 'abusive notice' and when awarding costs.

Article 2 of the Swiss Civil Code provides that a misuse of rights will be a breach and the employer will not, in this situation, be able to rely upon the general right to dismiss an employee without any reason. The Swiss legislator has specified some cases where the termination of a contract of employment constitutes a misuse of rights. This is where an employer terminates an employee's contract because:

- of a characteristic inherent in the employee's personality such as age, race, gender, origin;
- the employee has lodged, in good faith, a claim in relation to his/her contract of employment;
- of the employee's membership, or non-membership, in an employee association or because the employee lawfully takes part in union activities; or
- there is a collective redundancy and the employer has not complied with the requisite consultation procedure.

This list is not exhaustive. It is possible, in other cases, to argue a misuse of rights based on the general provision of Article 2 of the Swiss Civil Code. In addition, there is protection against the termination of an employee's contract of employment where it constitutes discrimination (against women). Unlike notice given by the employer during a Prohibited Period, where the employer has given an 'abusive notice' the termination is effective. However, in this situation, the employee may claim compensation from the employer. The amount of compensation is determined by the court but, in any event, cannot exceed the equivalent of six months' wages or, in the case of dismissals in the context of collective redundancies, two months' wages.

2.1.1.4   *Dismissal with Immediate Effect*

Where an employee's employment is terminated, without a valid reason, with immediate effect, the dismissal is still effective. However, the employee may claim damages representing:

- where there is a fixed term contract, what he/she would have earned up until the expiry of that fixed term; or

– where there is a contract for an indefinite period, which is terminable on notice, damages for what he/she would have earned if the notice period had been observed.

Furthermore, the employee can claim compensation which, unless otherwise agreed with the employer, will be fixed by the court taking into account all circumstances, but which may not exceed the equivalent of six months' wages. The employee cannot apply for reinstatement.

2.1.2   Collective Redundancies

The Federal Act of December 1993 on the Participation of the Employees amends the Swiss Code of Obligations (SCO) by incorporating into it rules governing collective redundancies. The rules were introduced, largely, in response to Directive 75/129 of the European Union on collective dismissals. The amended SCO, whilst entitling the employer to dismiss employees for economic reasons, obliges the employer to comply with certain formalities before doing so. Collective dismissals are deemed to be notices of termination under legally defined conditions.

To fall within the definition of collective redundancy:

– the dismissals must always be for economic reasons; and
– the employer making the redundancies must employ either:
    i. more than twenty, but less than 100, employees if at least ten employees are to be made redundant;
    ii. more than 100, but less than 300, employees if ten per cent or more of the employees are to be made redundant; or
    iii. more than 300 employees where at least thirty employees are to be made redundant.

For the purposes of calculating these figures, the employer must look at how many dismissals are declared within thirty days.

2.1.3   Notification to the Cantonal Labour Office

In addition to the requisite procedures set out in section 2.1.2 above, where the employer proposes to make collective redundancies, the employer must notify the Cantonal Labour Office of the same. The notice must include details of the outcome of the consultation with the employees or their representatives, as appropriate. A copy of the notice must also be given to the employees or their representatives, as appropriate.

2.2   INFORMATION AND CONSULTATION

2.2.1   Collective Consultation

Prior to making any dismissals, the employer must first consult with the employees' representatives or, if there are none, with the employees themselves, in order to give them an opportunity to make suggestions on how to avoid the redundancies or to reduce the number of redundancies. The employer is required to give the following information about the proposal to the employee representatives or the employees, as appropriate:

- the reason(s) for the proposed collective dismissals;
- the number of employees it is proposed to make redundant;
- the number of employees usually employed by the employer; and
- the period over which it is proposed to dismiss the employees.

2.2.1.1 *Effective Date of Termination*

Where there is a collective redundancy situation, the employees' employment terminates thirty days after the Cantonal Labour Office has been informed of the collective redundancies, unless the contracts of employment, or other legal provisions, provide that the employment will terminate at a later point in time.

2.2.1.2 *Timing and Consultation*

The consultation with the employees or employee representatives, as appropriate, must take place before notice of termination is given to employees. Thus, the consultation period and the time it takes to notify the Cantonal Labour Office of the proposed terminations will result in an extension to the notice period of the employees.

2.2.1.3 *Cantonal Labour Office*

Whilst the employer must notify the Cantonal Labour Office in advance of any collective redundancies, it is not required to obtain its consent to make such redundancies. The office's sole role is to ensure that the employer has complied with the requisite procedure prior to making any redundancies.

2.2.2 Individual Consultation

Only if there are no employee representatives is the employer obliged to consult employees individually.

2.3 RISKS

2.3.1 Legal Requirements

According to Swiss labour law, the employer needs no specific reasons in order to give notice. However, there are some general and singular reasons that may make a termination abusive and that also apply in cases of redundancy (see section 2.1.1.3 above).

2.3.2 Selection Criteria

Swiss law does not provide any selection criteria or guidance on how the employer should select who should be made redundant. The most important provisions that have to be respected refer to notice at improper time and abusive notice, as explained in sections 2.1.1.2 and 2.1.1.3 above.

2.3.3 Notice Restriction

In general, notice given by either party terminates the employment relationship. In a few cases, however, the employment agreement continues despite the notice. This is when:

- the party giving notice has not complied with any statutory or contractual terms. In this case, the employment relationship will be prolonged until the expiry of such term; or
- the notice of termination has not been given in the prescribed form, e.g., in writing. In these circumstances a new notice has to be given in the correct form.

When an employee's employment comes to an end, all claims arising from the employment relationship crystallize. In particular, the following sums become payable: The net salary for the notice period, compensation for any other benefits due under the contract of employment and any voluntary severance payments. The employer should also pay any sums due under any social plan that has been set up for the benefit of employees who are made redundant, as part of any collective redundancy exercise and any additional payments it has agreed to make under any employment agreement, settlement agreement or collective agreement. At the same time, the employer will be obliged to pay any compensation due to any other claims the employee may have from the employment relationship.

2.3.4 Compensation

As stated above in section 2.1.1.4, if the employer terminates the employment relationship with immediate effect, and without a valid reason, the employer must compensate the employee for the resultant loss caused to the employee. In particular, the employee may apply for compensation for loss of the remainder of the fixed-term contract, where there is one, or, where there is a contract for an indefinite period of time but terminable on notice, for the period until what would have been the end of the notice period. Furthermore, and as stated above in section 2.1.1.4, additional compensation equivalent to up to six months' salary may be payable by the employer to the employee.

2.3.5 Discrimination

An employer is obliged to treat both men and women equally when terminating their employment and the penalty for failing to do so may be reinstatement. This, therefore, constitutes an exception to the principle under Swiss law that even abusive dismissal is effective and that the penalty is purely one of compensation.

2.4   Costs

2.4.1   Compensation

Where, during a collective redundancy exercise, an employer does not comply with the requisite procedure, the dismissal will be a misuse of rights, which entitles the employee to bring a claim against the employer. The notice of termination will be considered to be abusive if it is given as a result of a collective dismissal but without prior consultation with the employees or the employee representatives, as appropriate. Compensation that the employees can request from the employer may not exceed two months' wages for each individual employee. Where an employer fails to notify the Cantonal Labour Office of its intention to make collective dismissals, the dismissals will be invalid. The employer, though, has no legal duty to make any severance payments or to negotiate a social plan.

2.4.2   Social Plans

When collective redundancies occur, agreements between the employer and the employee's association or the employee representatives can be set out in order to alleviate the effects of redundancies, such as:

- assistance in finding a new job (out-placement service; appropriate time off to look for other work);
- longer notice periods as stipulated in contracts and law;
- additional salary payments depending on age, seniority, civil status;
- promise of reinstatement in case of financial recovery of the company;
- payments of difference between the actual wage and the lower wage accepted with a new employer because of collective redundancy;
- payments towards rents for new flats or travel tickets due to the change of working place; and
- early retirement and payment of the gaps due to early retirement.

A social plan may be put in place by the employer; however, it is not obliged to do so, nor is the content of such social plan provided by law. Most employers put in place social plans if there are enough financial means at their disposal and for reasons of reputation. The social plan then would be applicable to all employees of the company. The content and costs may vary according to the given situation.

3 PRACTICAL ADVICE

3.1 NOTICE

The most important advice with regard to termination notices is that redundancy schemes should always be well prepared. Especially it is important to examine the employment agreement of each individual employee in order to determine when the termination notice can be given. Furthermore, especially in connection with a collective dismissal, it is recommended to explain the reason for the dismissal to the employee(s). When deciding whether or not to make redundancies, and whom to make redundant, the employer should consider each contract of employment to determine whether there are specific terms for individual employees in relation to termination by reason of redundancy.

3.2 COLLECTIVE REDUNDANCIES

Although trade unions do not have any real strength in Switzerland, in order to avoid situations where trade unions seek to delay the redundancy process or look to cause strikes, the notice to the employees/employee representatives of proposed collective redundancies, and the information to be given to the representatives, and the process generally, should be followed as closely as possible. In particular, it would be wise to give the employees, or their representatives, sufficient time to consider the proposed collective redundancy exercise. Seven business days is generally considered to be sufficient. The employer should also carefully consider how many employees and what particular category of employees will be dismissed, as well as considering other options besides dismissal for redundancy and whether it is willing, and can afford to pay, a social plan or make severance payments.

3.3 CONSEQUENCES

As has been mentioned above, the cost to an employer when it has breached its obligations in a redundancy situation is fairly limited. However, it is always wise to carefully consider the circumstances in which the employer terminates without notice and ensure that, where this happens, dismissal can be objectively justified.

An employer should always remember that the dismissal of employees during a collective redundancy exercise, without following the requisite procedure, will render any dismissal a misuse of rights and compensation of up to two months' wages may become due to each employee.

UNITED KINGDOM

Ben Doherty
Catherine Johns

1   OVERVIEW

The process of making redundancies within the United Kingdom is complicated and is subject to statutory control from numerous sources; accordingly, this chapter serves to highlight the most important areas but is not intended to be a comprehensive guide to redundancies within the United Kingdom.

There are different considerations for individual and collective redundancies; however, employers are required to follow the provisions of the Employment Rights Act 1996 (ERA), which provides employees with the right not to be unfairly dismissed, irrespective of whether the redundancy is in respect of a single employee or on a collective basis. The main source of statutory material in respect of collective redundancy provisions is found within part 2 of the Trade Union and Labour Relations (Consolidation) Act 1992 (TULRCA), which implements within the UK the European Collective Redundancies Directive (Directive 98/59).

Before considering the provisions in respect of the timing of collective consultation (see section 2.2.1 below), it is important to note that the statutory definition of redundancy within TULRCA is wider than the statutory definition within the ERA. The ERA provides that an employer may only dismiss an employee who has accrued at least one year's continuity of service in the event of five potentially fair reasons, one of which is redundancy.

©2008 Kluwer Law International B.V., The Netherlands.
Maarten van Kempen, Lisa Patmore, Michael Ryley, and
Robert von Steinau-Steinrück (eds), *Redundancy,* pp. 257-267.

Redundancy can incur in one of three situations:

- a disappearing job (no need for that particular type of work);
- a disappearing workplace (work no longer done in that location); or
- a situation where the employer requires fewer employees to carry out work of a particular kind.

This is in contrast to section 195 of TULRCA, which provides that a dismissal by reason of redundancy means 'dismissal for a reason not related to the individual concerned or for a number of reasons all of which are not so related.' Accordingly, the definition within TULRCA includes those within the ERA, but also has wider application and will include situations where the employer amends the terms and conditions of employment by dismissing the employees and re-engaging them on new terms and conditions.

2   MAJOR LEGAL REGULATIONS

2.1   Timing

2.1.1   Notice

The period of notice that an employee is entitled to is normally contained within the contract of employment. This contractual provision is subject to the statutory minimum entitlement of one week's notice for each complete year of service, subject to a maximum of twelve weeks' notice (section 86 ERA). Subject to the statutory minimum, the parties are free to agree on the period of notice. Manual and low-paid employees will frequently be contractually entitled to the statutory minimum notice but no more, whilst those with more responsibility or those who are highly skilled may be contractually entitled to three months' notice (or longer) from the outset of their employment.

When dismissing by reason of redundancy, before giving notice the employer will also have to comply with the provisions of the ERA in respect of having a fair reason for dismissal, and will be bound to follow fair procedures in all circumstances, either following the collective consultation provisions within TULRCA or the statutory dismissal procedure.

2.1.2   Collective Consultation

Section 188(1) of TULRCA requires an employer that is proposing to dismiss as redundant twenty or more employees at one establishment within a period of ninety days or less, to consult about the dismissals with the appropriate representatives of any of the employees who may be either affected by the proposed dismissals or may be affected by measures taken in connection with the dismissals.

Section 188(1a) provides that the consultation should commence in good time and that it should continue for at least a prescribed period before the first dismissal takes effect. If the employer is proposing to dismiss more than twenty but less than ninety-nine employees, the minimum period for conducting consultations is thirty days. The period increases to ninety days where an employer is proposing to dismiss 100 or more employees.

2.1.3 Notification to the Secretary of State

Section 193 of TULRCA requires an employer who is proposing to make collective redundancies to notify the Secretary of State for Trade and Industry of that proposal. Notice must be provided before giving notice of termination, at least thirty days before the first dismissal takes effect, where the employer proposes to dismiss twenty to ninety-nine employees within a ninety-day period; or at least ninety days before the first dismissal where an employer proposes to dismiss 100 employees. The employer is also required to provide a copy of the notification to the elected or appointed employee representatives.

If the employer fails to provide a notification to the Secretary of State, it will have committed a criminal offence and will be liable to a fine.

2.1.4 Individual Redundancies

On an individual basis, an employer should consult for a 'reasonable period', the length of which will depend on all the circumstances of the particular case. However, the employer should commence this process in good time and before it has decided to dismiss particular employees.

2.2 INFORMATION AND CONSULTATION

2.2.1 Collective Consultation

As mentioned above, section 188(1) of TULRCA requires the employer to consult with appropriate representatives. 'Appropriate representatives' are not limited to trade-union representatives, and where there is no trade union, the employer can either hold elections (in accordance with section 118A-1) or consult with a works committee which already has authority to consult in respect of redundancies.

Section 188(2) provides that the consultation process should include discussions about ways to avoid dismissals, ways to reduce the numbers of employees to be dismissed and ways to mitigate the consequences of the dismissals.

Section 188(4) provides that the employer should inform the representatives in writing at the outset of the consultation process of:

- the reasons for the proposals;
- the number and descriptions of employees whom it is proposed to dismiss as redundant;
- the total number of employees of any such description employed by the employer at the establishment in question;

- the proposed method of selecting the employees who will be dismissed;
- the proposed method of carrying out the dismissals, with due regard to any agreed procedure, including the period over the course of which the dismissals are to take effect; and
- the proposed method of calculating the amount of any redundancy payments to be made to the employees who may be dismissed.

2.2.2   Notification to the Secretary of State

The notification must be provided by letter or on form HR1. Notification must include the identity of any employee representative consulted and the date on which such consultation began.

2.2.3   Individual Consultation

Unlike collective consultation, the matters that should be discussed during the consultation process with an individual are not prescribed by statute. However, case law provides that, typically, proper consultation will require the employer to inform and consult with the employee about the following factors:

- the employee has been provisionally selected for redundancy;
- the reasons for the redundancy;
- the selection criteria;
- suggestions for ways to avoid the redundancy;
- any alternative employment positions that may exist; and
- an opportunity for the employee to address any other matters or concerns that he/she may have.

2.3   RISKS

2.3.1   Employment Rights Act 1996, Part X: Unfair Dismissal

A dismissal will be deemed unfair if it is not for one of the potentially fair reasons set out in sections 98(2) or 98(1)(b) and/or is not 'fair' in accordance with the general fairness test under section 98(4).

In relation to individual redundancies, section 98A provides that a dismissal will be 'automatically unfair' if the minimum statutory dispute resolution procedures contained in part I of schedule 2 to the Employment Act 2002 have not been completed and this failure is attributable to the employer (see also section 2.3.3 below).

2.3.2   Employment Rights Act 1996, Part XI: Redundancy

Section 139 includes the statutory definition of redundancy. This definition will apply in considering whether the reason for a dismissal is redundancy, and therefore a potentially fair reason under section 98(2)(c) for the purposes of an unfair dismissal claim.

2.3.3 Employment Act 2002, Schedule 2: Statutory Dispute Resolution Procedures

As referred to in section 2.3.1 above, the standard three-step dismissal and disciplinary procedure would apply to individual redundancies. This procedure does not apply where the information and collective consultation obligations governed by section 188 TULRCA apply (see section 2.2 above). The statutory procedure essentially requires that the employee is invited in writing to a meeting to discuss the proposed dismissal (step 1); that a meeting takes place and the employee is informed of the employer's decision (step 2); and that the employee has the right to appeal against the dismissal (step 3).

2.3.4 Discrimination

Regulations prohibiting discrimination on the grounds of gender, race, disability, sexual orientation, religion and belief, age, gender reassignment, pregnancy or maternity leave will apply as normal and standard. In particular, an employer may be at risk of discrimination claims arising from a redundancy exercise which involves the use of selection pools and criteria to identify the employees to be made redundant, where those criteria have a discriminatory effect. The relevant legislation relating to discrimination is to be found in the following statutes or statutory instruments:

- Sex Discrimination Act 1975;
- Race Discrimination Act 1976;
- Disability Discrimination Act 1995;
- Employment Equality (Religion or Belief) Regulations 2003;
- Employment Equality (Sexual Orientation) Regulations 2003; and
- Employment Equality (Age) Regulations 2006.

Section 105 of the ERA also specifically provides that selection for redundancy on a number of prohibited grounds will make a dismissal automatically unfair. These include the employee's role as an employee representative for the purposes of a collective redundancy exercise or Transfer at Undertakings Protection on Employment (TUPE) transfer; the assertion of a statutory right by the employee; a reason relating to the employee's trade-union membership or activities; and a reason relating to part-time or fixed-term status of the employee.

2.3.5 Maternity Leave

A further specific right applies to women absent on ordinary or additional maternity leave during a redundancy exercise. Regulation 10 Maternity and Parental Leave etc. Regulations 1999 provides that where a suitable vacancy exists within the company, the woman in question is entitled to be offered alternative employment under a new contract of employment, the terms and conditions of which are not substantially less favourable than her previous contract.

2.4   Costs

2.4.1   Employment Rights Act 1996, Part XI: Redundancy Payments

The right to a redundancy payment is governed by sections 135, 141(4) and 162-165 of the ERA. A statutory redundancy payment is calculated by reference to an employee's age and length of service (up to a maximum of twenty years). Half a week's pay is due for each full year of service where the employee's age is less than twenty-two. One week's pay is due for each full year of service where the employee's age is between twenty-two and forty-one. One and a half weeks' pay is due for each full year of service where the employee's age is greater than 41. The maximum amount of a week's pay for dismissals on or after 1 February 2007 is 310 Great British pounds (GBP). A written statement of how the redundancy payment is calculated must be given to the employee; failure to do so is a criminal offence (section 164 ERA).

Employers may elect to make more generous redundancy payments than under the statutory scheme; however, an enhanced scheme is likely to be indirectly discriminatory on the grounds of age unless it falls within the specific exemption contained within Regulation 33 Employment Equality (Age) Regulations 2006. This limited exemption allows employers to dis-apply the cap on the amount of a week's pay or increase the amount allowed for each year of employment (within the same statutory age bands) by multiplying it by a figure of more than one.

2.4.2   Protective Award

Section 189 TULRCA provides employee representatives the right to make a claim in respect of a breach of section 188 or 188A (Collective Consultation). If successful, the Employment Tribunal (of England, Wales, or Scotland) will make a declaration to that effect and may also make a protective award that the employer shall pay remuneration to employees for a 'protected period.' The maximum period, and therefore the maximum award, is ninety days' pay per employee. Although the complaint is brought by representatives, the award is made in respect of the affected employees of any description concerning whom the employer has failed to comply with any requirement of section 188.

2.4.3   Unfair Dismissal

In most cases, the amount of compensation payable in the event of a successful unfair-dismissal complaint is made up of a basic award (section 119 ERA) and a compensatory award (section 123 ERA). The basic award is calculated in the same way as a statutory redundancy payment (see section 2.4.1 above) and since any redundancy payment received by the employee is set off against the basic award (section 122(4) ERA), this usually means that in practice, no additional amount is payable in respect of the basic award in redundancy claims.

The compensatory award (section 123 ERA) is such amount as the tribunal considers just and equitable in the circumstances, having regard to the loss sustained by the employee as a consequence of the dismissal. Where a dismissal is automatically unfair due to a failure to comply with the statutory minimum procedures by the employer (see section 2.3.3 above), section 31 of Employment Act 2002 requires the employment tribunal to increase the compensation awarded by between 10% and 50%. The amount of the compensatory award is limited under section 124 ERA. The current limit for dismissals on or after 1 February 2007 is GBP 60,600. This limit does not apply where the reason for dismissal or selection for redundancy is that the employee acted as an employee representative.

2.4.4   Notice

As referred to above in section 2.1.1, section 86 of ERA provides for a minimum period of notice to be given to employees upon termination. Where employers seek to terminate employment immediately by paying in lieu of notice (under a contractual provision or otherwise), then the amount of notice due to an employee translates directly into an additional cost of redundancy to the employer and an increased redundancy payment to the employee in lieu of notice (see also section 3.1.1 below).

3   ADVICE FOR LEGAL PRACTITIONERS

3.1   TIMING

3.1.1   Collective Redundancies

The requirement to consult collectively is triggered once the employer 'proposes' dismissing as redundant the prescribed number of employees. Therefore, the employer is required to commence consultation before it has already decided to make redundancies; accordingly, the consultation must begin whilst the proposals are still at a formative stage.

Section 188(3) of TULRCA provides that no account is to be taken of dismissals in respect of which collective consultation has already begun. For example, if the employer has previously commenced collective consultation in respect of twenty-five employees and then proposes to dismiss an additional fifteen employees with the dismissals falling within a ninety-day period, there will be no requirement to collectively consult in respect of the additional fifteen employees.

Where the employer was originally proposing to make fewer than twenty redundancies but then proposes to make additional redundancies that will go above the twenty-employee threshold, there is a requirement for the employer to consult about all of the proposed redundancies.

If an employer is required to consult for ninety days and then serve a further twelve weeks' notice on its employees in order to terminate employment, this results in the proposed redundancies not happening for a period of six months from the time at which the employer starts consulting. This period can be shortened in two ways:

- The employer can include in the contract of employment an express right to make a payment in lieu of notice. Even when there is no express right, the employer may normally elect to do so. This will reduce the time period by the length of the notice period.
- Section 188 states that the consultation period should begin in good time and more than either thirty or ninety days before the first of the dismissals takes effect. As the time periods relate to the period which must elapse between the start of the consultation process and the first dismissal, the law does not provide a minimum time period for the length of consultation. Under English law, the dismissal takes effect on the last day of employment, which is typically the last day that the employee attends work. It does not take effect on the date that the notice is served unless the employer makes a payment in lieu of notice. Therefore, if the employer and the representatives have reached an agreement and have concluded consultation or if they agree that they cannot and will not be able to reach agreement (no matter how long the period of consultation), the employer may elect to serve notice within the thirty- or ninety-day consultation period. Provided that the notice does not expire within the consultation period, the employer should be able to satisfy its consultation obligations under section 188.

It is also possible to combine the two methods above, by serving notice within the consultation period and making a payment in lieu of notice for that period of notice which runs after the consultation period has concluded.

3.1.2   'One Establishment'

At its simplest, a specific geographical location will count as one establishment. However, practitioners should be aware of the issues surrounding proposals to make redundancies at more than one geographical location. The domestic courts have been prepared to find that separate geographical locations can be treated as a single establishment for a number of years.

3.2   INFORMATION AND CONSULTATION

In the situation where there is no recognized trade union, the employer can choose to hold elections to appoint appropriate representatives for the purposes of the collective consultation or to consult with employee representatives who have been elected for some other purpose. We recommend that the employer holds elections rather than consult with a pre-elected works council, as it may not be clear whether the works council has authority to consult in respect of the redundancies and there may be issues over whether the works council represents all of the affected employees.

Given the detailed information which the employer is required to provide to the employee representatives and bearing in mind the topics that the consultation is expected to cover, it is important that the employer undertakes detailed planning in respect of the consultation process. We recommend that the employers turn their attention as soon as possible to issues such as: formulating their proposals for the range of affected employees; whom they will identify as representatives; how they will identify the selection pools of at-risk employees; how they will select from those pools; and whether they are prepared to make any additional redundancy payments over and above the statutory minimum.

As information that is required to be given to an employee representative includes a breakdown of the proposed dismissals by categories of employee and the identity of the total number of employees in each category, the employer will need to have identified appropriate redundancy pools and established selection criteria to select out of those pools. In the situation where all the employees in the selection pool are to be dismissed, no selection criteria are required; however, if the intention is to reduce the numbers in the pool, then selection criteria will need to be considered and should be the subject of consultation with the employee representatives. Identifying the appropriate redundancy pool is important not only in relation to section 118 of TULRCA but moreover with a view to ensuring that any dismissal is fair, within the terms of the ERA. As a rule of thumb, it is safer not to define a selection pool too narrowly nor confine it to the most obviously affected group of employees.

3.3   RISKS

3.3.1   Planning

In terms of avoiding the risks of successful employment tribunal claims arising out of a redundancy exercise, the key advice to practitioners is to conduct detailed planning to ensure that the employer adheres carefully to the legal requirements in respect of timing and consultation, as set out above. In particular, in all redundancy processes, an employment tribunal will consider whether appropriate warning and consultation has been carried out; whether the correct pool for selection (where appropriate) was properly identified; whether the selection criteria (where applied) were fair and objective; and whether the employer took reasonable steps to avoid or minimize redundancy, including the offer of suitable alternative employment.

3.3.2   Minimum Service

One option to employers to minimize the risk of unfair dismissal claims is to terminate the contracts of employees with less than twelve months' service as a first step, since these employees will not have the minimum qualifying service required to bring an unfair dismissal claim. However, there is no minimum period of service for claims of discrimination; for example, if the reason for termination is disputed.

3.3.3   SOSR [Some Other Substantial Reason]

Where there is a question over whether a redundancy situation falls within the statutory definition of redundancy, an alternative defence to an unfair dismissal claim is to argue that the reason for dismissal (if not redundancy) was a business reorganization, falling short of redundancy but constituting some other substantial reason of a kind such as to justify dismissal under section 98(1)(b) ERA.

3.3.4   Statutory Dismissal Procedure

For individual redundancies, where the statutory dismissal procedure applies, we recommend that the three-step procedure (see section 2.3.3 above) is carried out at the end of the consultation process. This ensures that the decision to terminate employment is not made until meaningful consultation has taken place. Care should be taken to ensure that a formal letter of invitation is sent to the employee, regardless of the fact that by this stage in the process he/she should be well aware of the redundancy situation. The employee should be offered the right to be accompanied by a trade-union representative or a work colleague at the meeting. Completion of the statutory procedure is mandatory, even where (in the absence of alternatives to redundancy) dismissal appears inevitable. A right of appeal should always be offered, regardless of whether the redundancy process included an earlier right of appeal; for example, against provisional selection for redundancy.

3.3.5   Absent Employees

To ensure that all employees are included in consultation, it is advisable to check for employees absent from work for any reason – especially sick leave, maternity leave or other family leave – during a redundancy procedure and to take steps to ensure that they are included in the consultation exercise. Priority must then be given to any maternity returnees for suitable alternative employment where a vacancy exists (see section 2.3.5 above).

4   COSTS

4.1   ALTERNATIVE EMPLOYMENT

Where an employee has unreasonably refused an offer of suitable alternative employment, he/she will lose his/her entitlement to a statutory redundancy payment (section 141(2) ERA).

4.2   Protective Award

Recent case law (*GMB v. Susie Radin Ltd* [2004] *IRLR* 400) has made it clear that the purpose of the protective award is to provide a sanction for breach of the section 188 (TULRCA) obligations by the employer and not to compensate employees for the actual loss suffered. The starting point for the employment tribunal is therefore the maximum of ninety days' pay. The tribunal will then examine any mitigating circumstances to justify the maximum period being reduced. Particular care should therefore be taken by the employer to comply with the section 188 requirements as far as possible, in order to minimize the risk of protective awards being made, which is one of the largest potential costs of an unfair redundancy process.

Index

1. Maarten van Kempen, Lisa Patmore, Michael Ryley & Robert von Steinau-Steinrück (eds), *Redundancy Law in Europe,* 2008 (ISBN 978-90-411-2764-8).